Changing Histories KS3

Connected Worlds

c.1000 – c.1600

Christine Counsell
- Kerry Apps • Will Bailey-Watson
- Hannah Cusworth • Alex Ford
- Rachel Foster • Katie Hall
- Tim Jenner • Nicolas Kinloch
- Paula Worth

HODDER Education

Why and how we collaborated with historians on this book

The authors are all very experienced history teachers and history teacher trainers. Many chapters have been trialled in the classroom so as to ensure that they resonate with students. The authors all have wide historical knowledge as well as up-to-date specialist knowledge in many areas. Nevertheless, we felt that it was very important to work closely with historians so as to benefit from their years of experience in specialist fields and to ensure that the book is responsive to recent scholarship.

Historians have been involved at various stages of the development of this book. They have advised us on where we could incorporate or reflect recent historiography and they have read drafts of chapters relevant to their expertise. This book is much stronger as a result of this collaboration.

We would like to thank all the historians who helped us, including:

- **Professor Stephen Baxter**, Professor of Medieval History, St Peter's College, Oxford
- **Dr Helen Castor**, historian of medieval England, and a Fellow Commoner of Sidney Sussex College, Cambridge
- **Professor Eamon Duffy**, Emeritus Professor of the History of Christianity at the University of Cambridge
- **Professor Peter Frankopan**, Professor of Global History at Oxford University
- **Professor Toby Green**, Professor of Precolonial and Lusophone African History and Culture, King's College London
- **Professor John Hatcher**, Professor of Economic and Social History at the University of Cambridge
- **Professor Sabine Hyland**, Professor of World Religions, University of St Andrews
- **Dr Miranda Kaufmann**, Senior Research Fellow at the Institute of Commonwealth Studies
- **Dr Claire Kennan**, Senior Lecturer in Medieval History, Queen's University (Canada)

Note: this book contains historical sources which may use words that were widely used at the time of the source, but are derogatory, offensive and are not used today. These words may include 'coloured', 'Negro', and 'non-white'.

Although every effort has been made to ensure that website addresses are correct at time of going to press, Hodder Education cannot be held responsible for the content of any website mentioned in this book. It is sometimes possible to find a relocated web page by typing in the address of the home page for a website in the URL window of your browser.

Hachette UK's policy is to use papers that are natural, renewable and recyclable products and made from wood grown in well-managed forests and other controlled sources. The logging and manufacturing processes are expected to conform to the environmental regulations of the country of origin.

To order, please visit www.hoddereducation.com or contact Customer Service at education@hachette.co.uk / +44 (0)1235 827827.

ISBN: 978 1 3983 0703 2

© Christine Counsell, Kerry Apps, Will Bailey-Watson, Hannah Cusworth, Alex Ford, Rachel Foster, Katie Hall, Tim Jenner, Nicolas Kinloch, Steve Mastin, Paula Worth 2023

First published in 2024 by
Hodder Education,
An Hachette UK Company
Carmelite House
50 Victoria Embankment
London EC4Y 0DZ
www.hoddereducation.com

Impression number 10 9 8 7 6 5 4 3
Year 2027 2026 2025 2024

All rights reserved. Apart from any use permitted under UK copyright law, no part of this publication may be reproduced or transmitted in any form or by any means, electronic or mechanical, including photocopying and recording, or held within any information storage and retrieval system, without permission in writing from the publisher or under licence from the Copyright Licensing Agency Limited. Further details of such licences (for reprographic reproduction) may be obtained from the Copyright Licensing Agency Limited, www.cla.co.uk

Cover photos: Main figure: © Ivan Vdovin / Alamy Stock Photo; Map: © Universal History Archive/Universal Images Group via Getty Images

Illustrations by Elena Selivanova, Nick Harris, Janos Orban, Martin Sanders, Ellie Lonsdale, Daniel Rogers, Martin Bustamante, Carlo Molinari and Barking Dog Art

Typeset in Montserrat Regular

Layouts by Ian Foulis Design

Printed in the UK by Bell and Bain Ltd, Glasgow

A catalogue record for this title is available from the British Library.

Preface

I fell in love with history at school. Each history lesson was a story, full of surprise and mystery. It was full of people who fascinated, annoyed or amazed us.

Each history lesson made me wonder. I wondered how long a journey took with only horses or oars for power. I wondered how different people lived and worshipped, loved and laughed; or why when empires rose and fell, some lives shattered and others flourished.

Yet so much was missing! We learned how Edward I stormed into Wales. We didn't know that, meanwhile, in Mongolia, North Africa and South America, different conquerors also expanded their lands. We learned how Elizabeth I fought the Spanish but we didn't know that it was Moroccan sugar which rotted her teeth. We didn't learn how science and mathematics, art and language were shaped in Greek, Arab, Persian, Indian and Italian worlds, nor the quests, determination and accidents that connected them.

Many history teachers have written this book for you. We want you to enjoy wondering about past worlds, both in and far beyond Britain. We want you to revel in the stories and to discover how they connect.

And as you read, look out for the different ways in which we tell these stories. Then see what happens when you start to retell them yourselves! Part of the wonder of history is that stories change, depending on the questions we ask, the sources we use and the voices we find.

Christine Counsell

Series Editor, *Changing Histories*

Contents

Part 1 🌐 World views in 1000 CE — 2

1 Constantinople in 1050 — 2
Empress Zoe surveys her Mediterranean world *Tim Jenner*

2 The connected world of Islam before c1000 — 4
What drove Baghdad's thirst for knowledge? *Christine Counsell*

3 The French village of Conques before 1000 — 16
What light can one saint's story shed on western Christian worlds? *Rachel Foster*

Part 2 ⚔ Contested power, contested land — 28

4 A conquered England — 28
How disruptive were the Normans? *Christine Counsell and Tim Jenner*

5 Meanwhile, in Norman Sicily — 41
A story of one island, many worlds *Tim Jenner and Christine Counsell*

6 Unexpected allies for the Byzantine Empire — 45
Why did Alexios's empire survive? *Alex Ford*

7 Meanwhile, back in Norman England — 52
Struggling for control after 1087 *Christine Counsell*

8 The power of a queen — 54
What does the life of Eleanor of Aquitaine reveal about the medieval world? *Katie Hall*

9 Meanwhile, in the world of ideas — 62
A twelfth-century Renaissance story *Christine Counsell*

10 Meanwhile, in the Near East — 66
The story of the Third Crusade *Will Bailey-Watson*

11 Nightmare kings — 68
Why did the barons keep rebelling against their English rulers? *Alex Ford*

Part 3 👑 Empires: expansion and collapse — 76

12 Soldiers on the steppe — 76
How did the Mongols end up destroying Baghdad? *Will Bailey-Watson*

13 A golden country: the empire of Mali — 83
What does the story of Mansa Musa reveal about medieval west Africa? *Paula Worth*

14 Conflict and connection in the British Isles — 91
What were the effects of English expansion? *Katie Hall and Christine Counsell*

15 Order and disorder in Walsham — 100
How did one village respond to the Black Death? *Rachel Foster*

16 The consequences of the Black Death — 112
A story of changing histories *Will Bailey-Watson*

Part 4 ⚖ Stability and instability — 115

17 Meanwhile, somewhere in northern France — 115
The story of the Hundred Years War *Katie Hall*

18 Challengers and defenders of the late medieval crown — 118
What do the Wars of the Roses reveal about power and instability in fifteenth-century England? *Paula Worth*

19 Meanwhile, in Norfolk — 129
Changing family fortunes *Paula Worth*

20 Meanwhile, in Henry VII's court — 133
A story of strong monarchy returned *Kerry Apps and Christine Counsell*

Part 5 ☸ Revolutions in religion and ideas — 135

21 The Reformation begins in Germany — 135
How did Luther's protest become so big, so fast? *Steve Mastin*

22 Meanwhile, in England — 142
Henry VIII breaks with Rome *Christine Counsell*

23 Meanwhile, in Poland — 145
Nicolas Copernicus studies the beauty of the heavens *Christine Counsell*

24 Sofonisba Anguissola studies the beauty of the Earth — 150
What shaped the art of a Renaissance painter? *Paula Worth*

25 Reformation and rebellion in an English village — 154
What changed in the village of Morebath between 1520 and 1574? *Steve Mastin*

26 Meanwhile, in the Tudor court — 164
The story of Mary Tudor, Queen of England *Will Bailey-Watson*

Part 6 🪙 Silver and gold — 166

27 The Inkas — 166
How do historians use sources to study the Inkas? *Paula Worth*

28 Elizabethan worlds — 175
What connected Elizabeth and the Elizabethans to wider worlds? *Kerry Apps*

29 Meanwhile, in the National Archives — 187
Uncovering the lives of African Tudors *Hannah Cusworth*

30 Meanwhile, in the Mediterranean — 190
Travelling through connected worlds *Nicolas Kinloch*

Glossary — 194
Index — 195
Photo credits — 195

1 Constantinople in 1050

Empress Zoe surveys her Mediterranean world

The year is 1050. Zoe walks outside from an upper door in her imperial palace to stand on a grand platform. The platform juts out from a vast stadium. Now aged 72, Zoe remembers standing here before. Often, her presence had calmed the heaving crowd below. She remembers her people thronging the streets, chanting in support of her or her sister, or one of her husbands; or baying for her nephew's blood.

Zoe is a great empress. Standing here, she can see right across her magnificent city and beyond. Zoe has been empress of the **Byzantine empire** since 1028. This, her capital city, is Constantinople.

Standing here, Zoe can look into the past. Hundreds of statues glorify the memories of past emperors. Across the city, on tall columns, they rise to the sky.

Zoe remembers stories, learned in childhood, about her empire's glorious past. It is a past stretching back to ancient Rome. By the fourth century, Rome's empire covered much of Europe, north Africa and western Asia.

But this huge empire was divided.

It was the emperor Constantine who had finally defeated his rivals to bring the whole empire under his control by 324. And with this huge empire to rule over, Constantine had selected this ancient Greek city, once known as Byzantium, to build a new, eastern capital, greater even than Rome itself. The city had become known as Constantinople ('city of Constantine', in Greek).

Looking out to sea, Zoe sees boats weave through the harbour. These boats carry goods across the Mediterranean. From the east, as far away as China, merchants trade in silks and spices, paper and perfumes. Constantine had chosen this site for a reason; it was a place that connected worlds.

From these worlds, goods arrive in the bustling markets that Zoe can hear below. Merchants will return home and say that they have seen the richest city in the world. This wealth is carefully managed to keep Zoe, and her empire, rich.

But Constantine had done more than build a dazzling city. He had made his capital the heart of the Christian world. Rising above the great columns of the city, Zoe can see the impossible dome of the church of Hagia Sofia. It seems to be suspended from heaven. Nothing like it has been seen since it was built 500 years ago.

Zoe pictures the sacred wonders in that mighty church. **Pilgrims** flock around the finest collection of holy **relics** in the world. And in that church, stands this image of Zoe, in golden mosaic, next to those of past great emperors – each one God's representative on Earth. Zoe is one link in a chain never broken.

And as her eyes reach the towering city walls, Zoe is proud. Constantinople has never been conquered. As a child, Zoe heard how the Virgin Mary appeared on the walls to defend the holy city against all attackers – the Persians and Avars in 626, and later the armies of **Muslim** Arabs, of Bulgars and Russians.

Yet Zoe knows that greater threats to Byzantine rulers have come from within the city walls. This is why the most highly trained soldiers, the Varangian Guard, serve as her personal bodyguards. She needs them. She grew up with the stories of mutilation and murder, of endless rivals fighting for control.

And these are not just stories. Zoe has lived them. She remembers lonely days imprisoned in a convent, her head shaved, after her nephew seized her throne in 1042. She remembers how the people of Constantinople rose up and returned her to the throne, and how they demanded that her reluctant sister, Theodora, reigned with her – Theodora, who ordered their nephew's eyes to be gouged out.

But Zoe knows that the greatest challenges to her empire lie in its future.

She looks north, towards enemies who have challenged her empire for centuries. The Russians now follow her Church, the **Orthodox Christianity** of the Greeks. But she remembers their attack of 1043: Russian ships broke a century of peace.

The city's defences cannot be broken, but the empire beyond its walls is at risk.

Zoe looks east, towards Muslim lands. Zoe's ancestors lost vast lands to the Arab warriors who burst out of Arabia in the seventh century. Their Muslim empire declined in the ninth century and the Byzantines recovered much land. But now new armies of Muslim Turks threaten her empire from the east.

Zoe looks west, towards Rome, where the **Pope** seems determined to dominate Christianity in Europe. And she looks further west to a warrior people loyal to the Pope, the Normans. Now spread out from Normandy, and flexing their muscles in Italy and Sicily, these Normans threaten her empire's western edge.

Constantinople connects worlds. Goods, people and ideas, ever-moving, always changing, connect **Christendom** and Islam, Europe and Asia.

2 The connected world of Islam before c1000

What drove Baghdad's thirst for knowledge?

At two o'clock, on 30 July, in the year 762, a tall man with a long beard stood by the River Tigris holding a large brick. The tall man knew that this was the right moment. His royal **astrologers** had consulted the stars. The tall man's advisers, architects and engineers stood by. Along the banks of the Tigris, thousands of workmen looked on. Everyone watched. Everyone waited. Carefully, the tall man laid the brick. The building of the new city had begun.

The tall man was al-Mansur. This would be his new capital city – a capital fit for a great ruler of a Muslim empire.

To mark the great occasion, al-Mansur had special coins minted, like this silver dirham.

Muslim rulers were called caliphs. Al-Mansur had been caliph since 754. Since then, for eight long years, he had fought rebel after rebel. Even now, in 762, the task was not complete: it would be another five months before his soldiers would bring him, on a silver dish, the last rebel's head. But al-Mansur was hopeful. Surely, at last, he could bring the peace, security and prosperity that his supporters longed for?

Al-Mansur wanted to reassure all Muslims that this stability was finally on its way, so he called his city Madinat al-Salaam, 'city of peace'. It would soon gain another name – that of the tiny Persian village here before – Baghdad.

Before building began, al-Mansur had taken great trouble to test the brilliance of his city's design. It would be built in a perfect circle. Al-Mansur had asked his architects to mark out the plan of the whole city, on the ground, with cotton seeds. Oil had been poured over the seeds and set alight.

Now Al-Mansur could see his future city as a giant circle of fire – a visible plan, made of flames. What a sight it must have been!

Al-Mansur is said to have exclaimed, 'By God, I will live in this city all my life! It will be the home of my descendants. It will be the richest city in the world!'

Your enquiry

Baghdad soon became not just a beautiful city but one of the most important centres of learning that the world had yet seen. In this enquiry, you will gather together everything that led to Baghdad being a city of knowledge. At the end, you will present this on a large diagram.

Another city far away: Makkah

How did al-Mansur end up living by the River Tigris, founding a city in 762? To understand this, we must go back 150 years. We must head south, for thousands of miles. We must go to another city – an ancient one, in a desert.

Far to the south of Baghdad, in the land of Arabia, lay the city of Makkah. Let's picture that city, in the year 610.

The whole city seems to move. Through sun-baked sandy streets, long lines of camels pad their way. Some camels head north to the Christian lands of the Byzantine empire. Some are bound north-east, for Persian lands. Some move west to the Red Sea, where boats will carry their goods to Egypt. Some head south for the perfume markets of the Yemen, in Arabia's southern tip.

Here in the city of Makkah, wealthy merchants trade. Merchants sell perfumes from east Africa, cotton from Egypt, silks from China, linen from Persia and slaves from everywhere. Around the edges of the city, desert tribes camp. Everywhere we can see their tents of black goats' hair. These desert tribes will sell dates, oil, camels and leather goods.

Now look at the centre of Makkah. See the large, black temple: the Kaaba. Around it sit hundreds of sacred objects – Christian statues, Jewish pictures, pagan idols of gods and spirits. This part of the city, too, seems to move. Pilgrims circle this ancient desert shrine. They make sacrifices to the gods.

Something is about to happen in Makkah that will change the world.

Early in the seventh century, in that desert city, a merchant called Muhammad began to teach these traders and pilgrims. Muhammad had a startling new message. He taught that the old ways of worshipping at the Kaaba were wrong. Muhammad told his followers not to worship idols, nor to make sacrifices. Muhammad told his followers to surrender to the one and only god.

He also taught his followers to pray regularly, to live simply and to care for the poor, the sick, the weak. The religion became known as Islam and its followers as Muslims.

From Arabia to Khurasan

Through Islam, more and more Arabs were united as one people. Fired by faith, the Muslims began to spread their religion.

When Muhammad died in 632, the Muslims did not stop. On camels and horses, they formed armies of lightning speed. Bursting out of Arabia, they poured north and west into the Byzantine empire, conquering Syria and Egypt. No one was prepared for them. They swept north-east into the Persian empire, conquering the lands that we now call Iraq and Iran. By 750, they had reached so far east they had conquered Sind in Northern India. In the west, the Muslims made their way across north Africa, invading Spain in 711. Only in France, at the Battle of Poitiers in 732, were they finally stopped.

Find Khurasan on the map. Khurasan stretched from the deserts of central Persia to the borders of China. Weaving through Khurasan were the Silk Roads. These ancient trading routes took goods from China, through Persia, to the Byzantine lands of Syria, Egypt, northern Africa and eastern Europe. If the Silk Roads were the blood vessels of the world, Khurasan, where these roads met and flowed, was its heart.

In Khurasan, the Muslim Arabs met the fiercest resistance yet. Rich Persian noblemen, proud of their ancient culture, with its beautiful art, poetry and great learning, fought back. Tough Turkish tribes also refused to submit. To deal with this stiff resistance, more and more Muslim Arabs were drafted in.

As a result, something extraordinary happened. Thousands of Arabs, so recently living a simple desert life in Arabia, now poured into the Persians' cultured cities of art and learning. The Arabs were entranced. The Persian **nobility** lived in elegant houses. They ate exquisite food. They studied ancient Greek literature. They surrounded themselves with brilliant **scholars**, musicians and poets.

From this blend of peoples in Khurasan, a **new** Muslim culture emerged. Educated Persians merged with warrior Arabs. What a mix of cultures! Soon, a new governing class – Muslim in religion, but Persian in speech and customs – gradually gained control.

Here in this new Khurasan culture, support for a new Muslim revolution began to grow.

The expansion of Islam from 622 to 750.

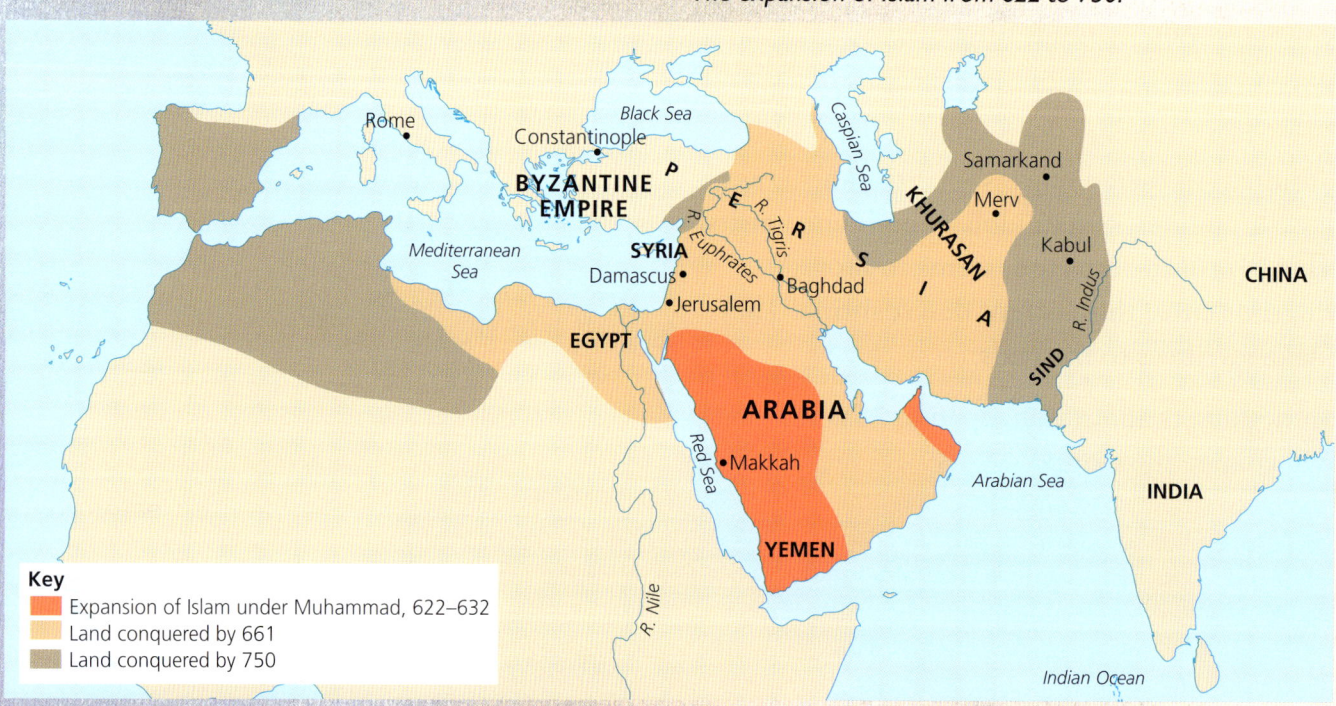

Key
- Expansion of Islam under Muhammad, 622–632
- Land conquered by 661
- Land conquered by 750

The Abbasids take control

During the 740s, across the new Muslim lands, especially in Khurasan, both the Muslim Arabs and their new Persian Muslim converts began murmurings of discontent.

At the heart of the desolate plains of Khurasan, lay the ancient Persian city of Merv. There, in 747, Muslim Arabs and Persians worked together to plan their revolution. Behind its strong walls, the leading rebels met to dye their robes black. Black was the colour of a new Muslim **dynasty** that these rebels supported. The dynasty was called the Abbasids.

Across the villages of Khurasan, the black banners of the Abbasid armies unfurled. Three years of fierce fighting followed. Powerful armies from Khurasan pressed down into Iran and Iraq, crushing the old dynasty's supporters. By February 750, this new and very different ruling family, the Abbasids, had gained control of most of the Muslim world.

The Abbasids left nothing to chance. The first Abbasid caliph hunted down and massacred almost every member of the old ruling dynasty.

Al-Mansur becomes caliph

Four years later, in 754, the second Abbasid caliph came to power. This was al-Mansur, the tall man whom we met earlier by the River Tigris. This was the caliph whose vision for a round city led to Baghdad.

Speech bubbles:
- "Where is the peace, security and prosperity we were promised?"
- "Why do our Muslim rulers not treat Persians as equals? Our Persian civilisation is ancient! It deserves respect!"
- "Why is the Muslim capital so far away from us? Syria is much too far away!"
- "Perhaps a different ruling family, one related directly to Muhammad, might restore a truer, purer Islam?"

There was no coronation. Muslims did not crown their caliphs. The leading Muslim nobles and soldiers simply filed past al-Mansur. One by one, they took his hand and swore their loyalty.

Loyalty mattered. For the first eight years of his rule, al-Mansur had many rebels to crush.

But all the time, al-Mansur was planning his new capital city.

He did not do this alone. Al-Mansur had a friend and adviser, an educated Persian from Khurasan, called Barmak. Barmak's learning dazzled al-Mansur. It was Barmak who guided al-Mansur to the perfect site, the ancient village of Baghdad, nestled in a tight curve of the River Tigris.

Perfect place for the perfect city

Let's picture al-Mansur and his learned Persian friend sailing down the River Tigris, searching for the best site. What would they have talked about?

They would have surveyed the rich farmland which could supply Baghdad with wheat, barley, rice and dates. All those wealthy farmers and traders could pay taxes, too. Al-Mansur would need this wealth to build the city and stock its libraries.

They would have discussed the latest poems of the court poets. Al-Mansur loved the traditions of Arabic verse, now enriched by Persian traditions too. (Al-Mansur once had a poet flogged for writing poor poetry.)

They would have talked of the tragic loss of ancient Greek books – on science, mathematics and **astronomy**. Like many Persian nobles, Barmak could read ancient Greek. They would have talked of the great Greek mathematician, Euclid, whose astonishing book on geometry was now a thousand years old. How al-Mansur loved Euclid's book! It contained the secrets of a perfect circle – secrets that had fired al-Mansur's dream of a round city.

They would have discussed the growing Muslim empire. Baghdad was closer to the new eastern borders than the old capital of Damascus, and closer to Khurasan.

They would have discussed the trade that could flow through Baghdad on the Silk Roads. Merchants from the East would pass through on their way to Africa, Arabia, Syria and the Mediterranean, bringing goods and new ideas.

Step 1

It's time to search for things that helped Baghdad become a city of learning. Make your own copy of this table. Then use pages 4 to 8 to make notes in the first three columns only. We have started two columns for you.

The role of the caliphs	Connections between Baghdad and elsewhere	Money and trade	The religion of Islam
	Baghdad was connected with Khurasan where many Persian noblemen read Greek.	Rich farmlands and trade gave the caliph money to build libraries.	

None of al-Mansur's Baghdad has survived, but the Ukhaidir Palace, built nearby, still exists. Al-Mansur's palace would have had grand entrances like these.

Building the perfect city

Al-Mansur sent out a decree to all corners of his empire asking for builders and labourers. Al-Mansur paid them well. Even ordinary labourers received one twenty-fourth of a dirham a day. With one dirham you could buy 30 kilos of dates or a whole sheep.

With no natural stone near the Tigris, bricks were made from mud, cemented with lime and baked in the sun. Millions of bricks were needed for the 24-metre-high circular walls. Al-Mansur made his workmen measure each brick. Workers wasting even a handful of clay were thrown into prison.

From miles away, travellers could see the green domes of the caliph's palace. Next to the palace was a mosque, where al-Mansur preached sermons during Friday prayers. It was said that his long beard soaked with tears, dripping onto the ground, as emotion overcame him.

The round city was finished in 766, but houses and workshops soon sprawled beyond its circular walls. Down by the Tigris, with private mosques and gardens sloping to the river, were the grand houses of al-Mansur's family. Whole sections of the city housed soldiers. Soldiers came from all over the empire, from Khurasan to Arabia.

Baghdad constantly attracted workers. Canals needed digging and houses needed plastering (the flooding Tigris kept dissolving the mud bricks). Two-storey hotels sprung up. Traders could stable a horse or camel on the lower floor. In the poorer quarters, newcomers squatted in shacks and tents. The city soon teemed with languages from Arabia, Africa, Persia, Greece. And everywhere, there were mosques. Above the street noise, five times a day, Baghdad citizens heard the call to prayer.

City of books

Mosques had always been places to learn. Muhammad himself had taught Muslims to seek knowledge. But books were rare, fragile and came in many languages. How could scholars find them? How would they preserve them? How could they understand them?!

Al-Mansur now threw himself into finding, translating and copying books. This thrifty caliph, who wouldn't waste a dirham on bricks, was about to spend a fortune on books.

Baghdad connects worlds

Books from the Greeks

Although his armies often raided the border with the Byzantine empire, al-Mansur had no plans to take more Byzantine land, let alone the distant fortress of Constantinople. No one had conquered Constantinople since Constantine founded it, over 400 years ago! Al-Mansur wanted something else from that city. Hidden behind Constantinople's walls were precious, ancient, Greek books.

Once safe in a vast library in Alexandria, these books had been lost through decay, fire and the chaos of collapsing empires. In northern Greek lands, however, books had been saved. Al-Mansur now wrote to the Byzantine emperor. He asked for books on science and mathematics. He especially asked for one, special book – Euclid's masterpiece on geometry, the *Elements*. Copies existed in Muslim lands but they were incomplete, damaged or fragile.

The books took months to arrive from Constantinople. They probably came in a heavy wooden chest. Imagine al-Mansur's servants heaving open the heavy lid. Imagine al-Mansur and Barmak peering in. There, among the scrolls, they would have seen it. The Byzantine emperor had sent them a copy of Euclid's *Elements*.

These are the earliest known fragments of Euclid's Elements, *written in Greek and dated to c.200 CE. That is already 500 years after Euclid's death (c.300 BCE). Look closely and you can see the lines of papyrus reeds.*

Mathematics from India

In 771, some Indian scholars visited Baghdad. They showed al-Mansur a book called the *Siddhanta*. Its style was puzzling. Mathematics and science seemed to be written as poetry.

Al-Mansur was entranced. The Indians used just nine digits and a zero, with columns for tens, hundreds and so on. How different this was from cumbersome Roman or Greek numerals! This system was already known in Syria, but in India it had transformed mathematics. Using zero, the Indians made huge numbers and could do complex calculations.

Brahmi (ancient Indian)	–	=	≡	+	ↄ	ҩ	7	ς	ʔ
Hindu	०	१	२	३	४	५	६	७	८	९
Arabic	·	١	٢	٣	٤	٥	٦	٧	٨	٩
Medieval European	O	I	2	3	ᒾ	ҁ	6	Λ	8	9
Modern European	0	1	2	3	4	5	6	7	8	9

The numerals we use today come originally from this Indian system, which was further developed by the Arabs.

The *Siddhanta* also had tables charting the stars, planets and moon. This was precious knowledge for Muslims. For their religious calendar, Muslims needed to know when a new moon would appear. For their prayers, they needed the stars to show Makkah's direction.

Paper from China

Ancient Greek scrolls of papyrus decayed quickly and needed constant recopying. Parchment lasted longer, but involved stretching, cleaning and drying animal skins. Only paper could speed things up, and the Chinese had made it for centuries. Baghdad scholars and officials now started to buy paper from Chinese traders.

Then, in the 770s, in Samarqand, the far north-east of the Muslim empire, two Chinese men shared the secrets of papermaking. Now the first paper mills could be built on Muslim soil.

Al-Mansur's legacy

On a hot afternoon in 775, al-Mansur sat in an upper room in the north-eastern gate of the round city. He often sat there. Enjoying the breeze, he could gaze towards the distant province of Khurasan, whose people had brought his dynasty to power. Here, he could think and plan. Already, he had achieved much:

Euclid's great work was not yet translated…

… but a group of scholars were now overseeing the translation of *all* ancient Greek texts.

The *Siddhanta* was not yet translated…

 … but al-Mansur's royal astronomer had begun.

Paper was not yet being made in Baghdad…

… but its secrets were creeping along the Silk Roads, from Samarqand.

Later that year, al-Mansur set off on his annual pilgrimage to Makkah. It would be his last. Along the journey, a royal doctor watched as al-Mansur slipped off his camel to defecate by the road. The doctor noticed how weak he looked as he re-mounted his camel. Al-Mansur was dead by dawn.

> ### Step 2
> Using pages 4 to 8, add more notes to your table. For example, for the religion column, think about astronomy. Why would the Muslims want ways of doing mathematics more quickly?

Baghdad's brilliant minds

City of paper

The year is 830. It is fifty-five years since al-Mansur's death. Four caliphs have reigned.

Along Baghdad's streets, a new kind of business has sprung up – booksellers, or 'paper traders' as they are known. The city has hundreds. In backrooms, teams of scribes copy out books. Out on hot roadsides, books lie on tables for browsing.

The books are starting to look like books. Instead of papyrus or parchment, books are made of paper and bound.

Apprentices learn new arts of bookbinding. They use fancy new products of glue and ink. And down by the Tigris is the technology driving it all: water-powered paper mills.

In the alleyways, voices are raised. Booksellers invite scholars to debate scientific ideas. Some even employ their own translators and writers to write more books! The *Siddhanta* and the *Elements*, now translated, are everywhere. Ideas flow through Baghdad's streets.

Across the Muslim world, these ideas travel in books, around campfires and through the new postal service. To find books, scholars will risk disease, sandstorms, robbers and wild animals. They band together for safety with those who know the inns and water-stops: pilgrims, messengers, soldiers and wandering preachers.

A new caliph: al-Mamun

In 830, leading this empire of swirling ideas, and living in Baghdad, is an extraordinary caliph – al-Mamun. He is energetic, demanding and unstoppable. Like his great-grandfather, al-Mansur, he craves knowledge.

Yet how different al-Mamun is from al-Mansur! At al-Mamun's banquets, dancing girls entertain guests, silver bowls of rosewater perfume the air, pomegranates tower on gold platters, pistachios drip with honey. Women and men sing, play and compose music. (Of course, the female musicians are enslaved – no free woman would disgrace herself by singing in public!)

Al-Mansur would have been shocked. He disapproved of music. He once broke a musician's instrument over his head.

Meanwhile, in the city, Turkish slave-soldiers now live in their thousands. Many of these slave-soldiers are about to join al-Mamun on a new military expedition. For in 830, al-Mamun has decided to attack the Byzantine border, and to lead the army himself.

The description above shows how things were in 830, but al-Mamun hadn't always been so secure. Al-Mamun's path to power was as blood-soaked as that of the first Abbasids. Before becoming caliph in 813, al-Mamun had had to defeat his brother in a **civil war**. Even then, he chose to stay in his power base in Khurasan until 819, when he finally felt safe to march a thousand miles to Baghdad and to claim it as his own.

Gathering minds

Al-Mamun's father had founded a place called the House of Wisdom, where scholars worked on ancient texts. When al-Mamun finally entered Baghdad in 819, the city was in ruins and the scholars had fled. Al-Mamun now revived the House of Wisdom. In this twelfth-century painting of it, you can see the books piled high on the shelves.

Historians are not sure what, exactly, the House of Wisdom was. Was it one building or many? Was it one library or many?

Twelfth-century painting of the House of Wisdom.

Thirteenth-century painting of Caliph al-Mamun sending messengers to the Byzantine emperor.

Historians are sure, however, of these four things:

Scholars in the House of Wisdom got better at translating.
They looked for the meaning of whole sentences, instead of single words. They worked in teams, checking each other's translations. They began to add their own comments to the texts, editing them and creating new versions.

Al-Mamun organised the search for more books.
He sent scholars everywhere, including north Africa, India, China and the Byzantine empire. The painting at the bottom of page 12 shows al-Mamun (on the right) sending messengers to the Byzantine emperor.

The House of Wisdom was properly organised.
Al-Mamun appointed directors and paid salaries to scholars and other workers.

Al-Mamun gathered scholars from everywhere, regardless of their faith.
Whether from Khurasan, Sindh, Syria or Egypt, whether Jewish, Christian or from Persian religions. Al-Mamun did not mind what faith the scholars held.

The House of Wisdom scholars often held many roles at once. A translator could be doctor, mathematician and government official, all at the same time. One doctor translated 129 ancient books by the famous Greek doctor Galen and travelled thousands of miles to find them. He wrote this about one of his searches:

> I sought for it earnestly and travelled in search of it in Mesopotamia, Syria, Palestine, Egypt and Alexandria. All I could find was half of it in Damascus.

Scientific minds

The ancient Greek astronomer Ptolemy had calculated the Earth's circumference. But had Ptolemy's methods been right? Al-Mamun was determined to find out. His astronomers set off for the desert. They carried an instrument like this, called an astrolabe, the Greek invention for navigating with the stars. At dead of night, when the stars shone most brightly, they formed two teams. One walked north, the other south. After travelling one degree of the Earth's curve, they stopped and walked back. They then took an average of the two distances travelled. They multiplied it by 360. The astronomers calculated that the Earth's circumference was 24,500 miles. We now know that they were only 400 miles out.

In this story about measuring the Earth, we see Baghdad scholars laying the foundations of modern science. Let's look more closely at this:

The story shows Baghdad scholars...	Where else was this happening?
...testing the claims in ancient texts.	The scholars in Baghdad tested and improved ancient Indian star tables from which they could tell the date and time.
...using scientific methods such as observing and measuring.	In Baghdad and in Damascus, Al-Mamun built observatories for viewing the stars. Now scholars could compare two sets of data about the stars.
...improving ancient technology such as the astrolabe.	Three Persian brothers from Khurasan wrote a *Book of Ingenious Devices*. Their inventions included a crankshaft, a windproof torch and a flute that played itself.

At this time, astronomers and astrologers were the same people. Astrologers needed precise measurements of the movements in the night sky. This is why astrology (trying to predict the future from the stars) spurred on the study of astronomy (the proper, scientific study of the stars).

A mathematical mind

Al-Mamun was not just *fascinated* by mathematics. He *needed* mathematics. He needed it to estimate the size of enemy armies, to measure canals, to calculate taxes. Traders needed mathematics to calculate prices. Muslims needed mathematics to calculate their inheritance, especially now that Islam's inheritance laws had introduced shares for daughters.

The man who was al-Mamun's answer to these challenges was a Persian, a devoted Muslim, and a mathematical genius. He was called al-Khwarizmi. Try saying it: *al-kwa-rithmi*. This is how his invention, the 'algorithm', got its name.

Al-Khwarizmi found the mathematics in the *Siddhanta* beautiful. The Indian number system was so simple and concise! Al-Khwarizmi now used this system to invent mathematical rules, known as algebra, for solving everyday problems. Al-Khwarizmi dedicated a book on algebra to al-Mamun:

> That love of science, by which God has distinguished our leader al-Mamun, has encouraged me to compose this work. ...I have kept it to what is easiest and most useful in arithmetic, such as men constantly need for inheritance, dividing estates, lawsuits, trade and their dealings with one another, or for measuring of lands, digging canals and other geometrical calculations.

From the preface to al-Khwarizmi's The Book of Restoring and Balancing.

A statue of al-Khwarizmi in his birthplace Khiva, Uzbekistan.

This picture of a doctor grinding herbs is from an Arabic translation, made in Baghdad, of a first-century Greek book.

Medical minds

Caring for the sick was an important Muslim tradition. From the Greeks, Baghdad doctors learned how to examine patients, how to use alcohol as antiseptic and how to prepare medicines. The famous Greek doctor Galen had proved that our arteries carry blood and that we have nerves. Encouraged by al-Mamun, Baghdad doctors now built on this knowledge.

Al-Mamun also poured money into building hospitals. To help patients recover, the hospitals had restful gardens and flowing water.

Step 3

Using pages 11 to 14, add more notes to your table.

Al-Mamun's last years

Al-Mamun's last years were busy. He led military expeditions to the Byzantine empire in 831 and 832. In 832, he visited Egypt and saw the pyramids.

Something else, too, made al-Mamun busy: getting cross with his religious scholars. He paid scholars to develop new ideas, but not on religion! Al-Mamun was always summoning religious leaders to his palace to ask them tricky questions. They were in trouble if their answers were wrong!

In August 833, al-Mamun set out for the Byzantine border, yet again. He never reached it. Resting by a mountain stream, he suddenly complained to his companions of feeling cold. A fever had gripped him. Within a few hours he was dead.

Before he died, al-Mamun wrote instructions for his burial:

> When I die, turn my face towards God, close my eyes and perform the rites of purification over me. See that I am properly shrouded. Then lay me on my side, and hurry along with me. When you set me down for prayers, let my eldest kinsman come forward to lead the worship.... Turn me on my right side, in the direction of Makkah.... Then wall up the niche with mud bricks and sprinkle earth over me. Then leave me to my fate.

From the will of al-Mamun, as recorded in an historical account by al-Tabari Muhammad ibn Jarir, a scholar who lived in Baghdad in the second half of the ninth century.

Baghdad's light shines on

After al-Mamun died in 833, Baghdad fell into civil war and declined. By 1000, the Abbasid territory was just a small area around Baghdad. Meanwhile, a new Muslim power had risen in the region – the Turks.

Yet Baghdad's quest for knowledge continued. The tenth century produced al-Razi – Baghdad's most famous doctor. Al-Razi wrote nearly two hundred books on medicine. Al-Razi often summarised the knowledge of Greek, Indian, Arab and Persian doctors and then gave his own view on whether each was right. With all this knowledge gathered and organised, Baghdad doctors could begin the first proper training of doctors. Al-Razi's fame spread so far that one medical student travelled from China to learn Arabic so that he could listen to al-Razi read aloud from Galen's books. He then translated them into Chinese.

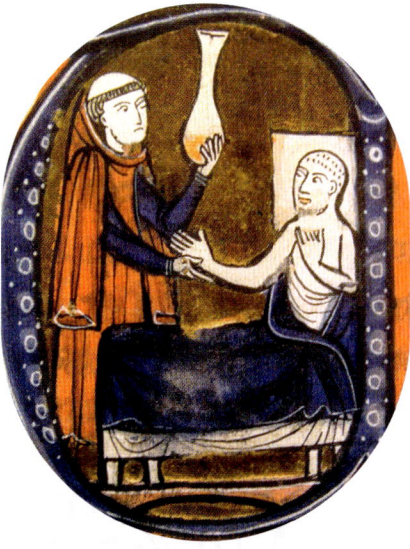

This is an image of Al-Razi from a thirteenth-century Italian book. Al-Razi is still honoured by doctors all over the world.

The fire of knowledge that burned in Baghdad was so bright that it burned on elsewhere after Baghdad fell into chaos. Slowly, all this knowledge flowed from the Arab Muslim world into Europe. When, in the thirteenth century, European countries started their first universities, they were powered by knowledge which had been rescued and developed in Baghdad.

Shaping your answer

Make a diagram to answer the question, 'What drove Baghdad's thirst for knowledge in the years 762–1000?' Follow these steps:

1) Draw the round city in the centre of a large piece of paper. Within it, write a little on each type of knowledge: astronomy, science, mathematics, medicine, technology and poetry.
2) Outside your round city, draw four boxes labelled with the four headings from your Steps. These are your four factors feeding the thirst for knowledge. In each box, summarise the role of that factor. Choose a colour for each box.
3) Using coloured arrows show which factors were especially important in driving which types of knowledge.

3 The French village of Conques before 1000

What light can one saint's story shed on western Christian worlds?

In 1013, two travellers slipped into the cool quiet of the church. They were monks – Christian holy men who had dedicated their lives to God. They had travelled hundreds of miles to a tiny village called Conques in what is now south-western France.

Now, finally, they would meet her, the girl they had come so far to see. The two monks inched their way forwards through the crowd. The church heaved with people. Finally, straining their eyes against the gloom, they caught a glimpse of her, shimmering in the candlelight.

Covered with gold and precious stones, she was seated on a throne. In the small box, resting on her lap, were the remains of a young Roman child. The two travelling monks were staring at a statue. For the girl that had brought the travellers so far was not living. She had been dead for over 700 years.

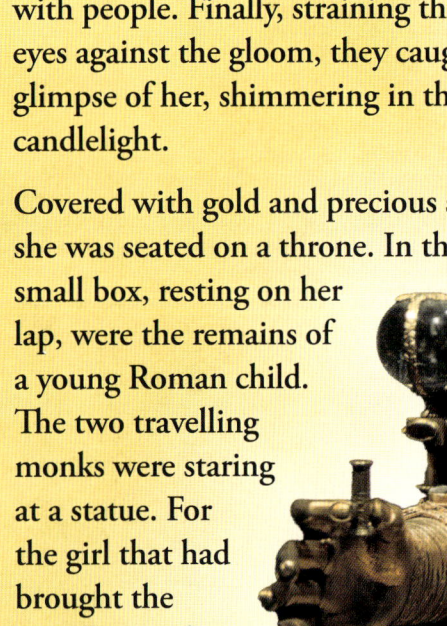

Her name was Foy, meaning faith, and she was a **saint**.

The monks had heard the stories about the statue, about the girl who had lived centuries before them, and about the miraculous powers of her bones. She could heal the sick, make the blind see and bring the dead back to life. She also had an eye for trinkets and jewels, a particular fondness for donkeys and a liking for practical jokes.

As those around him knelt in awe, one of the travellers turned to his companion and smirked. Much later, when writing about the visit, he recalled his thoughts:

> thinking it absurd, of course, and far beyond the limits of reason, that so many rational beings should kneel before a mute and insensate thing

From the Book of Miracles, written by Bernard of Angers in the early 1000s.

Uncovering western Christian worlds before 1000

The monks who travelled to visit Foy lived in western, Christian Europe. On the map, western Christian Europe in the year 1000 is shaded in red. In western Europe, Christians looked to the leadership of the Pope, who was based in Rome. These Christians were members of the Catholic Church. Further east, Christians followed a different kind of Christianity, sometimes called Eastern Orthodox. That Church was led from Constantinople, the city we saw in Chapter 1.

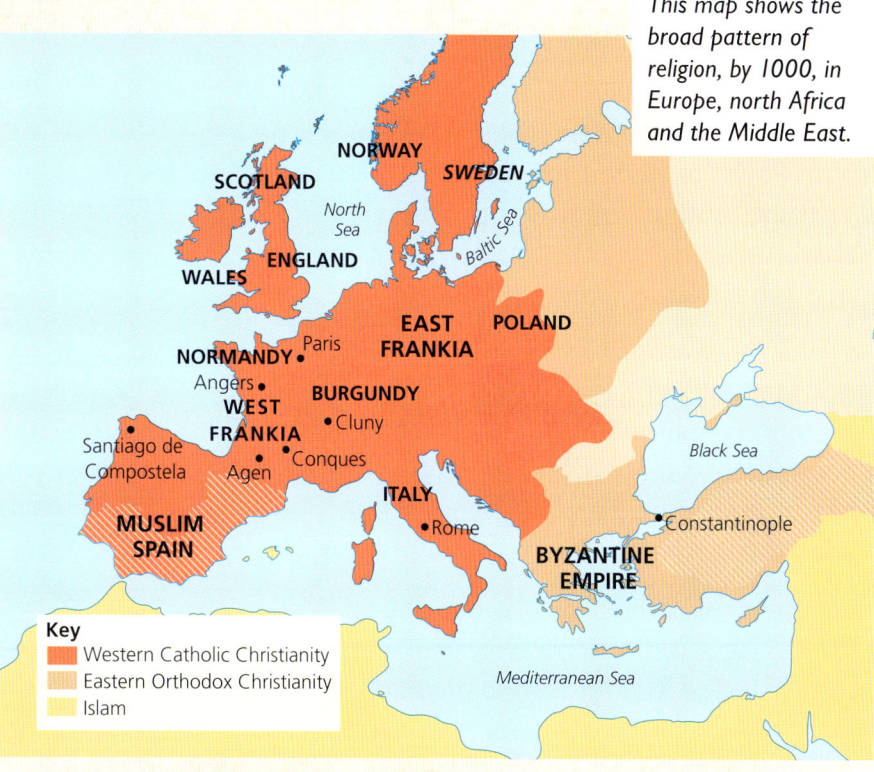

This map shows the broad pattern of religion, by 1000, in Europe, north Africa and the Middle East.

The monks were visiting Foy in 1013. This was the end of what used to be called the Dark Ages. Historians now call it the early medieval period. Lasting from the fifth century until 1000, this period gained the name 'Dark Ages' because of the chaos after the collapse of the Roman empire. In the last chapter, you read how the Arab Muslims tried to recover all the knowledge that was in danger of being lost in that chaotic time.

Historians studying western Christian Europe know less about this period than about other periods of European history because fewer sources from the period survived all the chaos. Nonetheless, historians do have various methods for studying the period. Many sources shed light on the so-called 'Dark' Ages.

One way that historians learn about the Christian worlds of western Europe in the period 500–1000 is by studying the stories which people told at the time about saints. Foy is a good example of this.

Fortunately, many of the stories told about Foy have survived. In fact, many were written down by one of the monks whom you have just read about. His name was Bernard of Angers. These stories can be puzzling. Some contain details that are almost certainly not true. Yet from these written sources about saints, together with buildings, statues and precious objects, historians can learn much about what Christians believed, how they practised their faith, how they showed devotion to the saints and what it all meant to them in their medieval world.

Your enquiry

You are going to learn how historians can use small stories to shed light on much bigger ones. You will use the story of Saint Foy to understand western Christianity during the early medieval period. As you read about Saint Foy, you will record information about western Christian worlds in a spider diagram. Then you will reorganise your notes to answer the enquiry question: What light can one saint's story shed on western Christian worlds?

The story of Foy's life and death

Foy was probably born in around 290. She lived in Agen – now in south-west France but then part of the Roman empire. We know little about Foy's life. According to later stories, she was the beautiful daughter of a Roman official. What made Foy special, however, was not her life, but her death.

Foy's family were pagans. They worshipped Roman gods. But Foy did not. As a child, she had made a dangerous decision. She had become a Christian. At that time, Christians were often persecuted. They were hunted down, tortured and killed.

Historians think that Foy was caught up in one of these persecutions, possibly in 303. Brought before a judge, she refused to give up her beliefs. She refused to take part in pagan rituals. When she refused to make a sacrifice to a Roman goddess, Foy was tortured by being held over burning coals. She was then dragged to a nearby temple and beheaded. She was twelve.

From cult to church: Christianity changes

After Foy died, the Roman empire changed dramatically:

The **first dramatic event** came in the early fourth century. For the very first time, the Roman emperor Constantine allowed Christians to worship freely. By 380, Christianity was the official religion of the Roman empire.

The **second dramatic event** came in 395. The Roman empire split in two! The western empire was ruled from Rome. The eastern empire (later known as the Byzantine empire) was ruled from Constantinople.

The **third dramatic event** came in the fifth century. The western Roman empire collapsed! Non-Roman tribes, known as barbarians, attacked Rome itself in 410. After 476, there were no more western Roman emperors.

Then something surprising happened. Although the western Roman empire collapsed, the Christian church did not. Instead, it continued to spread. And as Christianity grew, it changed.

1 Changing buildings

Early Christians had met secretly but once they could worship freely, they built churches. They built churches on the sites of Roman temples or over saints' tombs. So many churches covered western Europe that in the 790s one Christian scholar boasted, 'Europe is as bright with churches as the sky with stars'.

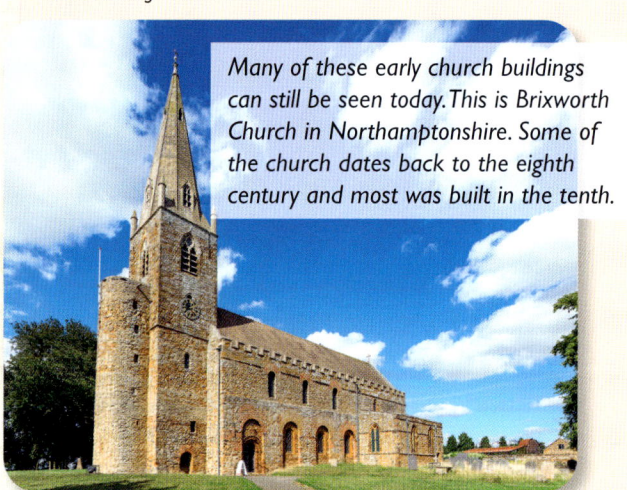

Many of these early church buildings can still be seen today. This is Brixworth Church in Northamptonshire. Some of the church dates back to the eighth century and most was built in the tenth.

2 Changing organisation

As Christianity spread, it became more organised. By 800, western Europe was covered with parishes. A parish was a small area, usually a village, led by a priest. Priests had special powers and duties. Only priests could lead the ritual known as the Mass. In the Mass, Christians believed that bread and wine, although still looking and tasting like bread and wine, became Jesus's body and blood. Only priests could hear Christians confess their sins and assure them that their sins were forgiven. Bishops led groups of parishes, called dioceses. Leading them all was the Pope in Rome.

This thirteenth-century painting shows a priest celebrating Mass. He offers up the bread to God. Christians believe that the night Jesus shared his last meal with his friends, he said, 'Take this bread. This is my body'.

3 Changing ways of life

During the fourth century, in Egypt, Palestine and Syria, a new way of living as a Christian emerged. Monks and nuns gave up ordinary family life. They lived simply, following strict rules and spending their time in prayer and work. Some, called hermits, lived alone. Others lived in communities known as monasteries or convents. Monks and nuns cared for travellers, the sick and the poor. Many were also scholars who encouraged learning. By 800, monasteries and convents were scattered across western Europe.

In the early sixth century, a monk called Benedict wrote rules for monks, which later became known as 'the Rule of St Benedict'. This picture, made in 1129, shows him giving his rules to his monks.

4 Changing beliefs

When people converted to Christianity, they didn't always forget all their old ways. Pagan and Christian ideas and rites mixed together to form new religious beliefs and practices. Ideas about saints are a good example of this.

People who died for their faith, like Foy, were known as martyrs. By the fifth century, Christians began to call these martyrs, saints. People who lived unusually holy lives were sometimes called saints, too. Over time, Christians started to believe that saints had supernatural powers, including:

- the power to talk to God directly on other Christians' behalf
- the power to work miracles.

For all these reasons, Christians began to pray to the saints, and revere them. To revere someone is to honour, admire and respect them. Books called hagiographies were written about the lives of saints. The story of Foy's death comes from her hagiography. Hagiographies were used to teach Christians how to live. Saints' deaths started to be remembered on special feast days. Saints' tombs soon became shrines, special places where Christians could show their devotion. Christians would go on long pilgrimages to visit shrines of favourite saints. At the shrine, pilgrims offered jewellery, money or land in return for a saint's help or protection, just as they had once made offerings to pagan gods.

These relics were kept in jars or, later on, in ornate boxes called reliquaries, like this one.

Step 1

It's time to start collecting information about early medieval Christianity. On a large page, draw a spider diagram like this. Decide which of these boxes your information should go in. Then record it in that box using notes and drawings. We have started one box, on 'heaven and hell', for you.

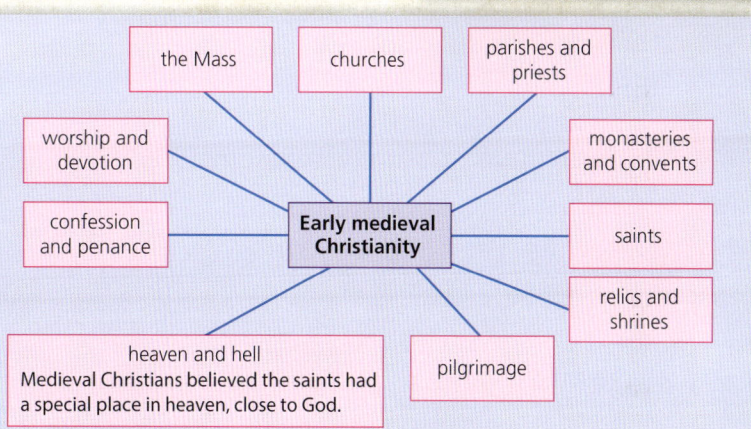

Early medieval Christianity:
- the Mass
- churches
- parishes and priests
- worship and devotion
- monasteries and convents
- confession and penance
- saints
- relics and shrines
- heaven and hell — Medieval Christians believed the saints had a special place in heaven, close to God.
- pilgrimage

The ninth century: monks come to Conques

200 kilometres away from Foy's resting place in Agen lay the little village of Conques. Historians think that the first settlers in Conques were probably Roman Christians.

But in the **fourth** century (around the time that Foy was martyred) **disaster struck**. Conques's little church was destroyed by pagans, who massacred the small Christian community.

In the **sixth** century, **disaster struck** again. The rebuilt church was destroyed by the Franks, one of the barbarian tribes who had overrun the Roman empire from the fifth century onwards.

In the **eighth** century **disaster struck again**! The church was destroyed by Arab Muslim invaders from north Africa who had conquered Spain in the seventh century and were now pushing north into southern France.

And so it was that, sometime at the beginning of the ninth century, a lone traveller gazed at the valley spread out below him. It was perfect.

Lush vegetation, fed by a small freshwater spring, covered the steep hillside. Far below, thick mist hid the valley floor. On one side of the valley, bathed in bright sunshine, he could just pick out the ruins of a few buildings.

The traveller's name was Dado. How had he come to be in this place? Dado had been fighting the Muslim invaders in southern France. The Muslims had captured his mother and offered to trade her for his war horse, but Dado had refused to sacrifice his horse. His mother was killed in front of him. Overcome with shame, Dado had given up everything, including home, friends and family, and become a hermit. He lived alone in the forests, praying and doing penance for his terrible sin. Now he wanted to serve God even more, by founding a **monastery**.

Dado breathed in the fresh, cool air of the valley. It was just the place that he was looking for. He would call it Conques, because the valley was shaped like a mussel shell – a *conche*. It would be a place of peace and beauty, work and learning, reverence and devotion. It would be a place of safety in a violent and uncertain world.

Struggle for survival

Dado founded his monastery at Conques in around 801. Like many monasteries, it was small and struggled to survive. By the ninth century, churches were supported by a tax called the tithe that everyone paid. But monasteries relied on gifts of money and land to survive. With so many monasteries seeking gifts, how could Conques compete?

Conques needed to become **famous**.

Map showing pilgrimage routes across Europe.

If only Conques were famous, thought Dado. If only. Rich families would give money and land! They would send their children to become monks! Pilgrims would travel there, bringing gifts with their devotions. The more famous Conques became, the bigger the gifts it could attract. And the one thing that would make the monastery really famous? Relics.

The monks of Conques already boasted that Charlemagne, the most powerful Frankish king of the age, had helped found their monastery. They had this special relic made, which the monks claimed that Charlemagne had given them. Pilgrims travelled from far and wide to see it.

A search for a special relic

But to survive, Conques needed to attract the pilgrims passing through on their way to the famous shrine at Santiago de Compostela in Spain. Pilgrims would stop off at well-known shrines along the route. You can see on the map that one of these pilgrimage routes ran right through Conques. But its relics were not special enough for pilgrims to stop there.

There was another reason the monks at Conques wanted a special relic. During the ninth century, the countryside of southern France had become a lawless place. Kings had grown weak and so powerful local lords did largely as they pleased. And what pleased them was fighting. They built castles, attacked other castles, raided the land for crops, stole treasures from churches and monasteries and held people to ransom. But while peasants could flee, and churches could beg bishops for protection, monasteries could not. They needed supernatural protection. They needed a saint.

The monks hatched a plan. If they could not find the relics of a saint, they would just have to steal them. And the relics they had set their sights on...? Foy's.

Step 2

Using pages 20 to 21, choose more details for your spider diagram. For example, you can add detail on tithes to the 'churches' box. You can write about gifts in the 'monasteries and convents' box.

Foy comes to Conques

The monks at Conques believed that if Foy wanted to come to Conques, she would allow her bones to be stolen. But her tomb in Agen's church was well-guarded, so the monks had to plan their theft with great care. They chose Arinisdus, a clever and careful monk, to be their thief. In 866, Arinisdus travelled to Agen, disguised as a priest. He joined the local religious community that served the church. For ten years, Arinisdus worked in the church. For ten years, he worked to win the locals' trust. For ten years, he waited.

Finally, Arinisdus was made guardian of the church's treasure. Finally, his chance had come. 200 years later, a monk from Conques wrote down the story. As you read, look for all the words which show Arinisdus's devotion to Foy:

At daybreak, the alarm was raised. Someone noticed that the guardian of the treasury was missing. The tomb was empty! The people of Agen turned on their priests in fury. How could they have trusted a stranger with their most precious treasure?! They swore a terrible revenge: when the thief was caught, he would be blinded, then hanged.

A search party set out in hot pursuit. The terrified Arinisdus fled homewards. When news reached Conques that he was on his way, the monks and people of the village walked out to meet him. As soon as they caught sight of Arinisdus, they rushed towards him. Amid a great throng of people, praising God in hymns and psalms, Foy's bones were borne into the church in a joyous procession.

> While they lingered over their festive meal for a long time, Arinisdus, who placed his trust not in himself but in the Lord, approached the sacred virgin's burial place. But the covering stone remained immobile because it was held firmly in place by iron seals. Arinisdus didn't know how to lift it intact, so he struck it at the foot. The tomb partly opened and he very carefully gathered up the most sacred body. Lifting it out of the tomb very reverently, he put it into a small sack that was very clean, exalting and magnifying God. After this, Arinisdus waited tensely for the silence of the night. Then he summoned his companion for the journey and, taking their divine gift, they set out swiftly for home.
>
> From Sainte Foy's Translation, written by a monk from Conques between 1020 and 1060.

Foy gets a new home

The monks at Conques wanted a spectacular home for their special saint. At the end of the ninth century, they made the beautiful **reliquary** statue that you saw on page 16. The body was made of wood, possibly by a local shoemaker. The head was taken from an old Roman statue. Both were covered in gold. Pilgrims gave Foy jewels, which were later added to the reliquary.

As the news of the daring theft spread across France, crowds of pilgrims began to throng the old monastic church. Donations of money and land came pouring in. The monks had achieved their goal: Conques was famous.

Now there was a new problem. The abbey church was too small! So, between 940 and 980, the monks built a bigger church. But it was *still* too small for all the pilgrims who wanted to see the bones of the famous child saint. So, between 1050 and 1100 an even bigger church was built. You can see it on this page.

At the same time as Conques church was being rebuilt, many churches in western Europe were being built in the same new style. It is called Romanesque because builders copied the round arches of the Romans. This design made it possible to build bigger, taller buildings.

Step 3

Using pages 22 to 23, add some more details to your spider diagram. Which boxes are relevant this time? Can you add any detail to boxes in which you have already written?

Later, in the early 1100s, a stone carving was added above the entrance door. Most people could not read, so churches used images like these to teach Christian beliefs. The carving shows what early medieval Christians believed. To them, the spiritual world was as real as the everyday world in which they lived.

This side shows **a world of peace and order**. Those chosen by God to spend eternity in Heaven are approaching Jesus on his throne. Among them are the Virgin Mary, St Peter, Dado the Hermit, an **abbot**, and the emperor Charlemagne. Find St Foy, kneeling. God's hand reaches towards her.

On the far right of the picture, we see a **world of chaos and terror**. This is hell, where devils and demons torture the damned. Find the greedy monks and a war-like lord.

In the centre, separating the saved from the damned, is Jesus himself. Below him, an angel and devil weigh the souls of the dead. This picture conveyed both terror and hope. It reminded people that by hearing their confessions and praying for their souls, the Church could save sinners from a terrible fate.

Before they visited the shrine, pilgrims would have marvelled at the nave, supported by 212 graceful arches, soaring towards heaven. At the far end of the nave, pilgrims strained forward to catch a glimpse of the reliquary. The reliquary was protected by an iron gate. This gate was made from the chains of former prisoners who had been freed with Saint Foy's miraculous help. At her shrine, pilgrims lit candles, prayed, and left gifts.

Foy's fame spreads

Yet it was not the reliquary or abbey church that brought so many pilgrims to Conques. It was Foy's miracles. In 983 one miracle made Foy *really* famous. A poor servant, blinded by his cruel master, had his eyes put back in after Foy visited him in a vision.

News of the miracle spread. More pilgrims flocked to Foy's shrine. She cured sick animals, raised the dead and broke the chains of slaves. She was known to love jewellery and so pilgrims brought her gold and precious stones. But Foy was also feared. She punished those who wronged her, haunting them in visions or even bringing about their death. People who sinned by being greedy, or unfaithful, were especially likely to be punished. Not all her miracles were life-changing, however. She helped and punished people in much smaller ways. Local people called these miracles Foy's jokes. Here is one story:

A merchant came to Saint Foy to offer prayers. He noticed that there was a very brisk trade in wax, and, with such a throng of pilgrims offering candles, the price seemed too low to him. At once, the merchant remembered the skill for which he was known as a businessman and thought to himself, 'What an easy profit! How stupid I am! If I had learned this before I could have put my business on a sound footing and made myself rich! But now I'll make up for my ignorance! Frequent trips to and from Conques will make me a wealthy man in no time! It's time to act like a man and get this business underway.'

And so the merchant approached the wax seller, made a hard bargain for a great quantity of wax, and paid just ten gold coins for it. Then he took possession of all the wax and stored it in sacks. And he was already rejoicing, for he saw that his profit would be at least four times what he had paid.

But now let's get to the ending quickly. A beautiful candle had been left out because it didn't fit in the merchant's sacks. The greedy man slipped it into his clothing in such a way that the larger part of it projected below his belt and the smaller part jutted up toward his beard through the opening in his garment. But the avenging power of all-seeing God didn't allow the robber's wicked deeds to stay hidden. For the wax taper held beneath his belt was suddenly set afire by divine flame and began to scorch him badly beneath his garments. Steam, belching flames and billows of smoke poured out. Then a ball of flashing sparks hurled itself upward, his huge beard blazed, and, with a crackling sound, the hair on his head was consumed. Nor were the flames confined to the front of his body: they encircled him and burned his backside. Calling out loudly, he ran at once to Foy's tomb and dumped all his wax there. Just as swiftly, the fire vanished.

A story from the Book of Miracles, *written by Bernard of Angers in the early 1000s.*

Step 4

Using pages 23 to 25, add some more details to your spider diagram.

Foy's story is told

By the eleventh century, Foy's shrine was famous across France and beyond. But not everyone was convinced by the stories of her miracles. One person who had doubts was the monk whom we met at the beginning of our story, Bernard of Angers. Look back at the source on page 16. What did he think about all the people showing devotion to Foy?

Bernard was a monk and a scholar. At the time, there were no universities. Instead, monastic and church schools were the main centres of learning in western Europe. Bernard had studied at an important church school in Paris. Like many educated monks and priests Bernard worried that ordinary people's ideas about God were incorrect. When he heard about the crowds of pilgrims showing such reverence to Foy's reliquary statue, Bernard was horrified. He feared people were turning back to the old pagan ways:

> To learned people this may seem to be full of superstition, if not unlawful, for it seems as if the rites of the gods of ancient cultures, or rather the rites of demons, are being observed.

From the Book of Miracles, written by Bernard of Angers in the early 1000s.

Bernard decided to find out what was going on. He set out with a companion for Conques in 1013. As we have seen, at first, Bernard mocked those who knelt before Foy's reliquary. Then he changed his mind.

He started to regret having doubts:

> In truth my empty talk and small-mindedness at this time did not arise from a good heart. For the holy image is consulted not as an idol that requires sacrifices, but because it commemorates a martyr. Since reverence to Foy honours God on high, it was despicable of me to compare her statue to statues of Venus or Diana. Afterwards I was very sorry that I had acted so foolishly toward God's saint.

From the Book of Miracles, written by Bernard of Angers in the early 1000s.

The monks of Conques invited Bernard to stay with them. They brought him witnesses to Foy's miracles and begged him to write down their stories. Bernard did: 49 in total. After he died, two other monks added to the stories. They were collected together in a book called *The Miracles of Saint Foy*. The picture and source extracts on this page are from this book. Can you find Foy in the picture? She is shown as St Fides, which is Latin for 'faith'. Books like this were made in monasteries across Europe. Stories from the books were read aloud during church services, and on special occasions such as the saint's feast day. Priests used them to

Detail from the Book of the Miracles of Saint Faith, Bibliothèque Humaniste de Sélestat.

remind Christians of God's power in the world, and of how to live a good Christian life.

In many ways, the fourth-century Saint Foy and the eleventh-century Bernard of Angers shared the same Christian world. Both lived in the same region of western Europe. Both were Christians. But the worlds in which they lived were not exactly the same. The western Christian world at the end of the first millennium was different from the western Christian world of the late Roman empire. (And both were different again from the Christian world of the Byzantine empire!)

These worlds are hard to uncover. They are interesting but strange. Historians need to use many types of source and to keep asking questions about what things meant at the time. How many different kinds of sources have we used in this chapter to tell Saint Foy's story?

Shaping your answer

Saint Foy feels like one very small story. Yet learning about how medieval people treated Foy has helped you understand something much bigger: western, medieval Christian worlds. Through our focus on Saint Foy – the places she was taken and the people who loved or feared her – you have thought about what Christians did and believed, what they could see around them and what it all meant to them. You are now going to re-organise your notes in short summaries which answer our enquiry question: What light can one saint's story shed on western Christian worlds?

In each 'ray of light', write a short summary about that aspect of the medieval western Christian world. Then for each one, choose two or three relevant examples from your spider diagram which are connected with stories about Saint Foy.

In each 'ray of light' you might include sentences such as these:

- From stories about Saint Foy, we can learn how Christians… . For example …,
- This written source (or this building, relic, statue…) about Saint Foy tells us that…
- From Saint Foy's story, historians could work out how Christians…

…how the western Christian world was **organised**?

…how Christians **behaved**?

…what the western Christian world **looked like**?

…what Christians **believed**?

What light can one saint's story shed on…

4 A conquered England

How disruptive were the Normans?

Duke William prepares

The army of William Duke of Normandy poured out of 700 ships onto a wide shingle beach. Thousands of soldiers and hundreds of horses had crossed the rough sea. The place was Pevensey, on England's south coast. The day was 28 September 1066. The invasion of England was underway.

The Normans soon found the perfect spot to build a castle. They chose the site of an old Roman fort. They had even cut the wood, in preparation, before leaving Normandy.

No preparation was complete, however, without God's blessing. Just before leaving Normandy, William and his wife Matilda had given a precious gift to the Church. The gift would secure God's support for the invasion.

The gift was William and Matilda's own daughter. They had given her to a monastery. For William, invading England was a holy mission. The Pope himself had blessed it.

The Normans recorded this story in a long piece of embroidery – the Bayeux Tapestry. In this image, the Normans chop wood and build boats. The image below shows their landing at Pevensey.

William wanted England very badly. One of the richest and most organised lands in western Europe, England was a great prize for whoever could take her. And so many had tried! For two hundred years, Viking armies, sailing from Scandinavia, had invaded England.

But this time, the invaders came from the south, from Normandy.

King Harold prepares

England's King Harold, like William, was also a brilliant military leader. When William invaded, Harold had only been king for nine months. He had been crowned in January, straight after the death of the old and childless king, Edward the Confessor. As a highly respected leader, Harold was the nobles' natural choice for king.

Like William, Harold had a superb army. Like William, Harold was well prepared.

Your enquiry

When the Normans built on that old Roman fort, they were already using what they found in England. Again and again, in this enquiry, you will see how the Normans built on things which existed before 1066. So in some ways, the Normans changed little. Yet in other ways, they changed a great deal. This is why historians argue about how disruptive the Norman Conquest really was.

As you read about Norman England between 1066 and 1087, look both for change and continuity. You can then build an answer to the question: How disruptive were the Normans in England?

English spies had told Harold that William was coming. Harold now gathered the largest army that England had ever seen.

All summer, along the south coast, Harold's army waited. But William did not come. Without the right wind, William's 700 ships could not sail.

Then suddenly, Harold had terrible news. A Viking army had landed near York! This Viking army was led by yet another remarkable military leader, the Norwegian Harald Hardrada. Hardrada meant 'hard ruler'. Harald Hardrada had served the Byzantine emperor in Constantinople, leading the highly-trained Varangian Guard. This was a threat that Harold could not ignore. Harold had to march 300 miles north.

On this map, follow the story of what happened next.

1 Harold marched his army northwards to meet the Vikings.

2 Harold met the Vikings at the Battle of Stamford Bridge. It was a great victory for the English. The Viking leader was killed.

3 Straight after the battle, Harold received news. The Normans had landed on the south coast. With no time to recover, Harold's forces had to march south. Many English foot-soldiers were too exhausted to keep up.

A shocking battle

Shortly after sunrise on 14 October, two huge armies met in a marshy area, north of Hastings. The English army stood high on a ridge. The Bayeux Tapestry shows the English in a strong position behind a solid wall of shields.

All day, the armies clashed. For hours, the English held their ground. Then the battle turned against the English. According to some sources, a rumour that William had been killed caused the Normans to retreat. Some English soldiers then left their shield wall and chased the retreating Normans down the hill. That gave the Normans an idea: the Normans *pretended* to retreat again. Now more English left their shield wall to chase the Normans. Having left their strong position on the hill, the English were fatally weakened.

Even after Harold was killed, the English fought on. As darkness fell, thousands lay dead, including many of England's most powerful noblemen.

The English lords submit

For two weeks, William waited for the surviving English lords to submit to him. When many refused, William marched his troops around the outside of London, violently crushing all opposition as he went. He was trying to convince the English to give in.

By December, they had. A sad little band of English bishops and earls met William outside London. There they surrendered. The chief citizens of London handed over the keys of the city.

A new king, a new England?

Crowning the king

William wanted to be crowned King of England in the traditional English way. He wanted to show that he was the true successor to Edward the Confessor.

On Christmas Day 1066, accompanied by his leading Normans, William rode solemnly through London to Westminster Abbey. As they rode through the streets, some London citizens showed their anger. Others stood sullenly by.

Westminster Abbey was the magnificent new church built by the old king, Edward the Confessor. Perfect for the occasion, Edward had built it in the new Romanesque style that was becoming popular back in Normandy. Harold had been crowned here only a year before. Westminster Abbey would have looked something like this image of Durham Cathedral. Huge columns supported rows of round arches.

Inside the abbey, the leading Normans and Englishmen had gathered. The **Archbishop** of York made a speech. He asked the English if they would have William as their king. The English all shouted, 'We will!'. Then a Norman bishop asked the Normans the same question. They, too, shouted for William. The Archbishop then made William swear a solemn **oath** that he would rule England fairly and respect its laws. Finally, he placed the crown on William's head.

Outside the abbey, Norman soldiers heard the shouting. They thought that William was being murdered. In their panic and rage, they began to kill Londoners and to set fire to houses.

Spreading the word across England

To complete his conquest, William had to bring his new lands fully under his control. Some great English lords had survived the Battle of Hastings, so William quickly invited them to join his royal court.

William also got to work writing charters. Charters were promises that William would rule England fairly, with as little change as possible from Edward's reign. At the foot of this page, you can see the London Charter. This granted London citizens the same rights that they had enjoyed under Edward.

These charters were written in English, by the same people who had written charters for King Edward. They were spread around England by the same officials that had helped Edward and Harold to rule – the sheriffs. William wanted English people to see the old ways of government continuing. William hoped that all this would reassure the English, so that he could control England without too much more violence.

He was wrong. The violence had barely begun.

Step 1

Make some notes in your own copy of this table. For Column 1, find examples of how the Normans disrupted England. For Column 2, find examples of how Norman rule continued English ways.

What was disruptive?	What was not so disruptive?
England's King Harold was killed.	William used charters, just as Edward had done.

Gaining control

Taxing the English

At the start of 1067, William sailed back to Normandy. There William was reunited with Matilda, his wife. Matilda had governed Normandy while William was away. Meanwhile, William left England in the control of his most loyal supporters, his half-brother, Bishop Odo, and his cousin, William FitzOsbern. The English hated both of them.

The English were already angry because William was imposing very high taxes. It was his way of making the English buy back their own land. High taxes were common before the Conquest, but we know from a long record kept by monks, called the Anglo-Saxon Chronicle, that English people expressed great anger at William's taxes.

This map shows the major castles built by 1086. Sites for big castles, such as Chepstow, were carefully chosen. You can tell from this map which areas William considered the most dangerous.

Building castles

The Anglo-Saxon Chronicle also recorded English anger at all the castles that the Normans started to build. A castle was a military base from which soldiers controlled the land. Sometimes, hundreds of English homes were destroyed to build these castles, leaving English people homeless. Towering over local buildings, castles became hated symbols of Norman power.

At first, castles were built quickly from earth and timber. But in dangerous places, in the larger towns and at important river crossings, the Normans built in stone.

Early in William's reign, stone castles like this one in Chepstow were springing up. Chepstow Castle was built high on a cliff above the River Wye. At its centre was a strong stone keep. Horses and soldiers were kept in the outer courtyard, or bailey.

The English resistance

In 1069, the resistance began. Many English lords felt that William was not sticking to his promise to keep the laws of King Edward. Rebel English lords began to plan their resistance.

Each time the English rebelled, the Normans sent soldiers to crush them. The Normans then built yet more castles. But big **rebellions** were still a huge threat, and the bigger the rebellion, the more brutal William's response.

Most brutal of all was his response to what happened in Yorkshire …

The Harrying of the North

In 1069, in York, an uprising began. The rebels quickly took control of York's new Norman castle. Soon, a Viking army joined with the rebels. Together they killed hundreds of Normans. It seemed as though the whole of the north was about to throw William out.

First, William paid the Vikings to go away. Then, he did something so brutal that it became known as the 'Harrying of the North'. Even by the violent standards of the time, it was horrifying. Across Yorkshire, Norman soldiers burned villages and crops. They slaughtered thousands of people. They even destroyed farm animals and tools so as to stop villages recovering. Thousands starved to death. Some areas took decades to recover.

The Normans now built so many castles that they formed a vast network of control that would be very hard to undo. In rebellious areas, the Normans built enough castles to have them just one day's march apart (about 22 miles). William also now replaced even those English lords, whom he had once trusted, with Norman ones. William's control of the north was now even stronger than Edward's or Harold's had been.

But one last corner of the country fought on. This last rebellion took place in the watery land of the Fens. We cannot be sure what happened, but here is one story:

Here is how one famous monk, Orderic Vitalis, described the Harrying of the North 50 years later:

> Never before did William commit so much cruelty. He set no bounds to his fury, but ordered corn, cattle, tools and every sort of food to be collected in heaps and burned to ashes. Innocent children, young men and old, died of hunger. I have praised William often, but I dare not praise him for a deed which brought all, good and bad, to one ruin. God will punish him.

Orderic Vitalis wrote this in the early twelfth century. Born in 1075, in Shropshire, Orderic Vitalis was son of a Norman and an Englishwoman. He was given to a French monastery, aged 10. He used Norman sources but wrote from an English perspective.

Capturing the Fens

The Fens of East Anglia were dangerous. For miles lay nothing but marshy lakes and rivers. Only those who knew the secret tracks could cross. Amid these wild wetlands lay a small rocky hill called the island of Ely. Here, in an ancient abbey, the monks lived out their lives in prayer.

And it was here that the last English rebels gathered. Many were famous fighters. Songs told of their bravery. The most feared of all was Hereward the Wake. In later years, Fenland people told stories of Hereward fighting twelve men at once with his sword 'Brainbiter'.

The first time the Normans came, they were not ready for the Fens. They built a wooden path across the marsh, but it sank under their weight. The Normans drowned in the dark, soft mud. Behind abbey walls, the monks thanked God.

The Normans tried again, but Hereward set fire to the dry reeds.

Yet some monks became frightened. Secretly, they helped the Normans find a way in. When the Normans reached Ely, they slaughtered all Hereward's men.

Hereward fled without trace.

Step 2

Re-read pages 31 to 32. Choose more points for the columns in your table. For example, how was farming disrupted in the north? What would this have meant for food? (Tip: you may want to write something about taxes in both columns!)

Owning the land

The monarch and the land

After the big rebellions in Yorkshire and Ely, William was much less willing to let great English lords keep their lands. Those English earls who had shouted for William in Westminster Abbey were not welcome to share power now! William gave nearly all their land to his chief Norman **barons**, bishops and abbots. If anywhere else were to rebel, these leading nobles could help crush rebels fast. He also reduced the number of powerful landowners. He wanted to give land to so few people that he could look into their eyes and decide to trust them.

These leading nobles were William's 'tenants-in-chief'. They were called '**tenants**' because the land was still William's. He could take it back at any time. William gave himself much more power over land than previous kings of England. If a powerful lord died, his son even had to pay William to receive his lands.

Tenants-in-chief provided **knights** and other soldiers whenever William needed them. Of just over 1000 tenants-in-chief, fewer than 60 were English by 1086. Very few were women, but some English women did marry Norman lords.

These tenants-in-chief parcelled out land to sub-tenants, such as knights, leading townspeople or senior churchmen. The sub-tenants gave loyalty, rent and services, especially military service, to the tenants-in-chief.

Many sub-tenants were still English but, overall, the English had lost control of their country. By 1086, English landowners owned just 8 per cent of all England's wealth.

Just how big a change was this?

Historians have long argued about this. The link between lordship and land, at every level of society, was certainly not new! The historian Stephen Baxter, however, who has studied landholding in detail, argues that in one important way the change was huge. King Edward had owned vast amounts of land, but now the entire kingdom belonged to the king and every single person held their land from that king. This, says Stephen Baxter, was new.

The peasants and the land

If we want to decide just how much change English people experienced overall, however, we must move beyond the lords. The sub-tenants managed the land, but they did not do the back-breaking daily work. That work fell to the other 97 per cent of the population, the peasantry. Of roughly two million people in England, the vast majority were peasants. Did the Normans disrupt peasant lives, too?

Let's look closely at one village, the village of Bourn, which lies to the west of Cambridge, a day's ride from Ely. After studying the sources, Stephen Baxter concluded:

Stephen Baxter at work in the archives.

> The twenty years from 1066 to 1086 was one of the most calamitous periods in the history of medieval Bourn.

We have used Stephen Baxter's research to tell Bourn's story...

People of the land

The village of Bourn, February 1067

Nine miles south of Cambridge, hamlets sprawl across a gently sloping valley. Across the lower slopes, teams of oxen and horses drag their ploughs through clay soil. Higher up, where elm, ash and poplar trees crown the hilltops, no ploughs can be seen. Here and there, the trees peter out, revealing patches of rough pasture where sheep, horses and cattle feed.

Down below, along the valley bottom, runs a ribbon of water. This is Bourn Brook.

Bourn is home to about 360 people. These people's ancestors did the back-breaking work of settling the land. They felled trees and dug root-tangled soil, clearing the land for planting crops on the lower slopes and for grazing higher up. To survive, a village needs both land for crops and pasture for animals. Animals bring power. Animals pull carts and ploughs. Bourn has about 100 oxen, enough for 12 plough-teams.

No hedges divide the vast fields where crops are grown. Yet the land dips, in places, for tiny streams, each draining into Bourn Brook below. One stream turns the heavy wheel in a mill where grain is ground into flour.

The plough-teams move up and down, up and down, on little strips of land. About 40 such strips are arranged side by side, in blocks called furlongs. In spring, some will be sown with wheat, others with dredge (a mix of oats and barley) and others will be left fallow to rest. People reach their strips on grassy tracks between the furlongs.

Each strip must be sixteen and a half feet wide. The village reeve has checked this with a long pole. Most strips point downwards towards Bourn Brook. Their patchwork pattern sinks, climbs and rolls with the lie of the land.

And just as the lie of the land shapes each field, so the land shapes each peasant's life. Living in humble cottages are slaves, bordars, cottars and **villans**. Slaves own nothing and have no freedom at all. Each bordar or cottar farms just enough strips to feed a family but must also work their lord's land for three days a week, for no pay. Villans, too, work the lord's land, but some farm enough strips to make a little extra to sell.

Villans, bordars and cottars must ask their lord's permission for many things, from felling a tree to marrying. None may leave the village without their lord's consent. All are tied to the land.

Who are the lords of these peasant farmers? Owning almost half the village is a proud English lord, Almaer of Bourn. Almaer holds land outside of Bourn too. Almaer has a fine timber house, with a church. Almaer even has a kitchen.

Almaer relies on the protection of a great lady called Eadgifu the Fair. She is one of the wealthiest landowners in England.

But other English lords hold land in Bourn too. The Abbot of Ramsey (who lives thirty miles away) has a little land here, and so do two priests. These priests can read and write. The priests also know some Latin, the language of prayers said on Sunday, the only day of rest.

Yet Almaer and these churchmen hold only half the village's land. The rest is held by twenty freemen and sokemen. These, the highest-ranking peasant farmers, are free – free to leave the village, make money, sell land and marry whom they please.

Each of these free peasants has been 'commended' to an important lord. They must perform duties, such as lending their carts and ploughs, or representing their lords in meetings and courts, but in return, they and their land are protected. During the time of King Edward, these freemen of Bourn were commended to some of England's most powerful lords – the Abbot of Ramsey, the Earl of Mercia, the Archbishop of Canterbury, Eadgifu the Fair (the second richest woman in England) and even King Edward himself.

During the cold winter months, the villagers fell ash trees to mend the shafts and axles of their ploughs. They chop elm wood to repair their houses, cartwheels, benches and stools. With supple twigs of willow, they make baskets. Now that the warmth of spring beckons, they prepare to sow seeds.

Meanwhile, word reaches Bourn of trouble. Foreign soldiers, once again, march in England. Not Vikings from the north, but soldiers from the south. Normans.

What will this mean for Almaer?

For the priests?

For free peasants?

For slaves?

The village of Bourn, February 1087

Twenty years have passed. Land, water, trees and animals still shape the peasants' worlds. The ploughmen still know the tiny folds in each slope. The villagers still hew wood, draw water and take grain to the mill. Sunday by Sunday, they still hear familiar prayers in church.

But in February 1087, the villagers' memories are full of trouble.

First, the soldiers came, thousands of them, on their way to crush the north. It was terrifying to watch them march by. Villagers now call the track running north of the village, 'Herestraat', which means, 'Army Road'.

A few years later, villagers returned from Cambridge market with worrying news. A Norman sheriff called Picot had taken control of Cambridge. Picot had forced the people of Cambridge to help build a castle, destroying houses and mills in the process. With foundations four metres deep, the castle's grim walls soon towered high above the town.

Cambridge people also grumbled that they had to lend their ploughs to Picot three times more often than they had had to do so for their former, English lords. The people of Bourn could only hope that Picot wouldn't come to Bourn.

But Picot did come to Bourn. Soon, Picot walked in Bourn's fields, surveying its land.

Before long, Bourn's peasants were felling trees to build a castle in Bourn itself. Picot is now building churches, too, including a large, expensive one in Cambridge, with six priests! Who pays for all this? The peasants of Bourn.

And do you remember those twenty free peasants? Picot has seized their land. It now belongs to his **manor**. These peasants have lost their freedom. They must pay Picot rent.

What happened to their protectors, the powerful English lords and ladies? They are all dead. Only the Abbot of Ramsey and Almaer have kept their land, although Almaer now holds his land from Count Alan of Brittany, William's trusted nobleman.

Perhaps one thing has improved: Bourn has fewer slaves than in 1066. Picot gets richer by turning slaves into peasants who pay rent.

How do we know about Bourn?

In 1085, William ordered a huge survey. Its remarkable scope and detail have astonished historians. William wanted to know about anything that created wealth:

- peasants
- animals
- plough-teams
- mills
- meadows
- trees.

First, information was collected from tax records and from landowners. Then, in meetings called shire courts, representatives from towns and villages answered questions. There, twelve jurors (six Norman, six English) swore that the information was true. Bourn's representatives attended a shire court in Cambridge castle. The survey's information ended up in this big book, Domesday Book. It shows historians who owned land both in the time of King Edward *and* in 1086.

Here is one of the Domesday Book entries that helped Stephen Baxter to find out what happened in Bourn. Can you find the words 'Picot', 'hide', 'bordar', 'vill' and 'car'? 'Car' is short for 'carruca', the Latin word for 'plough'.

Here it is in English. Use the glossary below to help you.

> Picot himself holds Bourn. It is assessed at 13 hides. There is land for 15 ploughs. In demesne are 5 hides, and there are 2 ploughs, and there can be 2 others. There are 8 villans with 4 bordars and 7 sokemen who hold 4 hides. They have 4 ploughs, and there can be 7 more. There are 13 cottars and 6 slaves, meadow for 15 ploughs, pasture for livestock of the vill, and a wood to repair fences and houses. In all it is worth £13; when received, £18; TRE £22.

A hide was a unit of taxation. Demesne meant the lord's land. A vill was a village. TRE stood for 'time of King Edward' (R stood for 'Rex', the Latin word for 'king').

Stephen Baxter used other sources, too, such as a book written by the monks of Ely. It seems that Picot stole goods and lands from the monks. He even insulted their much-loved patron saint, Æthelthryth. No wonder the monks described Picot as: 'a hungry lion, a prowling wolf, a crafty fox, a filthy pig, a shameless dog'.

Yet Stephen Baxter tells us that these twenty years may not have been so disruptive for *everyone* in Bourn. One juror at the Cambridgeshire court in 1086 was none other than Almaer.

Like many powerful Englishmen, it seems that Almaer learned how to gain rewards by cleverly fitting into William's new ways and serving his new Norman masters.

How typical was the disruption in Bourn?

Of course, Bourn was just one village. Let's fit Bourn into a bigger picture. Let's take a look at other places and at other kinds of change.

Other counties
In some counties, such as Bedfordshire or Hertfordshire, villages were like Bourn: free, land-owning peasants were forced into a lord's manor and lost freedom. In other counties, such as Kent or Norfolk, peasants just paid higher rents than before.

Other local officials
Other counties had sheriffs like Picot. The English were used to sheriffs, but William made them more powerful. The Normans kept other local officials, too, such as tax collectors and reeves. Most English people therefore kept old roles. Like Almaer, they began serving the Normans.

Other laws
William kept many English laws but made harsh new ones too. If a Norman was murdered, local people had to find the murderer or else pay a big fine – the Murdrum Fine. William also stopped the English hunting in royal forests. Punishments for theft were severe, including execution or chopping off a hand or two fingers.

Other types of settlement
Not all peasants lived in farming villages. About 10 per cent of English people lived in towns. The Conquest led to new trade between England and Normandy. As more goods were sold, towns could grow. Southern towns, especially London, grew fast and their people grew wealthier.

Step 3
Re-read pages 33 to 37. Choose more points for your two columns.

A religious revolution?

The Normans had their own ideas about saints. You have read how Picot upset Ely's monks by insulting their patron saint. Picot dedicated his new Cambridge church to his wife's favourite saint, Saint Giles. In some places, much-loved holy objects, precious to English people, were destroyed. In these ways, religious change crept across England.

But just how disruptive were Norman changes to the Church? The bigger picture is complicated. After all, there was nothing new about Christian ideas arriving from France! Let's follow just one story. You decide how far the Normans were changing things.

In the year 675, in Shropshire...

… a local lord founded Wenlock Abbey, a religious community of monks and nuns. They followed the Rule of St Benedict. This meant that they prayed nine times a day and took three vows: to own nothing, to stay celibate (unmarried) and to obey their abbot or abbess. They helped the poor and sheltered pilgrims.

After a few years, a royal princess called Mildburga became abbess. Mildburga worked tirelessly to convert all of Shropshire to Christianity. When Mildburga died in 727, stories spread. It was said that she made the blind see, the barley grow and the birds obey her. When a prince tried to force her into marriage, a river rose up to keep him away. One day, her veil slipped off. She found it hanging on a sunbeam.

A local bishop announced Mildburga a saint. Farmers, worshipping at her tomb, asked her blessing on their crops. Women trying to avoid marriage sought her help.

Yet the nuns' community did not last. During the tenth century, the nuns' church fell into ruins. Mildburga's burial place was forgotten.

In the year 910, in Burgundy...

… the Duke of Aquitaine gave some monks a gift of forests, vineyards, fields, streams and mills. The land came with peasants and slaves to work it. The place was Cluny. The Duke was founding a monastery. In return, the monks of Cluny prayed for the Duke and his family, asking God to forgive them their sins. These monks, too, followed St Benedict's Rule, taking vows of poverty, chastity and obedience. These monks, too, sheltered strangers and pilgrims.

But Cluny was different. This monastery was controlled by the Pope. And although each monk possessed nothing, the monastery was wealthy. Workers were hired to farm and cook so that the monks could devote themselves to prayer. Christian rulers gave Cluny money in order to be remembered in Cluny's endless prayers. At the mass, monks wearing silk offered bread and wine from vessels of gold. The beauty of their fine abbey inspired their worship.

The monks gathered ancient manuscripts. They copied out bibles and wrote the lives of saints. Year in, year out, they filled thick parchment pages with flowing script. Cluny's library became famous in Europe.

Soon the monks of Cluny founded other monasteries, all following St Benedict's Rule, all loyal to the Pope.

In 1079, in Shropshire…

…a Norman earl, Roger de Montgomery, was enjoying his new lands. But Roger had a problem. He had killed so many people! Although the Norman invasion had been blessed by the Pope, Christians still had to do penance for the sin of bloodshed.

Norman bishops announced the penance. For each man killed, the penance was fasting on bread and water for one year. How could Roger do this? England would come to a standstill!

The solution for Norman nobles like Roger was a monastery. Monks could do the penance for Roger. Monks could pray that he would go to heaven. There were other benefits too. Founding a monastery did not just save your soul; it showed you were important.

In 1083, Roger founded Shrewsbury Abbey. The locals were soon watching its Romanesque columns soar upwards. But Roger wanted more. His dream was a monastery modelled on the great Cluny.

A few miles from Shrewsbury lay Wenlock Abbey. Roger had found his site! A community of monks still lived there, but Roger's new monastery was not for local monks, and certainly not for nuns. Monks from Cluny arrived to set up the monastery. They called it Wenlock Priory. Locals muttered: who were these monks with their proud French ways?

In 1101, these Cluniac monks were in trouble. Roger had died. His heir had had all his land confiscated for rebelling against the king. What would happen to Wenlock Priory? How could the monks prove their right to stay? They needed a sign of God's approval.

In 1102, they found it. Or rather, they found her… in the ground. Saint Mildburga's remains. The monks lost no time. They wrote about Mildburga's miracles. They shared her stories. They carried Mildburga to a new resting place in Wenlock Priory.

Pilgrims soon came from England, Wales and France. Thanks to an English saint, a monastery founded by a Norman could stay.

Let's see how this story fits into England's bigger picture.

The Church and the Normans

Did you notice *when* Roger founded his monastery? Up until the 1080s, Norman nobles still felt attached to their Normandy homelands and built monasteries there. From the 1080s, however, they founded many English monasteries, all connected to networks of monasteries across Europe.

In 1070, William appointed his friend, Lanfranc, as Archbishop of Canterbury. Lanfranc wanted monasteries (instead of greedy local lords) to control the many new parish churches that the Normans were building. Lanfranc also wanted priests to behave like monks – wearing robes, not marrying; not hunting or getting drunk. Lanfranc wanted priests to look holy.

Before 1066, we know of only nine nunneries in England. While Wenlock Priory did not have nuns, more nunneries were appearing from the 1080s. Why did women become nuns? Both before and after 1066, some were given to religious communities as children, while others chose to join. After 1066, a new reason arose: some women became nuns so as to avoid marrying a Norman! In a letter, Lanfranc wrote of women who 'fled to a monastery, not for the love of religious life, but for fear of the French'.

Saints and the Normans

Christians had always argued about which saints were the best. Lanfranc now interfered in these arguments by ranking the churches according to which saints the Norman Church thought important. No wonder that from around 1070, stories about saints' miracles multiplied!

At the same time, the Normans still used saints to gain English support. Soon after William died in 1087, Norman lords built this mighty cathedral in Durham. It houses a shrine to St Cuthbert, England's most popular saint.

How was the Church ruled?

To answer this, let's study William's friend, Archbishop Lanfranc, and bring him to life a little.

Lanfranc was born in Italy and he didn't start life expecting to be England's archbishop. Brilliantly clever, he studied law. Years later, he taught in a cathedral school in Normandy.

In 1042, Lanfranc gave all this up to enter a poverty-stricken Benedictine monastery. For three years, Lanfranc hid himself away. But the Abbot persuaded Lanfranc to raise money for the monastery by opening a school. As a brilliant teacher and scholar, Lanfranc became well known.

The Pope admired Lanfranc, and so did an ambitious young William, Duke of Normandy. William needed the Pope's permission to marry his wife, Matilda. Lanfranc helped him. Lanfranc also secured the Pope's blessing for William's invasion. William was forever grateful.

At this time, the Pope was trying to reform the Church. By conquering England, the Normans were strengthening the Pope's power. Lanfranc further strengthened the Pope's power by introducing special church courts, free of royal control. So whose side was Lanfranc on? The Pope's or William's? This is a little complicated! But in any hint of conflict between William and the Pope, Lanfranc supported William.

The Church and slavery

Under Lanfranc, England's churchmen began to be more critical of the English slave trade. The Normans had mostly abandoned the practice of slavery before the Conquest, but it was still normal in England. In Bristol's slave markets, children could be seen roped together, ready for sale to Ireland. Yet by 1102, a church council was condemning 'that shameful trade by which in England people used to be sold like animals'.

Step 4

Continue your table using pages 38–40.

Shaping your answer

How disruptive were the Normans in England? It is time to shape your argument.

First, write an introduction.

Tell your reader that historians argue about how disruptive the Normans were. Then, tell your reader which topics you will write about.

Then, use your notes for each Step to plan your main paragraphs.

For example, for Step 3, you could begin like this:

Some things changed for ordinary peasants. For example, in Bourn…

Finally, write a conclusion.

Summarise your answer to the enquiry question.

5 Meanwhile, in Norman Sicily

A story of one island, many worlds

The marble gravestone of Anna, in St Michael's Church, Palermo, Sicily.

If you stand on this high fort, on Sicily's coast, you can see Italy. In the twelfth century, ships easily sailed the calm waters of the Mediterranean to Italian cities, such as Venice or Rome. Glance at the map on page 44, and you'll see Sicily's closeness to other shores of the Mediterranean too. A journey south would bring you swiftly to Muslim north Africa. Head east, and you could sail right into Constantinople's harbour.

Sicily was central in the connected worlds of medieval Europe, Asia and Africa. But it was also unique. Here, on this tiny island, these connected worlds existed very close together indeed.

Many languages

The marble gravestone on this page was made in 1149. The woman buried in the grave was called Anna. Her son had the gravestone made. Look closely and you will see writing in four different scripts.

- On the left, we see Latin – the language of ancient Rome. In the twelfth century, western Christians still used Latin in religious services, in laws and in the business of government.
- On the right, Greek – the language of the Byzantine Christians.
- At the bottom, Arabic – the language of Muslim peoples.
- At the top, more Arabic, but not in the Arabic alphabet. This is the Hebrew alphabet, understood by many Jewish people.

In fact, Jewish and Muslim people had lived together in Sicily for so long that most Jewish people spoke both Arabic and Hebrew.

During parts of the twelfth century, Muslims, Jewish people and both types of Christian all lived and worked together, peacefully, in Sicily. We don't know which group Anna belonged to, but her son clearly wanted different groups to read about her. Many of these peoples kept their own traditions. By the time Anna's gravestone was made in 1149, Sicily's rulers allowed each community to practise its religion freely and even to run its own courts.

Norman king of many peoples

To understand the cooperation between these groups, there are few better places to look than the king's royal court. First, let's go to the king's royal chapel in Palermo. Begun in 1132, it took eight years to build. Look closely. The vibrant mosaics and tiles were made by Greek Christian craftsmen from the Byzantine empire. The shape of the church, however, is more like the churches being built at that time in Rome, and even England...

... except the shape of the central arch. It is an Arab Muslim design.

Now peer upwards. Wooden carvings hang like icicles from the ceiling. These geometric designs, based on plants and animals, are the work of Muslim craftsmen.

The king who built this chapel was a Norman. His name was Roger II of Sicily. Like the Norman rulers of England, Roger followed Christian traditions upheld by the Pope in Rome. Unlike the Norman rulers of England, Roger ruled over remarkable religious diversity.

Just as the builders of the royal chapel held different faiths, so did the royal officials who helped Roger rule. Hard at work in Roger's royal offices, writing laws and royal charters, were Greek Christians. These Greek Christians did not follow the Pope. Their Christian leader was based in Constantinople, in the Byzantine empire. Meanwhile, poring over the king's royal accounts, were Muslims. Some Muslims working on the royal finances pretended to convert to Christianity, just to please the king, but historians have found evidence that most privately kept their faith.

What were the Normans doing in Italy?

We need to go back in time to find out. 'Northmen' (Vikings) had settled in northern France in the tenth century. These 'Northmen' became known as 'Normans'. By the eleventh century, Normans were spreading all over Europe.

The first Normans to leave Normandy had been pilgrims visiting holy sites in Italy. These Normans were also skilled warriors. They soon found work as soldiers in wars between groups of western Christians, Byzantine Christians and Muslims. All these groups fought each other for control of Italy.

The Normans had their eyes on riches too. They were attracted by Italy's fertile land, its lemons, oranges and almonds, its crafts and trade.

Robert the crafty

In the year 1041 (twenty-five years before William of Normandy invaded England), a powerful Norman lord died leaving twelve sons. Since he had nowhere near enough land to give each son, the sons set off to seek their fortunes in Italy.

One of them, Robert, was such a skilful military leader that he earned the name 'Guiscard', which meant 'crafty'. Robert Guiscard began with no money and hardly any knights. In the Italian hills, his tiny band of followers barely survived. But crafty tricks paid off. Once, Robert pretended to hold a funeral. He disguised his soldiers as mourners, hid swords in the coffin and launched a surprise attack.

Robert Guiscard was soon terrorising towns all over Italy. By 1059, he controlled much of Italy. He was so powerful that the Pope promised to support him, but only on one condition. Robert had to fulfil one task. Robert had to capture the Muslim stronghold of Sicily.

In 1072, after years of bloody struggle, Robert Guiscard succeeded. Robert now possessed a large Norman kingdom including Sicily and many Italian lands.

The kingdom then passed to Robert's son, Roger I. It was his son, Roger II, who built the royal chapel on page 42. Roger II reigned from 1130 to 1154.

How Sicily connected worlds

People and ideas had long flowed into Sicily. Libraries in Sicily held books by ancient Romans and Greeks. When Muslim Arabs conquered Sicily in the ninth century, they brought their great learning with them. Do you remember all the scholars, doctors and translators in Baghdad? Their books came to Sicily. They spread north from there into Italy, too. Italy's famous medical school in Salerno held books written or translated in Baghdad. Travellers from as far away as England came to study medicine in Salerno or to find Arabic and Greek texts in Sicily.

This fourteenth-century painting shows the Pope blessing Robert Guiscard.

A map of the world from the Book of Roger. *We are so used to seeing maps with Europe at the top that you might need to turn the book upside down to recognise what the map shows. See if you can find the Mediterranean Sea, the Black Sea, the Red Sea and the Persian Gulf.*

One Arab Muslim scholar, called al-Hdrisi, lived in Sicily from 1136 to 1154. Born in north Africa, al-Hdrisi had travelled widely. His passion was geography. Al-Hdrisi set out to gather knowledge about the world, from India and China to England and Normandy. He did this by interviewing hundreds of sailors whose boats docked in Sicily.

Al-Hdrisi gathered this knowledge into an extraordinary book. The book became known as the *Book of Roger* because in 1154, al-Hdrisi gave it to Roger II.

This map from the *Book of Roger* has the Muslim holy city of Makkah at its centre. For others in Sicily, the centre of their world might have been Baghdad, Rome or Constantinople.

Peace... for a while

After the long years of fighting and conquest, the invading Norman rulers worked to restore peace in Sicily, mixing Christian cultures with those of Muslims and Jewish people who already lived there. Some Christians in Palermo began to wear Muslim dress and to speak Arabic. Books (like the *Book of Roger*), churches (like the royal chapel) and tombstones (like Anna's) all bear the mark of different peoples living peacefully together.

Yet peace was short-lived. Beyond Sicily, tension was growing between Christian and Muslim. In Sicily, by the end of the twelfth century, Christians were attacking Muslims. Many Muslims had to leave the island.

Still, for part of the twelfth century, Sicily was remarkable. Think how different the Norman story in Sicily is from the Norman story in England. In fact, the Norman territories springing up all over Europe were strikingly different. Some historians now wonder if we should call them 'Norman' at all.

Whatever we call them, for about three centuries, these Normans, descended from a band of Vikings, shaped European and Mediterranean worlds in peace and war.

These are the lands conquered by Normans by the twelfth century. Notice the Norman territory in the east of the Mediterranean, around Antioch. You will read about this in the next chapter. Prepare to meet Robert Guiscard again...

6 Unexpected allies for the Byzantine Empire

Why did Alexios's empire survive?

We are in Constantinople, the capital city of the Byzantine Empire. The Empress Zoe died 30 years ago. Now, in 1081, a huge cloud of smoke conceals the city's famous beauty. Smoke wreathes itself around the glittering domes of the city's great cathedral. Smoke fills streets and markets.

But there are no market stalls today. No traders selling cloth, glass, perfumes, jewellery and books. No people peddling fried foods. Today, soldiers tear through the town. Houses and churches blaze. Children scream.

This portrait shows the leader of the soldiers: Alexios Komnenos. Alexios is a general in the Byzantine army. Broad and muscular, he cuts a powerful figure. Alexios is a whirlwind of anger. He is angry with the Byzantine emperor. He is angry that the Byzantine Empire is crumbling.

Normans attack in the west. Pecheneg raiders burn the north. Muslims batter the south – not the Abbasid Muslims you met in Chapter 2, but a new Muslim empire, the Seljuk Turks. Yet the aging emperor seems more concerned with fine clothes. Tonight, Alexios has one goal: to remove the emperor and seize his throne.

Alexios's soldiers rampage through the streets. Their shields and spears catch the light of the flames. They drag the emperor's supporters from their homes and from their horses. The nobles are stripped naked and paraded through the scorching smoke.

The emperor realises all is lost. Stripped of his fine robes, he flees to the towering, golden cathedral at the heart of the city. Praying before the gilded images of Christ, he begs for guidance.

No guidance comes. It is all over. The rule of a new Byzantine emperor will now begin: the reign of Alexios I.

Your enquiry

As you know from Empress Zoe in Chapter 1, being the Byzantine emperor had never been easy. But in 1081, the Byzantine Empire was on the brink of collapse. The empire was under attack. Money was running out. People were angry and scared.

Yet the empire did not collapse. During his long reign, Alexios managed to restore, and keep, Byzantine power. So how was this possible? Which factors caused the empire's survival! In this enquiry, you will build your own argument to explain Alexios's success.

1081: Trouble at home

Alexios was a successful military leader. He knew when to send in the cavalry to attack head-on. He knew when to send his archers around the back of his enemies to attack them from behind. He knew when to fight and when to talk. He knew that a bag of gold could avoid a costly fight. He knew that good preparation revealed the best strategy.

Now that he was emperor, Alexios needed to size up his problems and choose strategies to solve them.

Study the map below. It shows just how bad the situation was by 1081.

As you can see, Alexios had to work quickly. First, he drove out the nobles who still supported the old emperor. Then, he made other nobles promise to be loyal. Next, he gave jobs to his own family and supporters.

But controlling Constantinople was just the start. Many powerful Byzantine nobles lived in Asia Minor. Alexios worried that these nobles could become a threat.

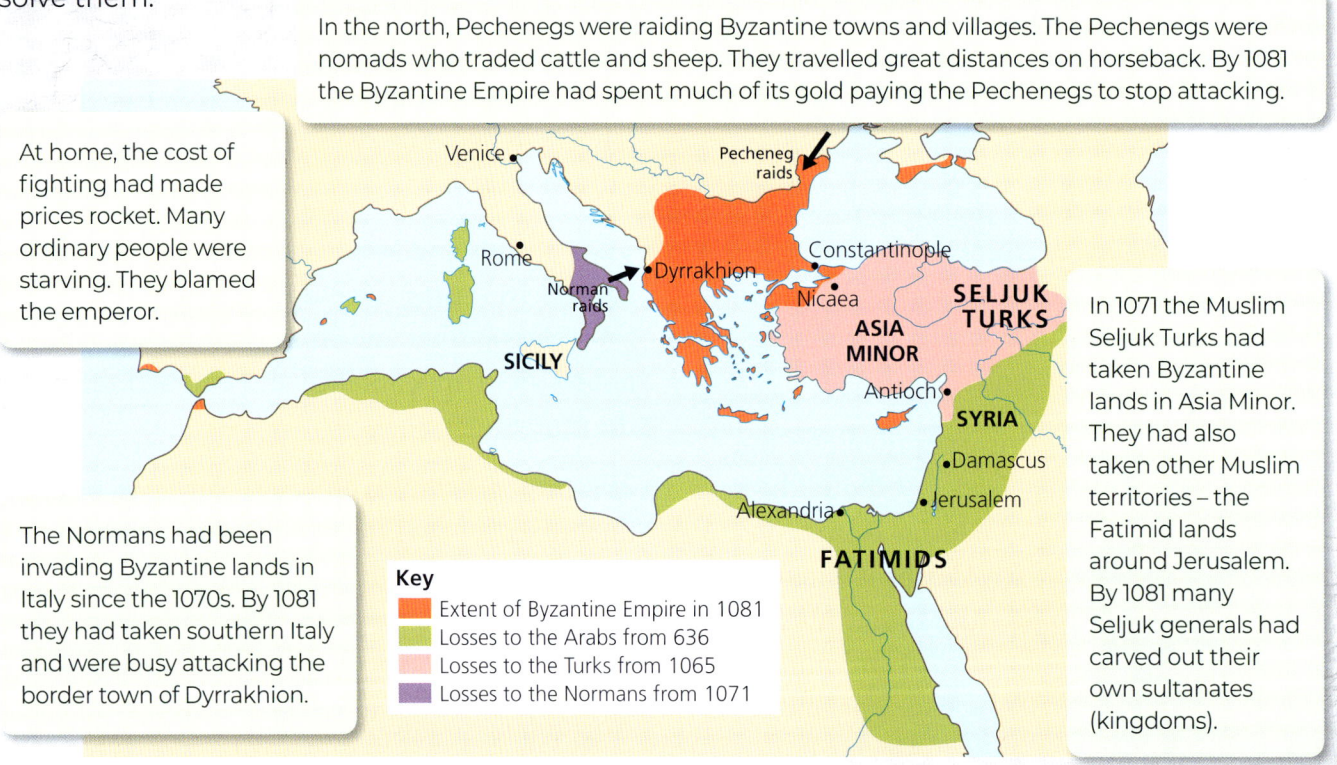

In the north, Pechenegs were raiding Byzantine towns and villages. The Pechenegs were nomads who traded cattle and sheep. They travelled great distances on horseback. By 1081 the Byzantine Empire had spent much of its gold paying the Pechenegs to stop attacking.

At home, the cost of fighting had made prices rocket. Many ordinary people were starving. They blamed the emperor.

In 1071 the Muslim Seljuk Turks had taken Byzantine lands in Asia Minor. They had also taken other Muslim territories – the Fatimid lands around Jerusalem. By 1081 many Seljuk generals had carved out their own sultanates (kingdoms).

The Normans had been invading Byzantine lands in Italy since the 1070s. By 1081 they had taken southern Italy and were busy attacking the border town of Dyrrakhion.

Key
- Extent of Byzantine Empire in 1081
- Losses to the Arabs from 636
- Losses to the Turks from 1065
- Losses to the Normans from 1071

Step 1

When historians work out why things happened, they look through the facts and stories to find themes which seem to make a pattern. We sometimes call these themes 'factors' or 'causes'. This table shows four factors which help to explain how Alexios was able to secure the Byzantine Empire.

Make a copy of the table. Re-read this chapter so far, once again. Find some details relevant to the first two columns.

How Alexios secured his empire			
Alexios was a skilful military leader.	Alexios got rid of political opponents.	Alexios made sure that he had a strong economy.	Alexios made alliances and got help.
	In 1081, Alexios drove out the nobles who supported the old emperor.		

Seljuk soldiers attacking Byzantine soldiers in a city. From the chronicle of John Skylitzis, an eleventh-century Greek historian.

1081–1085: Help from the south

Alexios needed success in battle. But he had no money. Seljuk attacks on Byzantine cities were stopping trade. But what could Alexios do?

A deal with the Seljuk Turks

Alexios hatched a plan. He struck a deal with the most powerful Seljuk general, Sulayman. Although not the **sultan** (ruler) of all Seljuk Turks, Sulayman still controlled powerful armies. Alexios gave Sulayman gold and jewels. He promised Sulayman control over Asia Minor. In return, Sulayman promised to support Alexios and to protect Byzantine trade. The deal worked. Seljuk attacks on Byzantine towns stopped. At last, trade flowed.

Fending off the Normans

Do you remember Robert Guiscard in Sicily? In 1081, Robert set sail from Italy to attack the Byzantine town of Dyrrakhion. Robert took with him 15,000 foot-soldiers and 1,300 knights (and their horses). Filling 150 ships, it was a vast, terrifying army. Robert's wife, Sikelgaita, and his son, Bohemond, came too.

The above image from the Bayeux Tapestry reminds us how fearsome the Norman cavalry were. Alexios had to plan carefully. At first, things went well. Alexios used his skilled Varangian Guard to slam into the mounted soldiers. The Normans fell back.

According to one source, it was Sikelgaita who rallied the Normans. When she saw the Norman soldiers running away, she shouted, 'Stand, and fight like men!' Grabbing a spear, Sikelgaita galloped after them until they turned back to fight. The Normans now drove their vast cavalry into the Byzantine army.

Alexios was badly defeated. The Normans took Dyrrakhion; then quickly sped on to seize more Byzantine land.

Alexios did not give up. Trade was improving, so Alexios devised a plan to use his wealth cleverly. He needed to push the Normans back to Italy, so he paid the German emperor to attack them there. This forced Robert Guiscard to return home, leaving his son Bohemond in charge.

Alexios saw his chance. He set out to meet Bohemond in battle. Alexios's Turkish ally, Sulayman, sent 7,000 Seljuk troops to help him. Now Alexios used all his military skill. This time, he needed to outwit those powerful, mounted Norman knights. Instead of attacking head on, Alexios tricked the Norman cavalry into chasing some Byzantine soldiers. The Norman knights became separated from the other soldiers. Alexios's troops surrounded and killed them.

Bohemond was forced to retreat. The Norman invasion was over.

When Alexios returned home, his wife had just given birth to their first child, Anna. In Constantinople's cathedral, Alexios thanked God for his victories and for his new child. The people of Constantinople celebrated for days.

1085–1095: Help from the east

1085 began well for Alexios. But before baby Anna had even learned to walk, disaster struck.

Alexios's powerful ally, Sulayman, was killed in battle. With Sulayman gone, other Seljuk generals began fighting for control of Asia Minor. Byzantine trade suffered. By 1086, Seljuk generals were closing in on Constantinople.

Meanwhile the battle against the Pechenegs in the north was also going badly. When the Pechenegs cut off the food supply, people had to eat snakes. With no money, Alexios couldn't even pay the Pechenegs to leave.

Alexios needed help. That help was to come from an unexpected place.

Another Muslim alliance

The man at the centre of the image below is Malik-Shah I. Around him are advisors and scholars. Since 1071, Malik-Shah had been the Sultan (a Muslim ruler) of the Seljuk Turks. Malik-Shah was extremely powerful. His empire stretched thousands of miles, across the Middle East and Asia Minor.

Just like the caliphs of Baghdad, Malik-Shah wanted to preserve and build knowledge. From art and poetry to science and astronomy, Malik-Shah was thrilled by the work of scholars. 600 miles east of Baghdad, in Istafan, Malik-Shah built an observatory. There, his astronomers sought to unlock the mathematics and physics of the universe.

A fourteenth-century painting of Sultan Malik-Shah.

For all his success, by 1085, Malik-Shah was worried. In Asia Minor, his generals were taking far too much land for themselves. What if they were to become too powerful and were to threaten his place as ruler of the Seljuk Turks? Malik-Shah therefore wrote to Alexios. He asked if they might work together, each to secure his own empire.

Malik-Shah also wanted his son to marry Alexios's daughter, Anna. Alexios laughed, but he didn't laugh at the idea of an alliance. That idea suited him. Malik-Shah and Alexios were both soldiers. They understood each other. They had similar problems. Alexios now sent Malik-Shah rich gifts – gold coins, precious stones, silk brocade woven with gold.

Quickly forming an alliance, the two men led armies into Asia Minor. Malik-Shah was able to capture Antioch and Nicaea from his generals. Alexios was able to reopen trade with these towns. Christians of the Byzantine Empire were delighted. They welcomed the stability that this new friendship brought.

Defeat of the Pechenegs

By 1090 Byzantine trade flowed again. Peace was almost restored. Feeling bold, Alexios planned a campaign against the Pechenegs. The Pechenegs had continued to plunder Byzantine lands, once even threatening Constantinople itself. In high spirits after victory over the Normans, Alexios's army headed north.

On 30 April 1091, Byzantine troops caught the Pechenegs by surprise in the hills. The Pecheneg soldiers had all their women and children with them. It was not a battle so much as a massacre. The Pechenegs were almost wiped out.

Sudden disaster

Security for the Byzantine Empire did not last. In November 1092, Malik-Shah died. Now no one controlled the Seljuk generals. By December, Alexios had lost all Asia Minor. The Byzantine economy collapsed. Across the empire, people starved. The nobles were furious.

> **Step 2**
> Using pages 47–48 add some more details to each column in your table.

1094–1099: Help from the west

A huge gamble

By 1094, things looked hopeless for Alexios. The new Seljuk Sultan was nothing like Malik-Shah. Instead of helping Alexios, he began attacking Byzantine towns! Now it seemed that the greatest threat was coming from the Seljuk Turks.

That summer a large group of nobles tried to have Alexios killed. The plot failed but Alexios knew that he had little support. Alexios needed another plan.

It was a huge gamble. Alexios brought his throne into the streets to face the angry crowds. He dressed in his soldier's uniform and surrounded himself with the Varangian Guard. This reminded the crowd that Alexios was a great military leader. It worked. The crowd backed down. Alexios survived.

Another gamble: help from the Pope

Alexios still needed to turn the tide, but how? In 1095, he sent a messenger to the leader of the western Christians, the Pope in Rome. He asked Pope Urban II for urgent help against the Seljuk Turks.

Pope Urban II responded quickly. He began to tell Christians that it was their Christian duty to drive the Seljuk Turks away from Constantinople. He also said that Christians should go further. They should seize Jerusalem from the Seljuks as well! He told them that they should claim the city of Jerusalem, where Jesus Christ had died, from the Muslims.

Alexios just wanted the Pope to help, but the Pope was turning help into a religious war.

The response was extraordinary. Over 80,000 Christians set out for Constantinople. The soldiers became known as 'crusaders' because they carried the symbol of the cross.

*Many preachers encouraged western Christians to go on **crusade**. This twelfth-century painting shows a famous priest and preacher of the crusade, Peter the Hermit, persuading men and women to 'take the cross' and go to Jerusalem. Before going on crusade in 1196, Peter the Hermit was one of several Church leaders who led anti-Jewish mob violence. Known as the Rhineland Massacres, thousands of Jewish civilians were killed.*

An even bigger gamble: help from the Normans

When the crusaders began arriving in Constantinople in 1096, Alexios was shocked to the core. He could not believe it. Many of the crusaders were his enemies, the Normans!

Worse still, one of their leaders was Alexios's old enemy, Bohemond. What on earth was Bohemond up to?

Alexios had to think quickly. As soon as the crusaders arrived, Alexios called the leaders to his throne room. He showered each one with sumptuous gifts. He made them promise to be loyal. He made them promise to return any lands that they conquered to the Byzantine Empire.

At first, things went well. In 1097, the crusaders and Alexios's armies pushed the Seljuks out of important trading cities. But it was so risky: Alexios was not leading these troops himself.

The gamble backfires: crusaders out of control

In 1098, things took a turn for the worse. The crusaders had made their way south to the city of Antioch. Antioch had been a major Byzantine city before the Seljuks conquered it in 1084 and Alexios wanted it back. The crusaders put Antioch under siege. The siege lasted for months. Thousands of crusaders died from starvation and disease.

Historians are not sure why, but Alexios did not help the crusaders at Antioch. This was the last straw for the crusaders. When Antioch finally fell, Bohemond refused to hand it over to Alexios. He even made himself the prince of Antioch!

The capture of Jerusalem

As Princess Anna celebrated her fifteenth birthday in Constantinople, the crusaders planned their next move. Early in 1099, they set off for Jerusalem itself and began a long siege. What methods of attack can you see in this fourteenth-century painting?

On 14 July 1099, the crusaders finally broke down the city's defences. They rampaged through Jerusalem's streets, butchering, beheading and burning men, women and children. Thousands of Muslim and Jewish people were killed. Eye-witnesses wrote of streets flowing in blood.

Soon afterwards, Jerusalem's Muslim holy sites were turned into Christian shrines.

Alexios secures his empire

Although parts of Alexios's empire were restored by 1102, many crusaders did not leave after the fall of Jerusalem. In fact, they set up their own kingdoms in the lands which Alexios wanted back! Bohemond even challenged Alexios for his restored lands. Faced with yet more problems, Alexios used methods which had brought him success in the past. He supported another crusader prince to keep Bohemond in check. He used gifts to secure support from a Seljuk general.

With his new wealth and power, Alexios gradually got the better of Bohemond. Alexios knew enough now about Norman tactics not to meet Bohemond head on. When Bohemond tried to attack Dyrrakhion, Alexios starved Bohemond's troops and defeated them. At last, in 1108, Bohemond was forced to grovel before Alexios. He promised to protect Alexios with his own life.

By the time Princess Anna was 25, Alexios's empire was almost completely restored. Alexios had done the impossible.

Step 3

Complete your boxes using details from pages 49–51.

Shaping your answer

Alexios's daughter, Anna Komnene, went on to become one of the most important historians of the Middle Ages. After her father died in 1118, Anna collected evidence about how Alexios managed to secure the Byzantine empire. She then wrote the history book that you can see below.

Over 900 years later, you are going to do something similar to Anna. You will answer the question, Why did Alexios's empire survive?

You have already sorted the story into factors which explain how Alexios succeeded against the odds. These four factors give you your four main paragraphs. We have suggested ways of starting each paragraph. Use your notes from your table to complete each paragraph.

Introductory paragraph

In your introduction, tell your reader when and how Alexios became emperor. Then set out the challenges that Alexios faced. Then explain the shape of your essay (its four main sections) so the reader knows what to expect.

Paragraph on the first factor

To secure his empire, Alexios needed to win wars. Alexios usually succeeded in war because…

Paragraph on the second factor

Alexios used alliances cleverly. For example…

Paragraph on the third factor

Alexios had to get rid of political opponents to secure his empire. As soon as he took power…

Paragraph on the fourth factor

Alexios needed money to secure his empire. Alexios gained money by…

Concluding paragraph

In your conclusion, tie the threads of your essay together. For example, you could show connections between the factors.

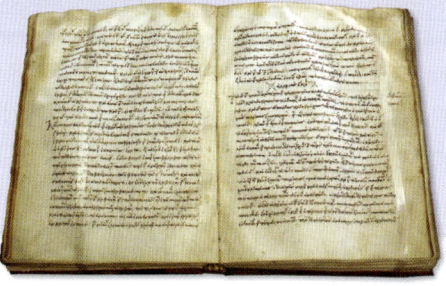

7 Meanwhile, back in Norman England

Struggling for control after 1087

An empire divided

In July 1087, William, King of England and Duke of Normandy, now aged 59, was trying to capture the French town of Mantes. Hot, exhausted and hugely overweight, he fell from his horse. As he fell, his enormous stomach caught on his saddle and burst open. He was taken to the Norman city of Rouen to recover.

William never recovered. When he died, his powerful supporters rushed off to defend their lands. They were certain that the king's death would bring chaos in England and in Normandy.

They were right. On his death, William's empire was split in two. One son, William Rufus, became King of England. Many Norman barons did not want William Rufus to be king, but with Archbishop Lanfranc's support, he took the throne. Meanwhile, another son, Robert, was made Duke of Normandy. The two sons were soon at war. Noman lords with land on both sides of the Channel were forced to pick sides.

An empire reunited

When William Rufus died in 1100, his brother Henry (later known as Henry I) became King of England. Henry defeated his brother Robert, bringing England and Normandy back together as one empire.

Henry I eventually restored stability to England and Normandy. He died in 1135, having re-established Norman rule. But the stability did not last. Terrible chaos was to follow Henry I's reign. Norman rule was to unravel, as quickly as it had begun.

The White Ship

In 1120 King Henry and his 17-year-old son and heir were on the coast of Normandy, waiting to sail to England. Henry's son, however, chose not to sail in the same ship as his father. He was excited and eager to sail on the newest, fastest ship in the king's fleet – the White Ship.

As the king's ship left harbour, the young prince joined his friends and the crew of the White Ship for several hours of heavy drinking. Later that evening, the priests who came to bless the ship were shocked by the drunken behaviour on board. They fled before giving the blessing.

In the middle of the night, the sleek new ship finally set sail. It picked up speed. The king's son, now very drunk, egged on the rowers to go faster. The White Ship had barely left sight of shore when it slammed into a rock.

The king's son managed to scramble into a small boat to row to safety. But through the waves he could hear his half-sister, screaming. He turned the boat around and rowed back. His little boat was overwhelmed with desperate people clinging to it.

We know these details because one person survived – a butcher from Rouen. Clinging to a rock, he was rescued in the morning by fishermen, and lived to tell the tale.

This image from a chronicle shows Henry I, looking very alone, contemplating the horror of the shipwreck. In losing his son, he had lost hope for the stability of England.

Civil War: Stephen and Matilda

Henry ruled for another 15 years. He never produced another male heir. He hoped to pass the throne to the woman shown here, his daughter Matilda.

Both Henry I and Matilda knew that Matilda would have to fight for the English crown. They were right. A woman would not be accepted easily. Shortly after Matilda heard news of her father's death in 1135, she heard further troubling news. Matilda's cousin Stephen was plotting with English barons to claim the throne for himself.

Matilda now had to fight a long and bloody **civil war**. This period was later called 'the Anarchy'.

How did the civil war affect ordinary people?

Local lords used the civil war as opportunity to build up their own power, and ordinary people were caught up in the chaos. Lords were not supposed to build castles without a king's permission, but now they built castles to protect themselves. When lord was fighting lord, no one was safe.

The Anglo-Saxon Chronicle recorded, 'there was nothing but disturbance and wickedness and robbery'. In many counties, crops were destroyed by armies, supporters of rival sides were terrorised, trade was disrupted and livelihoods were destroyed. Local lords saw the war as a chance to grab more land, control more peasants and build private armies.

Some evidence of this suffering comes from churchmen. One Cluniac bishop was so alarmed by his uncle's greed and violence, that he wrote a letter urging him to do penance. He told his uncle that he risked being swept into hell by the cries of widows and orphans.

Coins from the period also give us evidence that the civil war was extremely disruptive. No longer was there one system of coins. Both Stephen and Matilda minted coins, but so did other local lords!

Some parts of the country, however, such as Gloucester and Bristol, stayed relatively peaceful. The far north of England was unaffected, because here the King of Scotland had control.

Yet the power of the Norman monarchs was crumbling. It would take a strong king and a brilliant organiser to restore stability once again. That king, Henry II, was to arrive in 1154.

England and Wales were roughly divided into three parts during the Anarchy.

53

8 The power of a queen
What does the life of Eleanor of Aquitaine reveal about the medieval world?

This is the Palace of Poitiers. One of the wealthiest and most powerful women in Europe lived in this palace for parts of her life. Her name was Eleanor. We know her as Eleanor of Aquitaine.

Eleanor became the Duchess of Aquitaine in 1137, aged just 15. Later, Eleanor was to make this palace even more remarkable. She built the vast dining hall that you can see on the next page. 50 metres long, it was the largest dining hall in Europe. It was so big that the sound of footsteps was lost, earning it the name, 'Hall of Lost Footsteps'. Only great wealth made such a building possible.

Find Aquitaine and Poitiers on the map opposite. Aquitaine covered much of the south-west of what we now call France. Writing in their chronicles, monks marvelled at its wealth:

> Opulent Aquitaine, sweet as nectar thanks to its vineyards dotted about with forests, overflowing with fruit of every kind, and endowed with a superabundance of pastureland.

Heriger, Abbot of Lobbes, writing between 990 and 1007.

> [The land] abounds with riches of many kinds, so excelling other parts of the western world that it is considered one of the most fortunate and prosperous provinces…

Ralph of Diceto, from the Abbreviationes chronicorum, *probably written in about 1180.*

These sources reveal how wealthy the lands of Aquitaine were. It was wealth that strengthened the power of the dukes and duchesses of Aquitaine. Eleanor was born into this wealth. She was born into a powerful noble family. She would go on to be even more powerful. Much would be expected of her.

Your enquiry

The medieval worlds of war, religion and power were Eleanor's worlds. In this chapter you will follow Eleanor's story. You will draw out fascinating things that her life reveals about medieval worlds. You will use these things to plan a museum exhibition about her life.

Museum exhibitions often include boards with writing and pictures. You will plan four museum boards, each showing these themes in different stages of Eleanor's life.

Opulent Aquitaine

The language and laws of Aquitaine

The rich land where Eleanor grew up was not like England or Normandy. Aquitaine was closer to Spain than to England. The people living here had different ideas about religion and power from those in Normandy. They also spoke an old dialect – *la langue d'oc* – very different from the language of the north.

Aquitaine also had different laws from Normandy. Here, women could inherit land and titles. This was rare in the north. Eleanor grew up seeing women in control. In 1130, Eleanor's brother and sister died, making Eleanor heir to her father's lands. In 1137, Eleanor's father, the Duke of Aquitaine, died while on a long pilgrimage. On her father's death, Eleanor became Duchess of Aquitaine.

The sights and sounds of Aquitaine

Eleanor grew up in a colourful, musical world. She knew the love poetry of the **troubadours**, who wandered from noble court to noble court in southern France and Spain. Troubadours composed and sang for the delight of noble families. The Dukes of Aquitaine filled their courts with music, dancing, poetry and song. They filled their palaces with art and sculpture.

In Aquitaine, Muslim Spain never seemed far away. The cities of Muslim Spain were full of new learning in mathematics and science, of changing art and craftsmanship, of poetry and music.

Aquitaine hummed with the art, literature and architecture of Christian and Muslim worlds.

See how this medieval love poem is decorated. Young lovers meet in a walled garden. The art around them is inspired by nature.

Worlds of religious conflict

Eleanor grew up hearing how Muslims and Christians in Spain sometimes clashed in battle and sometimes collaborated. She also grew up hearing of battles between Christians. In 1130, the Catholic Church had split so badly that it elected two Popes! When Eleanor's father challenged one Pope's teaching, he was **excommunicated**.

This explains the long pilgrimage that her father went on. A pilgrimage did not just earn a place in heaven; it built power on Earth. Eleanor's father had gone on a pilgrimage to win back the Church's favour.

Step 1

You are now going to plan your first museum board. Choose examples from Eleanor's early life that you think reveal something about one or more of these four themes:

1. how rulers gained and kept power
2. how women could show their power
3. how very different parts of the world were connected
4. how powerful people used art and culture

Record your ideas in a table like this:

A detail from Eleanor's life	What it reveals about the medieval world	Either a source or a modern illustration that you could add to the museum board
Eleanor grew up in Aquitaine, which was close to Spain. She heard new music and poetry from the troubadours.	This shows how culture in France was influenced by Spain (Theme 3). It also shows how noble families encouraged new music and poetry (Theme 4).	Medieval love poems, beautifully illustrated. Map showing position of Aquitaine.

Queen of France

After the sudden death of her father, Eleanor's life changed quickly. The King of France decided that she would be married to his son, Louis. She was about to become very important indeed.

Eleanor gave this vase to her new husband on their wedding day. Rare and expensive, it was made of rock crystal and decorated with gold and jewels. The vase had been given to Eleanor by her grandfather, who had brought it back from travels in Spain. The vase had originally been made in Persia.

In August 1137 Eleanor arrived in Paris with her new husband, Louis. It was an even more important arrival than they expected. While they were making their journey back from their wedding in Aquitaine, the King of France had died. Louis and Eleanor were now King and Queen of France!

Eleanor had to adjust to this new life. A bustling city of 200,000 people, Paris was not like Aquitaine. The weather was cold. The royal court lived austere lives. Eleanor missed the rich sights and sounds of the south. Nobles in the French court looked down on people from Aquitaine. They called them 'better feeders than fighters'.

Eleanor also had to get used to her new husband, Louis. He was now Louis VII, King of France, but from an early age he had trained to be a monk, not a king. Louis had only become heir to the French throne when his elder brother died.

Life was difficult for Eleanor in Paris. In Aquitaine, she had exercised power. Now Eleanor was not allowed to be involved in politics, nor any important decision-making. Her role was to provide an heir to the throne. When she did not have a baby in the first few years of marriage, Eleanor was considered a failure.

But bigger worries would soon replace these. Trouble was brewing in the East.

Eleanor and the Second Crusade

To Jerusalem

The crusade that you read about in Chapter 6 later became known as the First Crusade (1096–1099). During the First Crusade, the crusaders established crusader kingdoms in the Holy Land, sometimes called crusader states. Edessa was the capital of a crusader state. In December 1144, rumours were reaching western Europe that the Holy Land was not secure. It was soon confirmed that the Turks had overrun the city of Edessa.

Louis VII saw an opportunity. Louis wanted to be the greatest Christian king in Europe. He also needed to do penance for a massacre (he had once burned down a church full of people). Louis decided to launch a new crusade.

On Easter Sunday 1146, Eleanor and Louis listened to a French abbot called Bernard of Clairvaux preach the crusade. Shortly afterwards, they took the cross. They were going to the Holy Land. Eleanor left her two-year-old daughter in Paris. She would not see her for three years.

This fourteenth-century painting shows Eleanor marrying Louis on the left and Louis leaving on crusade on the right. From Les Chroniques de Saint-Denis.

Helmets and buckles shining in the sun

Eleanor took 300 ladies-in-waiting. Her baggage train, carrying clothes, food and tents, was miles long. In June 1147, Eleanor and Louis reached the city of Metz.

In Metz, Eleanor and Louis met the German emperor, Conrad. There they made plans for their journey to the Holy Land together. Conrad was everything that Louis was not – physically strong and proven in battle. Louis, who had spent his early life preparing to be a monk, did not even know how to lead a military expedition. Some sources suggest that the crusaders respected Eleanor's leadership more than Louis's.

As the two armies left Metz and headed east for Bavaria, Eleanor made a remarkable impression. To the delight of cheering crowds, she wore a robe hemmed in gold and embroidered with the lilies of France. She rode a horse with a silver saddle. The long, colourful procession was full of hope. An onlooker described helmets and buckles shining in sunlight, and banners streaming in the breeze.

Bringers of trouble

Eleanor and Louis's next stop was the Bavarian city of Regensburg. There they met officials sent by the Byzantine emperor. The Byzantine emperor was worried that the crusaders might bring trouble when they reached Constantinople. Louis had to promise that he would conquer no Byzantine land.

Trouble certainly came, but it came before they reached Constantinople. Conrad's German forces left Regensburg first, a few days ahead of the French. When they reached Greece, the German crusaders plundered, murdered and raped. When Eleanor, Louis and the French reached Greece, the Greek towns refused them entry.

Then, Louis received news of a betrayal. The Byzantine emperor had agreed a ten-year truce with the Turks.

Constantinople

Eleanor, Louis and the French army reached Constantinople in early October 1147. The French were captivated by the splendour of Constantinople. The people of Constantinople were captivated by Eleanor. According to one story, she entered the city dressed as a man armed for battle.

As the French army left Constantinople in late October, they met the remnants of Conrad's German army, limping back to the city, wounded and starving. Nine-tenths of Conrad's army had suffered a massive defeat by the Turks.

Eleanor and Louis pressed on. At Christmas, the crusaders set up camp by the River Meander at Ephesus. As torrential rain flooded the valley, Eleanor sheltered in a tent. Supplies were so short that the crusader armies had to eat their horses. All were desperate to reach the safe city of Antioch, which had been ruled by crusader knights since the First Crusade. Eleanor's uncle Raymond controlled it.

End of a crusade... and a marriage

In March 1148 Eleanor, Louis and the French crusaders entered Antioch. Here, Eleanor and Louis's relationship fell apart. Louis wanted to press on to Jerusalem as a pilgrim rather than to focus on military goals. But Eleanor, influenced by Raymond, argued that they should wait. An exasperated Louis had Eleanor arrested and removed from Antioch by force.

The next six months were a disaster for the crusaders. The French army was alone. After failing to take Damascus from the Turks, many crusaders ran away. Others escaped starvation by converting to Islam and joining the Turks.

As for Louis and Eleanor's marriage, it was destroyed. Returning to Paris in the winter of 1149, Eleanor complained that she 'had married a monk, not a king'. In 1152, their marriage was annulled. Louis lost the lands that Eleanor had brought him.

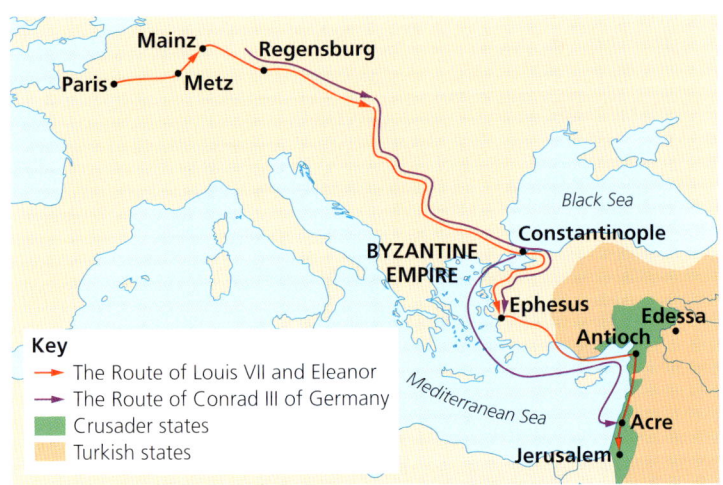

The routes taken by the crusaders on the Second Crusade.

Step 2

Your second museum board will be called Queen of France and the Second Crusade. Plan it by continuing your table with details from pages 56–58. Remember to use your middle column to show what each one reveals about one or more of the four themes.

1. how rulers gained and kept power
2. how women could show their power
3. how very different parts of the world were connected
4. how powerful people used art and culture

Queen of England

A new husband for Eleanor

Eleanor would never see Louis again. She was free. As Duchess of Aquitaine, she controlled castles and prosperous lands.

Eleanor decided it was impossible to use her power without a husband, but she had already thought of a solution. The year before, she had met Henry of Anjou, in Paris. A powerful French nobleman, he was also the son of Matilda – the troubled Queen of England fighting a civil war with Stephen (who we met in Chapter 7). In 1152, just two months after ending her marriage to Louis, Eleanor married Henry in a quiet ceremony in Poitiers.

To England

Henry of Anjou was determined to gain the lands of his grandfather, Henry I of England. In 1153, Henry saw his chance. He sailed to England with 26 ships, 3,000 men and 140 horses, hoping to force Stephen to give up the throne. Instead, they reached an agreement: Henry would be made Stephen's heir.

Only a year later, in 1154, Stephen was dead. Henry could lose no time in gaining the English throne. Already pregnant with her second child from this new marriage, Eleanor found herself sailing the English channel to be crowned Queen of England.

On 8 December 1154 they landed on the south coast of England and headed straight to Winchester to take control of the royal treasury. On 19 December Queen Eleanor and King Henry II were crowned in Westminster Abbey.

Henry's first job as king was to re-establish order in England. He did this by dividing the country into legal districts so that his judges could visit and make sure that order was being kept. He introduced trial by jury.

Eleanor took a very active part in government. She sat as a judge in courts across England. Eleanor supervised the accounts of the market at Oxford, the Cornish tin mines and her own mill at Woodstock. When Henry was in France for long stretches of time, Eleanor often acted as his regent.

This twelfth-century mural, in a chapel in France, shows Eleanor and Henry hunting with hawks. It is the only surviving image of Eleanor known to have been created during her lifetime.

In Eleanor's luggage were forty-two gowns of silk, fourteen pairs of shoes, embroidered with gold thread, and ten warm undershirts. Eleanor introduced new fashions and fabrics to England when she became queen. These reflected the rich, colourful court of Aquitaine.

This statue wears a bliaut – a gown made by puckering a huge piece of material, usually silk, and hanging it in folds from the waist.

This statue wears a barbette, a linen headdress that is passed under the chin and pinned on both sides. English nobles were eager to follow the fashions which Eleanor brought from Aquitaine.

The Angevin empire

Henry and Eleanor quickly established themselves as leaders of the empire which combined all their lands. We call this the Angevin empire. 'Angevin'

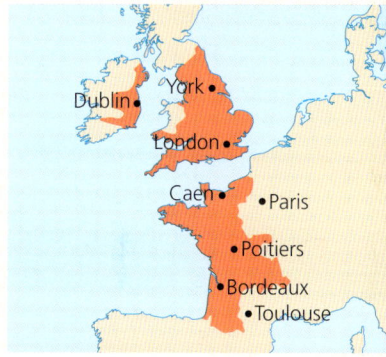

The Angevin empire.

takes its name from Henry of Anjou. It covered half of France, all of England and parts of Ireland and Wales. Like other medieval kings, he spent much time dealing with rebellions across his empire. Henry was frequently leading campaigns against the Welsh, but he always met fierce resistance.

Step 3

Now plan your third museum board, entitled Queen of England. Do this by continuing your table with details from pages 58–59.

Thomas Becket, the 'troublesome priest'

Shortly after being crowned, Henry II noticed a promising young clerk called Thomas Becket. Becket had studied law in France and Italy. Skilled in business and finance, he was just the sort of clever administrator that Henry II needed. There was so much work to be in done in England, reforming laws and reorganising the country. Henry appointed Becket to the high office of Chancellor.

Becket also became Henry's best friend. They spent whole days together, hunting, feasting, discussing state matters and enjoying witty conversation. And Becket was so useful! When Henry and Eleanor wanted to arrange the marriage of their eldest son (aged three) to the newborn daughter of Louis VII of France (Eleanor's ex-husband), it was Becket who went to France, charmed Louis and negotiated the marriage.

In 1162, Henry made Becket Archbishop of Canterbury. Henry was relieved to have his good friend lead England's Church. Together they could solve all sorts of problems. Or so Henry thought.

To Henry's horror, Becket now changed, almost overnight. Suddenly extremely religious, he prayed and fasted constantly. Becket now opposed Henry's reforms. He chose to protect the Church from the king's interference. They quarrelled bitterly for seven years.

What did Eleanor think?

We do not know Eleanor's thoughts on Becket. We do have two letters from churchmen advising Becket against seeking Eleanor's support. Perhaps Becket hoped that Eleanor might challenge Henry? It's possible. Some historians think that Eleanor and Henry were growing apart at this time. In 1166, Eleanor bore their eighth and last child, John, her tenth pregnancy. From 1168 she based herself in Poitiers. Perhaps she wanted more freedom, or perhaps this was just the best base from which to manage her own lands and to be the King's deputy in Normandy and Anjou.

A shocking murder

In 1170, Henry had his son crowned by the Archbishop of York. This was normally the Archbishop of Canterbury's role. Becket was furious. He excommunicated all the bishops who supported Henry.

That Christmas, Henry was in a hunting lodge in Normandy, probably with Eleanor. Discussing the problem with some visiting bishops, Henry flew into a rage. He is said to have cried, 'Will no one rid me of this troublesome priest?'.

Four knights overheard Henry's outburst. They set off for England and on 29 December arrived in Canterbury. Following behind the monks processing in for evening prayer, they walked into Canterbury Cathedral. There, they hacked Becket to death.

> Then he received a second blow on the head but still stood firm. At the third blow he fell on his knees and elbows, offering himself a living victim, and saying in a low voice, 'For the Name of Jesus and the protection of the Church I am ready to embrace death.' Then the third knight inflicted a terrible wound as he lay, by which the sword was broken against the pavement.

An eyewitness account written by a monk called Edward Grim.

Henry was horrified, and so was all of Christian Europe. As penance for his sins, Henry walked barefoot to Canterbury Cathedral and allowed the monks to whip him.

Becket was made a saint. As far away as Spain and Sicily, churches were dedicated to him.

Eleanor connects worlds

Art and trade

Eleanor's links with her homeland helped to make England prosperous. The French wine and silk trades made merchants in London rich. Writing in the style of the troubadours of southern Europe, many writers dedicated their works to Eleanor.

English churches began to be built in the new Gothic style using vaulted ceilings and arches. After a fire in 1174, Canterbury Cathedral was largely rebuilt in this Gothic style. (It also needed an extension to cope with all the pilgrims visiting Thomas Becket's shrine!)

Eleanor's children

Eleanor's three eldest sons, Henry, Richard and Geoffrey, each wanted more control over parts of the Angevin empire. In 1173 Eleanor encouraged them to lead a huge rebellion against their father.

Henry eventually brought the rebellion under control. Afterwards, he forgave his sons, but not Eleanor. He had her captured and kept under house arrest for nearly a decade.

In 1183, Eleanor's eldest son, Henry, died. This meant that when Henry II died in 1189, Richard became king. Eleanor's reign as Queen of England was over, but at 67, Eleanor was still busy. Richard needed her help.

How did Eleanor help Richard I rule?

1. Richard had been living in Aquitaine and Normandy for so long that English nobles did not know him. Eleanor summoned English nobles to swear an oath of allegiance to Richard.
2. Richard spent much of his reign crusading. Acting as Richard's regent, Eleanor took control. She relaxed Henry II's harsh forest laws. She arranged marriages of wealthy heiresses to loyal men.
3. Eleanor worked to keep Richard's empire together. She worked to stop her youngest son, John, from trying to grab control of England.
4. Eleanor arranged Richard's marriage for him.
5. She helped to negotiate Richard's release when he was captured after the Third Crusade.

When Richard died in 1199, Eleanor's youngest son, John, became King of England. Eleanor retreated to Aquitaine. She stayed there until her death in 1204. This map shows you how Eleanor's children influenced Europe. Eleanor's family continued to connect worlds.

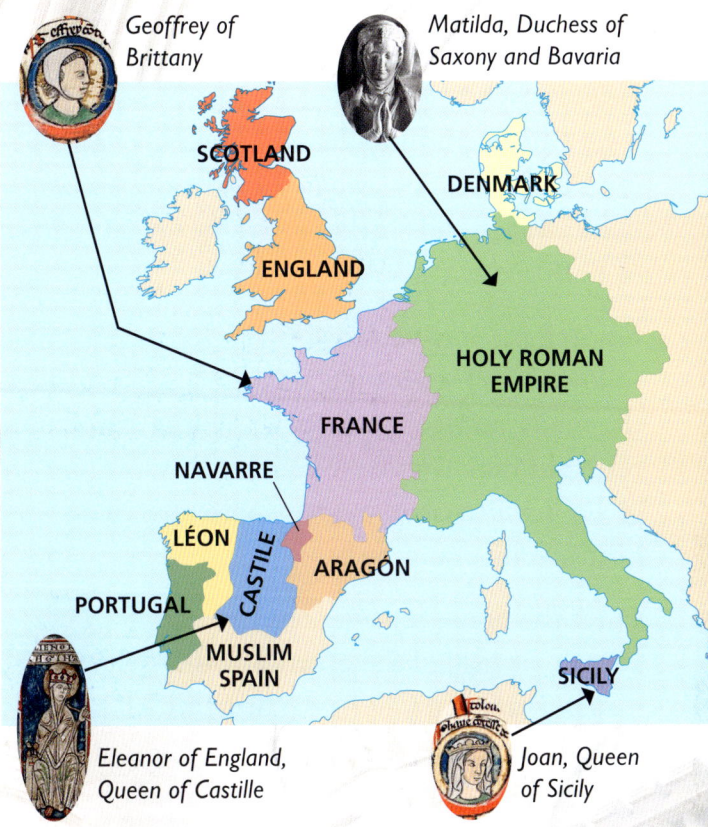

Step 4

Now plan your fourth museum board, entitled Eleanor connects worlds. Do this by continuing your table with details from this page.

Shaping your answer

You have now planned four parts of the museum exhibition. Your final task is to write an advert promoting it to members of the public who are fascinated by history. In your advert, explain what Eleanor's life reveals about medieval worlds. Remember to use all four themes and to mention each stage of her life.

9 Meanwhile, in the world of ideas

A twelfth-century Renaissance story

In 1116, while Henry I still reigned in England, a wealthy English nobleman began his long journey home. For seven years, the nobleman had travelled. His birthplace – the ancient city of Bath – was a distant memory.

Finding his way back to England, the nobleman followed well-worn pilgrim routes. He travelled the roads and sea-routes of crusading armies. He rested in monasteries. Wherever he went, his green flowing cloak made people turn their heads. Who could he be?

Once the noble traveller reached northern France, he visited the great cathedral schools in Tours, Paris and Chartres. Churchmen, monks and scholars remembered him from years before. They remembered how well he played the harp, how much he knew, how he loved to fly a falcon.

But was he the same man that they once knew?

He still had the same name – Adelard. But Adelard of Bath had changed.

In 1116, Adelard was returning home with new eyes and a changed mind.

Historians are fascinated by Adelard of Bath, and for three reasons:

1. They consider him remarkable.
2. They find his life revealing.
3. They see important consequences of his work.

As you read, decide which parts of Adelard's story show those three things.

Adelard's work was part of a big change in the world of ideas. Historians call this big change the twelfth-century Renaissance. 'Renaissance' means rebirth. Ancient ideas were being re-born…

… but differently.

Adelard the restless mind

When Adelard was a child, his wealthy parents asked the local bishop to secure him the best education possible. Leading churchmen taught Adelard Latin, theology and philosophy. But Adelard wanted more. The bishop suggested that Adelard continue his education in the famous cathedral school of Tours, in northern France. And so Adelard found himself being educated by the finest scholars in Europe.

But the more Adelard listened to endless debates about God and the Bible, the more he grew restless. Using the same old books, these scholars seemed to go round and round in circles. Adelard later said that they 'were making ropes out of sand'. Adelard was sure that other knowledge could be found.

Adelard had come across bits of mathematics and astronomy, but nothing like the great works of the ancient Greeks that the Arabs had translated in Baghdad. And now stories of different worlds were reaching Adelard's ears. The Normans had conquered Muslim Sicily. Crusaders had returned with stories from Muslim Turks and Syrian Christians, with knowledge of places such as Antioch and Constantinople.

And then there was Muslim Spain. As the Christians conquered more and more of Spain, word soon spread of astonishing Muslim libraries. Word spread north. It spread through Aquitaine. It spread into cathedral schools of northern France.

Adelard burned with curiosity. He burned for this knowledge. He left France and headed south.

Adelard the restless traveller

To find a safe route south, Adelard would have joined bands of pilgrims or merchants. After making his way through the Alps, he pressed down into the great plains of northern Italy, through its busy markets, then towards the coast and into Rome. From Rome, we know that Adelard headed for Salerno, where he met famous doctors and was delighted to find medical books by famous scholars like Galen and al-Razi. He discussed them with knowledgeable people, including Greeks, Arabs and Jewish people.

Then Adelard set off again, this time further south still, to Sicily. Adelard wanted yet more Arab knowledge, and only Sicily would do. Muslim Arabs had ruled Sicily until they lost the island to the Normans in 1072.

When Adelard reached Sicily, Roger II was on the throne, ruling over the three cultures of Jewish, Muslim and Christian people that we met in Chapter 5. Adelard marvelled at Sicily's volcano, Mount Etna. He met Sicily's bishop. He and the bishop discussed mathematics for hours.

But Adelard still wanted more. The First Crusade had opened up routes to the eastern Mediterranean, so Adelard journeyed on, this time to Syria.

Adelard in Antioch

Historians know that Adelard must have reached Syria by 1114 because he described Antioch's terrible earthquake of that year. He had sheltered under a bridge.

Travellers like Adelard had to be careful, and not just because of earthquakes. Crusader lands were violent. Antioch, however, was reasonably safe for Adelard. Antioch was ruled by a Norman (the grandson of Robert Guiscard) who had connections with Sicily. Powerful Normans probably gave Adelard protection.

And what a place Antioch was! By the time crusaders captured Antioch in 1098, it had been ruled by Arabs, Byzantines and, briefly, Turks. Jewish and Christian people had lived in Antioch for centuries. Goods and ideas from the Silk Roads flowed through its streets. From Antioch's harbours, ships weighed down with spices, sugar, wine, linen and silk set sail for Constantinople and Italy.

Such a ship would have carried Adelard back to Sicily.

Adelard the translator

From Sicily, Adelard made his way home to England where he secured a post in Henry I's government. But Adelard's adventures were not over. It was time for adventures of the mind.

Adelard carried two rare treasures home with him:

- an Arabic translation of Euclid's great work on geometry, *The Elements*
- an Arabic book on astronomy by the brilliant mind of Baghdad, al-Khwarizmi.

Somehow, somewhere – historians are not sure where – on his travels, Adelard had learned Arabic. Now, Adelard could at last unlock the secrets of Arab knowledge.

Where did Adelard find that copy of Euclid? Perhaps in Sicily. We know Arabic translations of Euclid had reached Sicily. Or perhaps the mathematics-loving bishop gave it to him. Or perhaps the bishop told him to search for a copy in Syria. We don't know. But we do know that Adelard set about translating. He translated both works **into Latin**.

Why does all this matter? When Adelard finished translating al-Khwarizmi's work in 1126, he was revealing to the western Christian world the riches of astronomy from the Muslim world. By translating Euclid into Latin, Adelard was putting the ancient Greek mathematics into a language that western Europeans could understand.

Picture Adelard's mind delighting in Euclid's great work. What must it have felt like to read Euclid? Euclid built his geometry from a few basic principles. Euclid made it all hold together so that each new idea grew from the last. This meant that Euclid's writing was not just useful for building, engineering or astronomy. Euclid showed how logic led to conclusions. Using Euclid's geometry, Adelard could show the power of reason.

How different this was from all that arguing round and round in circles that once frustrated Adelard in France!

Euclid had shown how to prove things were true. No wonder some Christians decided that God must be a mathematician. The fourteenth-century French painting on this page shows God as an architect, measuring the universe with a compass.

This is Chartres cathedral. Some craftsmen who worked on it were Muslims from Spain. Its lines and structures were made possible by Euclid's geometry. Its pointed arches (you saw these in Norman Sicily) were a feature of the new Gothic style of cathedral.

These arches allowed big distances between pillars. Architects could now design huge windows in what had once been long unbroken walls.

This painting of Adelard teaching was made in around 1400.

Slowly but surely, through Adelard's translations, this new mathematics found its way into the classrooms of the French cathedral schools. Soon the new knowledge affected cathedral buildings, too. When, in 1145, a terrible fire destroyed Chartres cathedral, the massive new cathedral owed much to new ideas coming in through Arab worlds.

From his hometown of Bath, Adelard would travel to meet the monks in the nearby monasteries in Wales and around the River Severn. Imagine the lively conversations about mathematics as scholars tried to make sense of the new learning!

Of course, not everyone agreed with Adelard. Adelard said that science needed reason and logic, not superstition. Adelard said that God should be left only for those mysteries that were impossible to solve with science. But Adelard won hearts and minds because he had a talent for explaining difficult things clearly. And he spread them to the powerful. When he wrote about the astrolabe, he dedicated his work to his pupil, the future king Henry II.

It is hard for modern historians to piece together Adelard's life. The sources are patchy. Nonetheless, for historians who write about him, Adelard feels alive. He scribbled witty comments in margins, sharing jokes with others who had worked on the same texts. Through Adelard's scribblings, we can almost hear the chatter of scholars at work in translation rooms, all those centuries ago.

At a time when hatred towards Muslims was deepening, and many Christians feared Islam, Adelard's life and work tell a different story. While fighting and fear between Christians and Muslims worsened, new ideas about the world, life, truth, mathematics, technology and building flowed steadily, changing minds and shaping worlds.

10 Meanwhile, in the Near East

The story of the Third Crusade

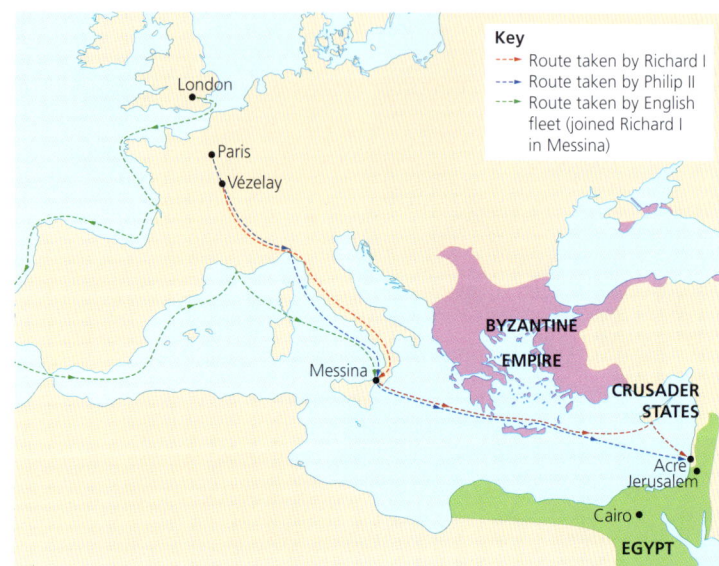

Routes taken by the crusaders on the Third Crusade

October 1187. The siege was over. Muslim forces had triumphed. They had taken Jerusalem.

And no wonder the Muslims had succeeded: the Christians were in chaos. Christian settlers in the Holy Land had argued about everything, including who should rule the Kingdom of Jerusalem itself. The Muslims had made the most of this. The Muslims had even convinced the Christian Byzantine emperor to help them.

Hearing the news, the Pope had a near-fatal heart attack. He was furious. Christian monarchs were supposed to work together.

The bickering had to stop!

Bringing Christian monarchs together would not be easy. And yet, two years later, in 1189, it would happen. The loss of Jerusalem had changed everything. Richard I of England would lead his soldiers up a steep cobbled path to this great abbey of Vézelay.

There, high above the French countryside, Richard I would meet Philip II of France. There, two kings would sit down to make peace.

For three months, the two kings talked. For three months, their armies ate and drank together. Eventually, the two Christian kings reached agreement.

They would launch another crusade.

Would the Christians remain united? Not for long. And they were not the only ones. Let us go back in time, by more than 30 years. There, we will learn how the Muslims came to secure that victory in 1187.

Muslims unite

Sitting in his palace in Syria, Nur ad-Din had spent days thinking. Like many Muslims, at first, Nur ad-Din had not grasped that the crusaders' aims were religious. Now he decided that for Muslims, too, recapturing Jerusalem should be a *religious* struggle. Nur ad-Din called this a jihad.

> Muslims should unite and reclaim Jerusalem! This quest is a holy war!

But there were so many Muslim groups! So many different priorities! What could be done?

Over in Egypt, another Muslim ruler, Salah ad-Din, heard about Nur ad-Din's idea. Salah ad-Din decided that he, Salah-ad-Din himself, would unite the Muslims and reclaim Jerusalem. Nur-ad-Din was furious. He decided to fight Salah ad-Din. The fighting continued until Nur-ad-Din died in 1174 and then Salah ad-Din seized his chance. Salah ad-Din now imposed his authority all over the Near East.

So it was Salah ad-Din who took advantage of the Christians' disunity. It was Salah ad-Din who was able to recapture Jerusalem. This was how, in 1187, the Muslims came together and won.

Christians unite

As you read earlier, Richard I of England and Philip II of France finally united. Christians flocked from across Europe to join them in a Third Crusade. At last, western Christians were united.

They started well. They knew that the hot, humid, bustling port of Acre was a gateway, by sea, to the Holy Land. If only Christian forces could capture Acre. In 1189, a long siege of Acre began.

By 1191, after a fierce battle, Richard's army managed to hold Acre. Now he could push towards Jerusalem.

Cracks in Christian unity

But nothing went to plan. Twice, Christian armies came within sight of Jerusalem. Twice, Richard judged it too dangerous to get nearer. Christian rivalries soon started to reappear.

By 1192, the Third Crusade had reached stalemate. The leaders agreed a truce. The Muslims would keep Jerusalem. The Christians would keep a strip of coastline. Both Salah ad-Din and Richard were delighted. Salah ad-Din, now in poor health, was struggling to keep Muslim forces united. Richard I faced trouble back in England, from his brother John.

Chaos

The truce did not last. In 1202, yet another crusade was launched. But this was not a religious quest. These crusaders wanted riches. The crusaders violently raided the Christian city of Zara. In 1204, the crusaders attacked the biggest Christian city in the world: Constantinople.

It was now hard to know who was fighting whom. It certainly wasn't East v. West or Christian v. Muslim.

In 1218, with Muslims controlling the Holy Land, new rumours began. A mighty army was crossing Asia. Who were they? Some Christians said that this was Prester John, a mythical Christian leader. Others knew the truth…

…the Mongols were coming.

11 Nightmare kings

Why did the barons keep rebelling against their English rulers?

It is spring, in the year 1130. King Henry I, son of William the Conqueror, lies asleep. Cool moonlight shines through the shutters of the king's bedchamber. Henry is restless. He tosses and turns. Great beads of sweat run down his brow. The king is in the middle of a nightmare.

First, the king sees a band of starving peasants. They stand over his bed with their scythes and pitchforks. Their eyes are filled with rage. They want the king to protect them from greedy and unjust nobles.

Henry wakes in terror. He leaps from his bed. His feet are bare. He seizes his sword, but the peasants melt away into the darkness. His room is empty.

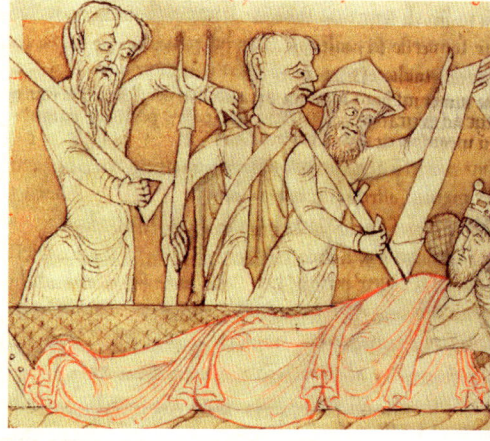

These remarkable pictures were created by a monk, John of Worcester, who told the story of Henry's three nightmares in a chronicle.

Henry drifts back into troubled sleep. Before long he is visited again. He sees a great band of knights and **barons**. Dressed in shining armour, they grasp lances, swords and spears. Their eyes, too, are filled with bloodthirsty anger. The king has been asking for too many taxes and ignoring their advice. They rush towards him.

Henry leaps up, crying, 'Help me!' Once again, he reaches for his sword, but no one is there.

Henry is dreaming of abbots and bishops. These churchmen accuse Henry of wickedness. He has failed to respect God's laws and stolen money from the Church to pay for his wars. Henry fears to look at them. He will certainly burn in Hell for his misdeeds. Closer and closer, they come, jabbing at him with their staffs.

Henry gasps and sits bolt upright. This time he sees a real and familiar face. His doctor is standing in the room. As Henry tells the doctor about his nightmares of rebellion, the doctor listens. He advises the king to do penance as soon as possible.

Just like Henry I, all medieval kings worried about rebellions. As you saw in Chapter 4, William the Conqueror spent years bringing English barons under control. Almost every English ruler who came after William faced challenges to their power.

What was more unusual, however, was for the barons' challenges to succeed; and that is exactly what happened in the reigns of two kings in the thirteenth century. These kings were John (1199–1216) and Henry III (1216–1272). These remarkable rebellions had lasting consequences for how England was governed.

Your enquiry

In this enquiry you will explore why barons *kept on* rebelling against their kings. You will explore the reigns of King John and King Henry III and look for the **causes** of different rebellions. Using these causes, you will create your own historical explanation of why barons *kept on* rebelling throughout the thirteenth century.

The ideal king

To explain why barons kept rebelling, you first need to know what people expected of kings in the thirteenth century. Historians think that as early as 1100, some English people were developing the idea that a king had to rule for the good of the community of the realm. That meant everyone who lived in the kingdom, from the most powerful barons to the poorest peasants. You have already seen, in Henry I's nightmare, what different groups expected of their king. Let's now look more closely at these **expectations** of a king.

Expectation 1:
Good kings were expected to defeat their enemies in battle and protect their own kingdoms. This meant having barons who were willing to fight, and plenty of money to supply knights and soldiers.

Expectation 2:
Raising money for armies meant that kings needed to tax their subjects. Barons and the leading churchmen expected kings to seek their advice and agreement before raising taxes.

Expectation 3:
Because English kings had to spend so much time in France, powerful barons were used to running the country for the king in his absence. They kept law and order and they collected taxes. Barons therefore expected to share in the king's power.

Expectation 4:
Fighting was not the only way to grow or secure a kingdom. Kings were expected to use marriage to make clever alliances and secure more land. Henry I had married his children carefully into powerful families. The map on the right reminds you just how much land the English Crown acquired through the marriage with Eleanor of Aquitaine.

Expectation 5:
As you saw in Henry I's dream, kings were expected to rule as good Christians. This was not easy! The Church had its own expectations. The Church expected freedom to collect its own taxes, to run its own courts and to have a say in appointing bishops. If a king upset the Pope, the king was in trouble. The Pope could excommunicate a king. This meant that other Christian rulers could attack the excommunicated king and take his lands.

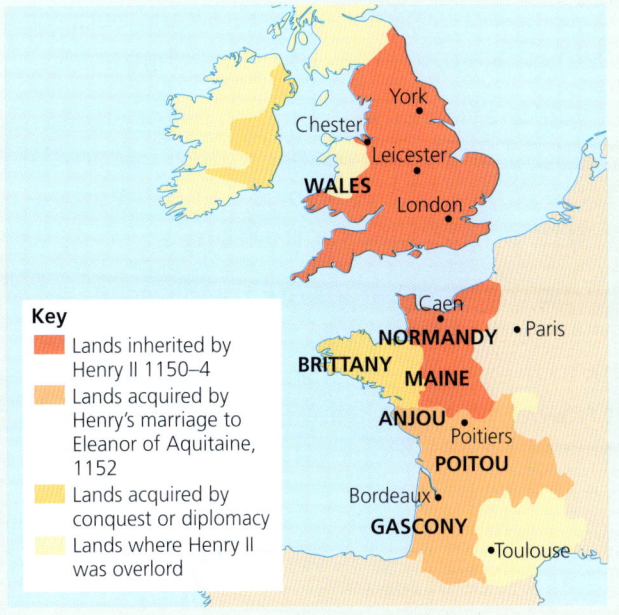

Key
- Lands inherited by Henry II 1150–4
- Lands acquired by Henry's marriage to Eleanor of Aquitaine, 1152
- Lands acquired by conquest or diplomacy
- Lands where Henry II was overlord

A map showing the Angevin empire.

John and Magna Carta

Look closely at this image. It is a modern artist's impression of one of the most famous events in English history. King John glares angrily at knights and barons around him. It is summer 1215, and leading barons are handing John a list of 63 demands. These demands would become known as 'Magna Carta': the great charter.

This was the first time in English history that the king's barons had used a written document to try to control the king. In so doing, they risked being executed for **treason**.

Why did the rebel barons risk their lives to challenge the king? To do this, we need to go back to the beginning of John's reign and find out how well he was living up to people's expectations of a medieval king.

A difficult start

John came to the throne in 1199 after the death of his brother, Richard I. But it was not straightforward! John's nephew, Arthur, also had a claim to be king, and the French king, Philip II, supported Arthur.

In 1200, John fought and defeated King Philip but he did not push on and take Philip's lands for himself. The English barons thought that this was cowardly. Before long, John's barons were calling him 'Softsword'.

In 1202 John captured his nephew and over 250 French knights. John almost certainly had his nephew murdered, and 22 of the prisoners were starved to death. From this point many French barons refused to fight for John. King Philip made the most of this. By 1206 John had lost almost all his lands in France. Only Gascony remained.

John flew into a rage and stopped calling on his barons for advice. Meanwhile, John gained another nickname, 'Lackland'.

Money matters

John desperately needed money to win back his French lands. His barons were too angry with John to agree to a tax, so John had to find other ways to get money. He turned to the knights. He decided to charge them 'scutage'. This was a special tax which knights would pay instead of fighting for the king. Other kings had occasionally done this, but John asked for scutage eleven times in just seventeen years.

John also looked for ways to make money elsewhere. He began using his own judges to hear cases around the country instead of leaving this to the knights and barons. This did make things a bit fairer for some people. For John it meant that court fees went to him instead of the barons.

He also made money by making knights or barons pay for the right to inherit their father's lands. All monarchs had done this since William the Conqueror. But John charged eye-watering amounts.

John upsets local communities

Without lands in France, John now spent much more time in England. This was not good news for many of his subjects. John moved around three times a week. Wherever he travelled, he expected local people and land holders to supply him with food, drink and even money. In 1204, one chronicler wrote that wherever John went 'there were burnings and killings and the people suffered'.

John upsets the Church (and ordinary Christians)

Like many kings, John saw the Church as a good source of money. To get to this money, he needed the archbishops to be loyal to him rather than to the Pope. In 1208, John decided to make one of his close friends the new Archbishop of Canterbury.

The Pope did not accept John's choice. He excommunicated John and put all of England under 'interdict'. This meant that no masses could be said, no one could have their sins forgiven, no one could get married and no dead people could be buried in a religious service. Do you remember reading about the religious lives of ordinary people in Chapter 3? To deprive the people of the role and comfort of priests and church services was the most shocking thing that the Pope could do.

Worse, King Philip of France could now invade England because the Pope was very happy to give his permission! In 1213, with Philip preparing to attack, John finally gave in to the Pope's choice of Archbishop. The Interdict was lifted. The invasion was stopped. However, John had to accept King Philip as his overlord.

John infuriates the barons

John had already upset the most important people in his realm, the barons. Now he pushed the barons over the edge. In 1214, when John tried to recover his lands in France, his expensive campaign was a disaster. John's armies were crushed.

Many of John's barons had finally had enough. In 1215, they rose up against their king. They seized London and defeated John in a series of battles. With the king beaten, they drew up a list of 63 demands. John had no choice but to give in.

On 15 June, in a water-meadow called Runnymede, on the banks of the River Thames, John had to agree to demands such as these:

1) The English church should be free from the king's control.
12) The king will not raise taxes without consent of the important nobles.
39) No freeman will be put in prison without a trial by his peers.
40) No one will sell or get in the way of justice.

Many other demands dealt with knights' and barons' other complaints about property rights and inheritance taxes. John also had to agree to appoint 25 barons who would check that he was keeping to the terms of Magna Carta. If he did not, the rebel barons had permission to take the king's lands.

John died in 1216 and the kingdom passed to his nine-year-old son, Henry III. The barons who supported the young king quickly reissued Magna Carta in Henry's name. The rebel barons agreed to give the boy king a chance.

The Crown was safe at last. Or was it?

Step 1

You now need to start looking for causes of rebellion against John. First, remind yourself, using page 69, what 'good kings' were expected to do. Then create three or four 'cause cards'. On each one, try to sum up one cause of the rebellion against John. Try to link your causes to the **expectations** of 'good kings'. For example, your first cause card might say this:

> The barons considered John weak for losing land in France

On the back of each card, add some specific details which fit under this heading.

Henry III and the Provisions of Oxford

A stumbling reign

This is Henry III sitting in front of Westminster Abbey. During his reign, Henry spent much money rebuilding this church. Henry tried to stay on good terms with the Pope and he tried to be a good Christian king. He went to church every day. He gave money to feed the poor.

This document is a surviving copy of Magna Carta that was made in 1225.

He also tried to listen to his barons. As Henry grew older, however, he argued with them more and more. In 1227, Henry began to rule without them. If he needed advice, he turned to family and friends. Think about how each of these points would have angered the barons:

Broken promises	Family favourites
Because Henry had started ruling without his barons, he tried to keep them happy. He promised them large gifts of money and land, but these often took months to arrive or didn't arrive at all.	In 1236, Henry married Eleanor of Provence. Over 170 of Eleanor's family came to England. They were given land and titles. A few years later, more relatives came, called the Lusignans. They were also given land, but they refused to pay taxes!
War and rebellion	**Money problems**
Henry tried, and failed, to regain John's lands in France. In 1240, Henry forced many Welsh barons to accept him as overlord. But between 1256 and 1258, one Welsh baron, Llywelyn ap Gruffudd, fought back. Llywelyn ap Gruffudd restored Welsh control to northern and central Wales. He called himself Prince of Wales.	Henry's wars cost huge sums of money. However, the Lusignans kept advising him to win new lands. In 1254 the Pope offered Henry the kingdom of Sicily. Henry's barons were shocked when Henry agreed because Sicily was ruled by a powerful German family. What made matters worse was that the Pope demanded over £90,000 to pay for its capture!

A peaceful rebellion

In 1258, the English barons were at the end of their tether. Some important barons, bishops and even some knights now held a meeting in Oxford. They created a document called the Provisions of Oxford. Like Magna Carta, this was a set of rules for the king to follow. The Provisions of Oxford, however, were much more extreme. These new rules said:

- A council of fifteen barons should run the country alongside the king.
- The king had to call parliaments three times a year.

Even Henry's son, Edward, supported the barons against his father. Henry was forced to give in. When the Lusignans opposed the Provisions, they were driven out of England.

Step 2

Make more cause cards using the section on Henry III and the Provisions of Oxford. Look for causes of anger against Henry III. For example:

> Henry III gave wealth and titles to his French relatives

On the back of each card add more details.

Henry III and Simon de Montfort

Henry III's problems did not end with the Provisions of Oxford. A Norman baron called Simon de Montfort was about to challenge Henry's right to rule.

Henry III claimed to be more afraid of Simon de Montfort than of thunderstorms. Simon de Montfort was a fearsome fighter with a stormy temper.

De Montfort was born into a crusading family in Normandy. As he grew up, he became determined to carve out his own place in the world. In 1229, he came to England to claim old family lands in Leicestershire.

At this time, because the Church forbade money-lending, many nobles and merchants borrowed money from Jewish people. Simon de Montfort now decided to make his mark quickly by expelling all Jewish people from Leicester. This horrific act released many merchants and nobles from their debts. De Montfort played on this fear and hatred of outsiders so as to become ever more popular.

Henry knew Simon de Montfort only too well. De Montfort was married to Henry's sister, Eleanor.

De Montfort helped Henry to stop rebellions in France and was well paid for his efforts. But de Montfort had little respect for the king. He thought that Henry took too much advice from foreigners and favourites. When, in 1242, Henry failed in a French campaign, de Montfort told the king that he should be locked up!

You won't be surprised to hear that Simon de Montfort played a key part in creating the Provisions of Oxford in 1258. He was quickly chosen to be part of the council of fifteen who were to help Henry rule. You also won't be surprised to hear that things soon went wrong. De Montfort fled to France.

In 1263, de Montfort was returning to England for a final showdown with the king. Read the thought bubbles below to find out why. Henry knew that de Montfort's arrival meant trouble.

> The king has agreed that we should have regular parliaments. But it isn't happening! There was meant to be one in January 1259 but Henry was in France! When I tried to hold a parliament, Henry arrived with 300 soldiers and accused me of plotting against him!

> The Lusignan family are back in England and advising the king again. The king should listen to his own barons! He should listen to knights and merchants as well. They all pay taxes!

> Henry has managed to wriggle out of the Provisions of Oxford. In 1261 he got the Pope to overturn them. The Pope said that kings do not have to listen to their own subjects. This is wrong! A king should seek the support of his people.

> The king has started raising money through his law courts again. It isn't fair. Magna Carta promised every free man the right to justice.

De Montfort's parliaments

De Montfort fights back again

When de Montfort arrived in England, he gained much support. He won over the barons who had rebelled in 1258 as well as many knights and London merchants. These supporters of de Montfort were furious with their king, and they showed it. When Henry's wife, Eleanor of Provence, sailed down the Thames to join Henry in a fight back against de Montfort, she was pelted with rotten vegetables. Things looked bleak for Henry III.

The King of France was called in to settle things. He said that Henry did not have to follow the Provisions of Oxford. This was a blow for de Montfort.

At this point, de Montfort made a big gamble. In May 1264, he raised an army, successfully attacked the king at Lewes (a town near the south coast), and captured both Henry and his family. De Montfort was now in charge. In June 1264, he called his own parliament without the king. De Montfort called knights and peasants across England to come and defend his parliament against foreign invaders. He also encouraged hatred of outsiders.

Knights and peasants came in their thousands, murdering Jewish people along the way.

De Montfort finally falls

By Christmas of 1264, de Montfort was losing the support of the barons. He called another parliament, but this time he asked knights and powerful town merchants to come too. De Montfort promised that his new parliament would be the model for the future.

But de Montfort had no future. In May 1265, Henry's son, Edward, escaped from prison. He defeated de Montfort at the Battle of Evesham. When de Montfort was finally cornered, his arms, legs and head were cut off and his testicles stuffed into his mouth.

Debates about de Montfort

Henry III returned to the throne and ruled until 1272. He continued to call parliaments, sometimes including knights and, on one occasion, men from the towns too.

Historians still debate what Simon de Montfort was really up to. Was he out for his own gain, or did he really want to share power? It is hard to tell.

De Montfort's efforts certainly had lasting consequences. Edward I, Henry III's son, agreed to call the 'commons' (those who were not lords) to his parliaments. Edward I also reissued a version of Magna Carta in 1297, although in Edward's version, the king remained firmly in charge.

Whatever de Montfort was up to, his actions played their part in the slow process of Parliament changing. Over time, rulers and people came to see parliaments as normal and necessary.

Step 3

Use pages 73–75 to make a final set of cause cards, this time explaining why Simon de Montfort rebelled against Henry III. Add details on the back of each card.

Shaping your argument

You now have a set of cause cards. You are going to use these to build an explanation of why the barons kept rebelling. Follow these steps:

1. In pairs or threes, look for themes that keep cropping up in your cards. Using these themes, sort your cards into groups. Look back at the 'expectations' of kings on page 69 to give you ideas for your themes.
2. Decide what to call your theme. Give it a heading. For example:

Kings not listening to barons

3. Now it is time to bring your explanation together in writing. Write out the enquiry question as your title. Then write a paragraph about each of your themes. The headings will help you to write each paragraph's opening sentence. Include plenty of details from this chapter's stories to support your points. Remember that all the time, you are explaining why the barons kept rebelling. Keep focused on that question!

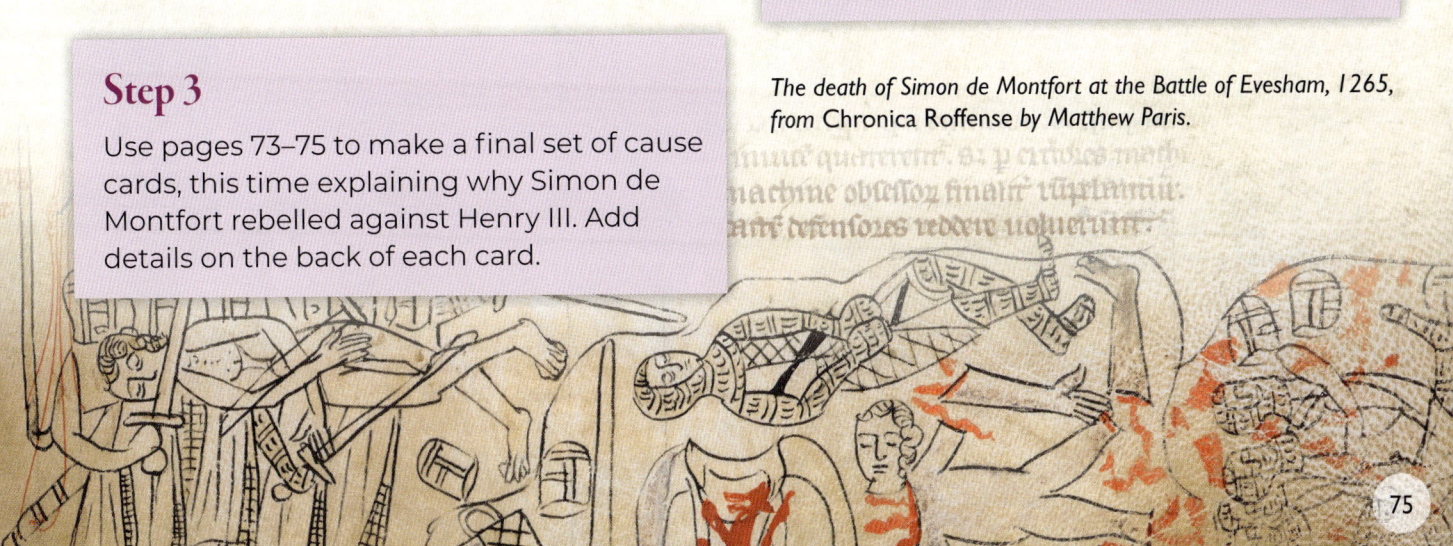

The death of Simon de Montfort at the Battle of Evesham, 1265, from Chronica Roffense *by Matthew Paris.*

12 Soldiers on the steppe

How did the Mongols end up destroying Baghdad?

'Go home to Mongolia, young man!'

In the year 1258, the caliph spat out these words. He sent a messenger to relay them to a man called Hulegu, who was right outside the walls of the caliph's round city. Hulegu was leading the Mongol army now surrounding Baghdad.

The caliph was confident that the soldiers defending Baghdad could defeat the Mongols. Four times in forty years, Mongol armies had approached the city. Four times, they had got no nearer. But the Mongols had ridden thousands of miles from central Asia. This time, they were not going back.

Hulegu launched attack after attack. With the blood of his grandfather, Chinggis Khan, in his veins, Hulegu was confident. Baghdad had never seen warriors like the Mongols before. For ten days, the Mongols rode their horses at terrifying speeds. For ten days, Baghdad cried for mercy.

In little over a week, one of the greatest cities ever built was reduced to rubble by Mongol soldiers from a distant corner of Asia. Centuries of knowledge were wiped out as books were burned or thrown in the river. 90,000 died. Irrigation was destroyed. Baghdad struggled to recover its influence and economic power.

This illustration of the attack on Baghdad is from the Jāmi' al-Tawārīkh, a history book, written by Rashid al-Din in the early fourteenth century. Published in Arabic and Persian, it covered so much history that it is sometimes called the first world history. How has the artist tried to show the roundness of Baghdad, and the richness of its culture? Can you find the catapults outside the city?

A boy on the steppe

Our story begins with a Mongol boy called Temujin. (It was Temujin's grandson, Hulegu, who later destroyed Baghdad.) Temujin would become one of the most feared warriors in history. Historians are unsure of most details in his life, but he was born in around 1162.

Before we learn how he made the Mongols a superpower, we need to understand the Mongols. Let us start with the world in which Temujin grew up – the Mongolian steppe. This largely treeless landscape stretched for hundreds of miles across Asia. It shaped every aspect of Mongol life.

The harsh climate, often with sub-freezing temperatures, toughened the Mongols. Mongols were always on the move, following their animals in search for new grazing. The lack of rainfall caused the Mongols to revere rivers.

Animals, especially horses, were vital to the Mongol way of life. Mongolian horses were smaller than western horses, and their hair grew to the ground. It was said that each Mongol needed five horses just to live on the steppe. Women and men each had roles to play tending to horses. From the earliest age, Mongols like Temujin were trained to shoot arrows while galloping on horseback.

Since everyone wanted the best grass for their horses, tribes formed to compete for land. But there was little loyalty. Mongols could be persuaded to join new, more successful groups. In such a world, it was possible for a charismatic person to build a band of soldiers very quickly. Once you had built your band, however, you had to keep fighting! And you had to keep winning. Winning was hard without any military bases, like castles (such as those that we saw the Normans build in England).

Your enquiry

Historians have to explain how such extraordinary events happen. You are going to use this chapter to find possible causes. At the end of the enquiry, you will organise these causes into a giant diagram that answers this question: 'How did the Mongols end up destroying Baghdad?'

Step 1

Our enquiry is about something which happened in 1258, yet we have just described Mongol life nearly a hundred years before. The information on this page won't help you answer the enquiry question yet, but it will become useful later. You need to record it and think about it. You will soon see why it was important. Make notes on:

- the steppe
- how the Mongols lived
- how the landscape and Mongol way of life shaped the growth of tribes.

Temujin becomes Chinggis Khan

Historians and the Mongols

Historians have found rich evidence for Temujin's life from objects and from oral tradition. A written account in Mongolian has survived but historians must rely on non-Mongol sources to check it. In order to do that, they need to understand many languages. Historians cannot be certain, therefore, about some Mongol stories. As is often the case with the distant past, historians must make cautious suggestions about what is *likely* to have been the case, rather than what definitely happened.

Historians *are* sure, however, how Temujin lived in his childhood. Like others living on the steppe, Temujin, his mother and siblings would have eaten berries, roots, milk products and fish. Temujin and his brothers hunted marmots for meat. The family owned only nine horses, which suggests that, compared with other families, they were poor.

Temujin gains followers

The stories that historians have found in the sources suggest that by age 12, Temujin had a ruthless streak. As a child, he killed his own half-brother for stealing a fish from him. Curious young men started to look up to him. Violent men admired him. Tales of Temujin's escapades spread across the steppe. Temujin led ambushes and raids. He overcame stronger opponents. And he always shared the spoils of his victories.

Temujin gained social status through the first of his wives, Borte, who was from a wealthier family. Stories from early in their marriage add to our picture of Temujin's character. One day, Temujin's camp was attacked by a rival tribe: the Merkit. Temujin and his followers fled.

But the sources say, 'there was no horse for Borte'. He had left his wife behind! Why was this? We cannot be sure. What we do know is that he returned to take revenge. Temujin slaughtered every single male involved in the raid. He took hundreds of women into slavery. Temujin would have no one stand in his way.

Temujin rewarded his followers for their skills and contributions. By 1186, his ever-growing band of loyal supporters swore to follow him into battle. The more he defeated other tribes, the more his followers adored him.

Soon Temujin started to dream big. Historians have been able to use the sources to find evidence for Temujin's big ambitions. It seems likely that Temujin wanted to become more than a local leader. At some point, he started to dream of becoming the most powerful person in Mongolia.

Temujin and Jamuga

A curious quirk of Temujin's life was that his best friend became his greatest rival. As two small boys, Temujin had made a pact called an 'anda' with Jamuga. The anda was a Mongol custom which made two friends closer than brothers. When he grew up, Jamuga became a tribal leader of another powerful tribe, the Naiman. By 1200, Temujin's new ambitions brought him into conflict with this other tribe, and therefore with his childhood 'anda'.

In 1203, Jamuga and his friends planned to poison Temujin at a feast. Two of Temujin's loyal followers uncovered the plot just in time for Temujin to escape. Temujin began to prepare his army for revenge. He promised his followers, 'I shall share with you the sweet and the bitter'.

After careful preparation and remarkable leadership, in 1205 Temujin defeated the Naiman tribe. But during the final battle, a strange thing happened. Jamuga deserted the Naiman tribe. Was it a childhood loyalty to his old anda? Historians are unsure. One thing they are sure of is that Temujin still showed no mercy to his old anda. Temujin had Jamuga executed.

Triumphant, Temujin headed to this river. It is the Onon River where he grew up – a fitting site for Temujin's crowning glory. He had destroyed every other threat to his power in Mongolia. Now, on the banks of the Onon, he received a new title: Chinggis Khan. Historians debate whether it means 'universal' ruler or 'fierce' ruler. But they all agree that Mongolia was now united.

This is a modern sculpture of Borte, next to her husband, Chinggis Khan.

Step 2

You can now start to build a picture of why the Mongols ended up in Baghdad. Knowing about the steppe helps you understand how Mongol strength grew. Re-read pages 77–78 and try to identify three or four causes which are long-term. A good way of doing this is to capture a cause in one word or phrase, and then explain it. For example:

- **Environment**
  Life on the steppe made Mongols very good at ...
- **Chinggis Khan's character**
  Stories about Chinggis Khan show that he ...

A terrifying empire

The Mongol army

Mongol soldiers were only loyal so long as they received rewards. So Chinggis Khan had a problem: if everyone in Mongolia was under his command, from whom would he take riches? He decided to do what no Mongol leader had done before. He would invade northern China.

China's population was a hundred times bigger than Mongolia's. So Chinggis Khan spent years planning. Every male under 70 received military training. Women did not fight in military campaigns, but they were expected to defend themselves, and some were skilled archers. Chinggis Khan surrounded himself with the best generals from Mongolia and beyond. He chose people for what they could do, rather than for their status or wealth.

Chinggis Khan made the Mongol army disciplined and versatile. It could defeat enemies in pitched battles or chip away at them with lightning raids. Sometimes each soldier carried five lanterns so as to deceive an enemy into thinking that the army was larger.

This army kept winning. China was successfully invaded in 1215. In England, people remember 1215 for Magna Carta. For the wider world, the Mongol success in northern China has had more historical significance.

Conquering the world

'Ruthless planning...organisation...strategic objectives'. These are the reasons that British historian Peter Frankopan has given for the Mongols' continuous success. But we must add something else: the Mongols were simply terrifying. In 1219, Chinggis Khan sent a friendly message to a Sultan who ruled the Khwarazmian empire, a vast Muslim empire by the Caspian Sea. In response, the Sultan killed 450 Mongol soldiers. To punish this insult to Mongol pride, Chinggis Khan ordered the massacre of tens of thousands of men, women and children.

Hearing stories that travelled down the Silk Roads, Muslims and Christians soon feared the Mongols more than each other. Even western and Byzantine Christians tried to patch up their differences.

After Chinggis Khan's death in 1227, the Mongols kept advancing. Look at the map. They did not stop in northern China. Over the next thirty years they invaded Russia. They took parts of what are now Pakistan, India and Tibet. They moved into eastern Europe.

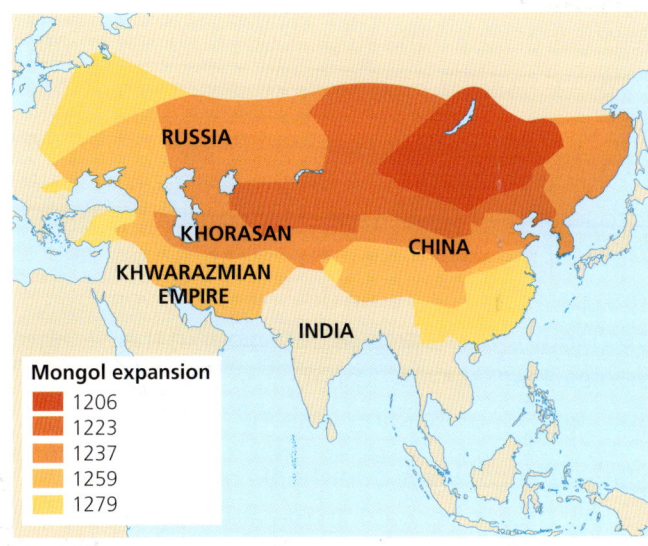

The Mongol empire by 1279.

Step 3

On page 79, find more words or phrases which could become causes of the Mongols' destruction of Baghdad. For example:

- ruthless planning.

Use some facts about each one to explain how it could be a cause.

Holding the empire together

Massive empires cannot be ruled only from horseback. Chinggis Khan had to govern his empire. He had to hold it together. What can hold an empire together? Like many rulers, Chinggis Khan chose to make use of shared values and rules. As early as 1206, he introduced something that was a bit like a legal code: the Yasa.

Historians dispute the exact content of the Yasa because most of it was never written down. Using other written sources and also oral sources, however, some historians suggest that the Yasa probably drew together Mongol traditions with the sayings of Chinggis. For instance, we know that the Mongols revered rivers. This helps to explain why the Yasa forbade people from washing in running rivers or from scooping water with hands rather than with a vessel. Washing clothes in a thunderstorm was also forbidden. It was also illegal to eat in front of someone without offering them food. What traditions or features of life on the steppe, do you think, might have led to a law such as that?

The Yasa seems to have set out rules around who could be enslaved. For example, Chinggis Khan forbade the enslavement of Mongol women. Much of the Yasa dealt with military issues. The Yasa promoted extreme discipline and very demanding standards of behaviour in the Mongol armies. The Yasa also forbade the hunting of animals in the breeding season.

Many offences were punishable by death, which usually meant beheading. Because royal blood could not be spilled on the ground, a royal victim (like the Baghdad caliph in 1258) might be wrapped in a carpet and trampled to death by horses.

Tolerance and diversity

The Mongols could be surprisingly flexible. Sometimes they let conquered people keep their own laws. The Mongols understood the importance of local cultures and traditions. Arts and crafts were encouraged wherever they conquered. In China, the Mongols paid for plays and paintings. In Russia they promoted the skill of goldsmiths and woodcarvers.

Archaeologists have studied the remains of the Mongol capital city of Qaraqorum. It lies right in the middle of modern-day Mongolia. In the 1230s, Chinggis Khan's son Ogedei ordered this city to be built. Qaraqorum has long since disappeared, but its archaeological remains show us that the Mongols tolerated customs and religions from around the world. Archaeologists have found the ruins of a Buddhist temple and coins with Arabic writing. Look at this huge stone turtle below from Qaraqorum, made in the thirteenth century. The turtle is covered with Chinese motifs. Qaraqorum was a melting-pot of ideas and influences. Historians have even found evidence that Mongol leaders sometimes argued about how far to be tolerant of other cultures.

After Chinggis Khan died, two powerful women fought over which of their sons should become the next Great Khan. Sorqaqtani Beki emerged victorious. One Iranian historian described her as the 'most able woman in the world'.

Like Eleanor of Aquitaine, Sorqaqtani Beki had four sons who all went on to be monarchs. She worked with others to build alliances and to allow local customs to exist alongside the Yasa. Her son Mongke became the Great Khan in 1251.

Connected by trade

As well as plundering China for booty, the Mongols now achieved control over the Silk Roads. Mongol rulers loved luxurious textiles. They liked to reward loyal followers with fine fabrics.

Because the Mongols were controlling the Silk Roads, for the first time in history there were stable connections between east and west. Ideas and goods spread quickly between worlds. Iranian chickpeas found their way into Chinese meals. Chinese designs found their way into Iranian pottery. Medicine improved because medical knowledge could now travel further and faster.

In the 1250s, the Mongols could have taken western Europe but they thought that far greater treasures were to be found in Asia. In his book, *The Silk Roads*, the historian Peter Frankopan writes that everything outside of Asia was a bit of a 'sideshow'. The Great Khan Mongke told his brother, Hulegu, to focus on conquering more of west Asia. It was this that brought Hulegu to Baghdad in 1258.

Scenes showing the siege of Baghdad from the Jāmi' al-Tawārīkh, written by Rashid al-Din in the early fourteenth century.

End of an era

For the Mongols, 1258 was the ideal time to arrive. The Islamic world was divided. The caliph was weak. Some Muslims were even secretly pleased to see Baghdad attacked.

Arriving in the outskirts of Baghdad, Hulegu did not plan to destroy the city. He just wanted riches and control. But the caliph's words (which you read on page 76) angered him. Hulegu decided to make an example of Baghdad.

Behind Hulegu was the largest and most diverse army that the Mongols had ever assembled: 150,000 men from all over the empire. It included Christians, determined to seek revenge on Muslims after the crusades. It included one thousand Chinese artillery experts. Using catapults, they launched a devastating attack on Baghdad's walls.

Step 4

As you look for more causes of the Mongol attack on Baghdad, think about how the Mongols made their empire stable enough to expand and survive. Use pages 80–81 to shape two or three more main causes.

What happened to the Mongols after Baghdad?

Some historians have called the destruction of Baghdad the end of the Islamic Golden Age. But it was the end of the Mongol empire too. In 1260, Hulegu's army was defeated by Egyptian soldiers – the first military defeat for decades. Chinggis Khan's successors now found it impossible to stay united. Soon, an empire that once ruled vast swathes of Asia was no more.

Shaping your argument

You will now make a giant causation diagram to explain how the Mongol attack on Baghdad happened.

You have already found a word (such as 'environment') or a short phrase (such as 'ruthless planning') to sum up each main cause. You have also supported each main cause with examples which help to explain or illustrate that cause.

Follow these steps:

1 Make large boxes for each of your main causes. Write your main causes in those boxes. If you think that any of those causes are very long-term, such as features of the environment which existed long before Chinggis Khan, you must place them around the edges of your diagram, rather than near the centre.
2 Near those cause boxes, make smaller boxes for your supporting examples.
3 Finally, draw lines to show any connections between your causes or between your examples.

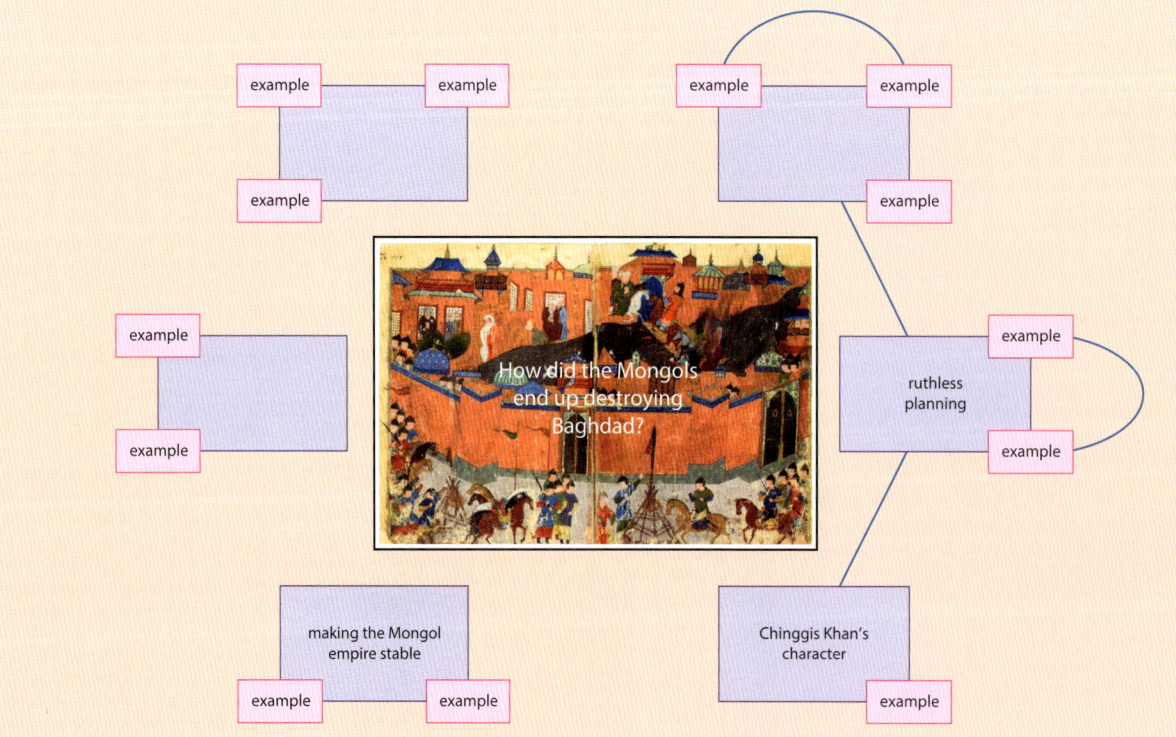

13 A golden country: the empire of Mali

What does the story of Mansa Musa reveal about medieval west Africa?

It is 1323. Mansa Musa, the emperor of Mali, sits on an ebony throne. Behind him, thirty enslaved people from Turkey and Egypt stand to attention. One of them holds a silk sunshade, topped by a golden falcon, over the emperor's head.

This is a land of gold and many will come to see Mansa Musa's rule as a golden age. South of the Sahara Desert, the African empire of Mali has grown rich from huge nuggets of gold mined from the goldfields of Wangara. One of the miners was at the palace today, bringing a camel laden with gold as a gift for the mansa. The word 'mansa' means 'emperor' or 'king'. Mansa Musa is the emperor of the biggest empire that Africa has ever known.

Two great elephant tusks stand beside the mansa's throne. On his raised platform in the palace courtyard, Mansa Musa can see the rounded roofs of clay houses stretching into the distance. Several horses stand calmly nearby. Mansa Musa will soon be inspecting them, ready for a long journey. This journey is a pilgrimage.

Mansa Musa cannot wait to get going, but he must. He must make sure that his empire is safe before he leaves. Today, he will discuss his plans with the emirs (chiefs), who each govern different parts of the empire.

Mansa Musa shifts a little on his throne. A bow and three arrows, each made of pure gold, rest heavily on his knees.

The mansa's musicians begin drumming. The buzz of balafons fills the air. The visitors must be here. Mansa Musa does not stand when the emirs arrive in the palace courtyard.

Your enquiry

Mansa Musa's pilgrimage made him famous. Stories of his wealth and his generosity became legends. People from as far away as England wanted to hear more about his kingdom. Historians, today, still find him remarkable. By studying Mansa Musa, historians have built fascinating new knowledge about the medieval world. In this enquiry, you are going to show what the story of Mansa Musa reveals about medieval West Africa.

Mansa Musa prepares for his pilgrimage

Decorated in silver and gold, the king's palace dazzles in the sun. From his throne, Mansa Musa strains to see his emirs. The emperor of Mali never speaks aloud in public. Instead, he whispers what he wants to say to a spokesman called a jeli, who makes the announcements.

On this day in 1323, the jeli is announcing the king's plans to go on a great pilgrimage or hajj to the holy cities of Makkah and Medina in Arabia. This journey will cross the Sahara Desert, the largest desert in the world. Crossing the desert will take over a year, so Mansa Musa will need provisions from all over the empire. He has already sent officials to the bountiful markets of his cities. Horses will be needed to carry the king and his great officials across the desert. There is so much work to do.

Mansa Musa rises to inspect his horses

Mansa Musa strokes the delicate strands of gold woven into his horse's mane. His mind turns to another important animal: the camel. Capable of carrying heavy loads in the heat of the Sahara, thousands of camels will carry food, water and equipment on the pilgrimage.

Mansa Musa's pilgrimage became so widely known outside Africa that the empire of Mali appeared for the first time on a European map. This map was made by Italian map-maker Angelino Dulcert in 1339.

Other camels will have a much heavier load to bear. Although Mansa Musa is on a religious pilgrimage to Makkah, where he will pray in front of the Kaaba, he can do other things along the way. Mansa Musa will present, in person, his gifts to the kings of other African states. This will help the mansa to strengthen alliances with these states.

Mansa Musa needs gold for these gifts. He gives the order for 80 camels to be laden with gold.

Step 1

In this enquiry, you will show how the story of Mansa Musa can reveal different things about medieval West Africa. Make a table like this one. Fill the columns with as many details as you can from what you have read so far. Your table will then show what the story of Mansa Musa **reveals**.

Kingship	Religion	Trade	Natural resources	The growth of cities
	Mansa Musa's great pilgrimage to Makkah reveals how Islam was established in West Africa.		Mansa Musa's order to load 80 camels with gold reveals how rich the Malian goldfields were.	

Mansa Musa sets out on his hajj

Mansa Musa and his entourage travel north, across the broad grasslands of central Mali. The mansa's caravan becomes a long line of glittering gold that stretches for miles across the landscape.

Herds of elephants, giraffes and gazelles stop and stare. Finding shade under a baobab tree, the mansa takes a drink of water from the tree's trunk. Water has collected here since the last rains came to the grasslands. The emperor knows that soon there will be no baobab trees, and very little water. Soon, he will reach the unforgiving dunes of the Sahara.

This is an extract from a book written much later, in the seventeenth century, by Timbuktu scholar Al-Sa'd. It shows how some of the stories which we are telling here lived on in the African source records. Al-Sa'd describes how Mansa Musa…

set off in great pomp, with a large party, including sixty thousand soldiers and five hundred slaves, who ran in front of him as he rode. Each of the slaves bore in his hand a wand fashioned from 500 mithqāls [nearly 2 kilograms] of gold.'

The route taken by Mansa Musa on the hajj.

Travelling with a caravan across the Sahara Desert is a dangerous business. The mansa has heard stories of entire caravans losing their way and dying in sandstorms. The mansa will need to rely on the traders who travel with him: their knowledge of oases in the Sahara Desert is vital for the pilgrimage to succeed. These oases will allow the caravan to replenish their stock of food and water. Without them, Mansa Musa and his followers will die.

There are no roads in the desert. Day after day, the mansa's scenery is the same. On some nights, the emperor stays up late, listening to men talk about the stars – their only guides across this barren land.

The emperor sleeps.

Mansa Musa reaches Cairo

One morning, about a year later, the emperor wakes up early. The sand-dunes are finally behind him. Today, he enters Cairo, a place which very few of his people have seen. The soldiers who guard the caravan are restless and excited. They are proud to stand guard over their emperor as he enters a new city.

Mansa Musa's arrival creates an instant sensation. People gape in amazement at this king from an unknown land, boasting hundreds of slaves carrying batons of gold. Rumours are whispered about the vast quantities of gold that the mansa has brought with him to Cairo. No one can quite believe how much! Yet Mansa Musa does not spend all his gold at the market; he gives it out freely. First, he sends gifts to the sultan of Egypt. Then he gives out gold to the poor, to important officials, and to people that he meets in the marketplace. He floods Cairo with gold.

The mansa gives out so much gold that the markets are flooded with it. Throughout Egypt and all the Middle East this precious metal will start to drop in value, all because Mansa Musa brought so much gold with him.

This is just one story of many which have been told about Mansa Musa's hajj. Historians admit that there is much that we still do not know. Many historians are fairly confident, however, that Mansa Musa stayed in Cairo for three months before continuing to the holy cities of Makkah and Medina in Arabia. After four months in Makkah, he returned to Cairo and then travelled home, passing through the city of Timbuktu. Mansa Musa had given away so much gold in Cairo that some historians think that he had to borrow money to fund his return home.

This is part of a medieval world map called the Catalan Atlas. It was made in Majorca, fifty years after Mansa Musa made his pilgrimage. It was commissioned by the King of France. Find Mansa Musa. Look carefully at him. Why do you think that the artist drew him like this?

Part of the Catalan Atlas, *made in about 1375, possibly by a Jewish book illustrator. The* Catalan Atlas *was made on parchment and painted in rich colours, including gold and silver.*

Step 2

It's time to add more details about Mansa Musa and his empire to your table, using pages 85–86.

Buried deep in the Mali empire

At the heart of the Mali empire were vibrant cities such as Niani and Jenne. At the time of Mansa Musa's rule (1312–1337), some of these cities held around 100,000 people. Niani was built on the wealth of the Buré goldfield – one of several goldfields in the Mali empire.

Some historians have estimated that in today's money, Mansa Musa was worth $400 billion. He was possibly the richest man in history. Each nugget of gold produced by Mali's goldminers went straight into the king's treasury. Gold connected the Mali empire with the rest of the world. Buying gold motivated merchants to risk their lives crossing the dangerous Sahara Desert.

Gold was central to Mali's success, but you cannot eat gold. To grow an empire, you need to feed and pay an army of soldiers. The empire of Mali grew on the savannah, a vast area of grassland, south of the Sahara Desert. Find the savannah on the map. This grassland was very good for grazing animals like sheep, cows and goats. It was also fertile soil for crops. The Mande people who lived here also fished in the river Niger, an important river for transporting people and goods to different parts of the Mali empire.

Fishing and growing crops gave the Mande people a reliable food supply. It meant that the first Malian kings could feed a larger population and form a bigger army. Making agriculture more efficient also led to the growth of cities. By the time Mansa Musa ascended to the throne in 1312, there were three cities: Niani, Jenne and Timbuktu.

On the back of the mansa's horses

Horses were unusual in sub-Saharan Africa, and each mansa cherished them. Emperors of Mali traditionally imported horses from Arabia. The horses formed a cavalry regiment, which served under the direct command of the mansa himself. Charging across the grasslands in tight formation, the cavalry was unstoppable. The horses became a symbol of royal power. This little terracotta figure of a horse and rider (now in a private collection) has been dated to the thirteenth or fourteenth century.

Long before Mansa Musa came to the throne, his great uncle had united all the Mande people into one kingdom. This was in around 1250. Mansa Musa's great uncle was called Sundiata Keita, but he also had a nickname – the Lion King. One Mande legend says that leaders were granted their power from a **spirit animal**. Another animal from the Mande legend, the bush buffalo, was a kind of guardian spirit with whom leaders had to make a contract.

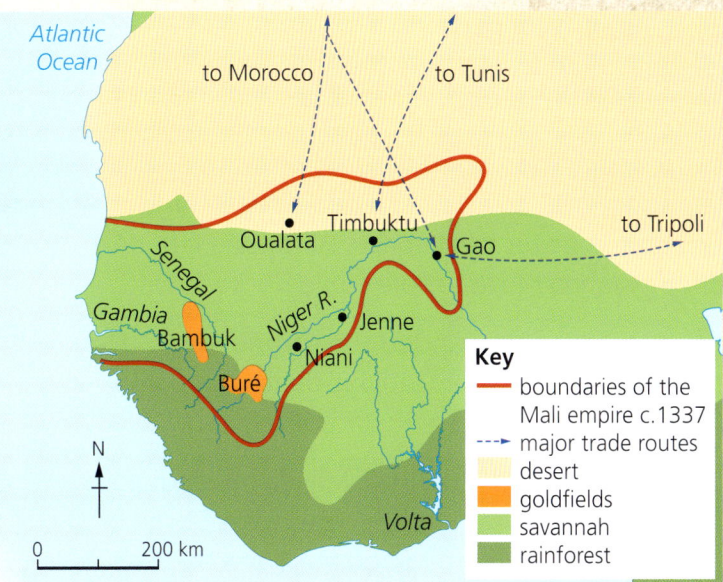

The Mali empire in around 1337.

Governing Mali

Sundiata died in 1255. After he died, seven kings struggled to keep control of Mali. None succeeded. Then one king, known as the Voyager King, decided to explore the Atlantic Ocean. He never came back. Before he left, he chose Mansa Musa to rule while he was away.

So Mansa Musa ascended the throne in 1312. He then stayed in power until his death 25 years later.

When he began ruling Mali, Mansa Musa quickly got to work strengthening the empire. Some of the land conquered by Sundiata Keita, such as Gao, had been lost. Find Gao on the map on the previous page. Notice that it was in a useful position, on a great river. Mansa Musa set about increasing the size of his army to around 100,000 soldiers, including 10,000 horsemen. He was then able to reconquer Gao. Mansa Musa also used the army to rid Mali of the bandits who interrupted trade across the empire. This allowed traders to travel and trade safely.

Sources suggest that Mansa Musa had twenty-four emirs (chiefs), each governing different parts of the empire. Mansa Musa invited his emirs to tell him of any complaints, earning their trust. One source suggests that he rewarded their loyalty with gold and a new honours system. The highest honour was the National Honour of the Trousers. It was said that 'the greater the number of a soldier's exploits, the bigger the size of his trousers.'

Mansa Musa was committed to Islam. He wanted everyone in his kingdom to become Muslim. He once tried to force his goldminers to become Muslim, but they resisted. Mansa Musa accepted this and allowed the miners to continue to believe what they liked.

Travellers, trade and trust

In Chapter 2, we saw how quickly Islam had spread in the seventh and eighth centuries. Bursting out of Arabia, the Muslim armies had poured north and west into the Byzantine empire. They had swept north-east into the Persian empire. By 750, they had reached so far east they were even touching India. In the west, the Muslims made their way right across north Africa to Spain.

But Islam then made its way further into Africa much more slowly. Now Islam moved more through trade and missionaries than through conquest. Eventually, Islam reached Mali. Islam was the faith of the long-distance traders. Shared Muslim beliefs created trust among travellers, making the dangerous journey possible.

Step 3

It's time to add more details to your table. We have helped you along with a couple of ideas.

Kingship	Religion	Trade	Natural resources	The growth of cities
Mansa Musa set out to re-conquer Gao as soon as he came to the throne. This shows that military success and control were a priority for African kings.	Mansa Musa's decision not to force his miners to convert to Islam reveals that ...			

The caravan routes were vital for keeping the doors of Mali open. Look again at the map on page 85. Notice how Mali was separated from the north by the vast Sahara Desert. To the west was another barrier: the Atlantic Ocean. Sailors had not yet learned to navigate the Atlantic coast. Malian trade was therefore only possible across the vast dry desert, and that meant that oases were vital. An oasis is formed in the desert where water bubbles to the surface and creates an island of green. With careful farming, the water could be used to grow crops. It was the oases which enabled the merchants travelling to and from the markets of Mali to find food and water.

By the time of Mansa Musa's reign, the caravans had grown very large – as many as 12,000 camels in one caravan. At this time, nearly all the gold in Europe's jewellery and crowns came from Mali. The caravans moving north across the desert carried not just Malian gold, however, but copper, cereals, fish, ivory and salt from the Sahara. Salt, which stopped food from rotting, was carried in huge tablets on the backs of camels.

Trade was regular both in and out of Mali. The Mande people living in the Mali empire expected to buy luxury items, such as silk, in their city markets. In a Malian market, goods could be found from as far away as China, India and Spain. The publicity that Mansa Musa created on his pilgrimage caused trade to increase even more. More and more merchants wanted to travel to Mali's golden lands, and Mansa Musa encouraged them to come.

Great minds shape great cities

Mansa Musa kept the doors of Mali wide open, not just to goods, but to ideas.

New ideas about art and architecture moved in and out of Mali. Mansa Musa asked architects to design hundreds of new mosques. Mansa Musa hoped that all these new mosques would help him to convert more of his people to Islam.

This is the Djinguereber Mosque, still standing today in Timbuktu. New mosques such as this made the city of Timbuktu exciting and attractive.

Caillie's Mali – a drawing of Timbuktu made by a nineteenth-century French explorer in about 1830.

Timbuktu became home to scholars, musicians and priests. Rather like the Muslim city of Baghdad in the eighth and ninth centuries, Timbuktu now became a great centre of learning. In its university, about 25,000 scholars studied in different 'schools'. With access to nearly a million books, they could become architects, astronomers, doctors and engineers.

Placed at the crossing of the Niger River and a major caravan route, Timbuktu saw goods and new ideas flowing in and out, every day. Many traders and travellers converted to Islam during conversations with the city's scholars and students. Busy and bustling, Timbuktu must have been an exciting place to learn.

Mansa Musa ruled Mali for about 25 years. After his death, in about 1337, Mali weakened. In the late fourteenth century, rival leaders fought civil wars. Then outsiders began to attack. In 1433, Mali lost control of Timbuktu. By the end of the fifteenth century, Mali had been taken over by the Songhay empire.

Step 4

Using pages 89–90, add some final details to your table.

Shaping your argument

This photograph shows Toby Green, a modern historian. He has shown that the story of Mansa Musa reveals a great deal about medieval west Africa – its trade, its government and its ways of life. Imagine that you are organising a history event with guest speakers. You have invited Toby Green to speak about medieval Mali. The event manager wants fewer speakers. He wants to cut Toby Green's talk. You are furious!

Write to your event manager explaining why you think that the story of Mansa Musa is historically significant. To do this, you must convince the manager that the story of Mansa Musa reveals much more than the story of just one ruler. Use the headings in your steps to organise your letter.

14 Conflict and connection in the British Isles

What were the effects of English expansion?

Wales and England: warfare and resistance

It is December 1176. We are in south Wales. At Cardigan Castle, Lord Rhys watches the preparations for Christmas. For five years, he has been rebuilding his old wooden castle in stone. Lord Rhys remembers his days as a young rebel leader, when he fought Henry II of England. But now he is a friend of Henry's and the undisputed leader of south Wales. Lord Rhys is secure in his power and authority.

This Christmas, the celebrations will be extra special. Lord Rhys has organised a cultural festival to reward his followers. From his Norman friends, Lord Rhys has heard about such festivals in France. But this festival will celebrate Welsh culture. There will be prizes for the best poets and musicians. There will be feasting and dancing for loyal followers.

This map shows Wales in the early thirteenth century.

	Life in Medieval Wales
Population	• c. 250,000 people
Type of land	• many mountainous and hilly regions • harsh, wet climate, especially in the mountains • soft, fertile lands in parts of the south and east
Ways of making a living	• farming sheep for wool, meat and milk • growing crops and preparing food • weaving wool • trade
Towns	• a few towns, such as Cardiff, with over 2000 people • trade with England, Ireland and France
Change in 12th and 13th centuries	• forests being cleared to create more farmland • more mills being built to make flour

Lord Rhys's festival would become known as an Eisteddfod. It was the beginning of a tradition, still running today, celebrating Welsh history and culture.

Look at the map of medieval Wales. The way Wales was ruled was not simple! Lord Rhys ruled the south in co-operation with the English. Meanwhile, the mountainous regions of the north were controlled by Welsh princes. The ancient earthwork of Offa's Dyke divided England and Wales. For many Welsh people this was a time of prosperity but it was also a time of fear – fear of what powerful English neighbours would do next.

Use the table and the map of medieval Wales to see how and where Welsh people lived.

A new king for England

In 1272, England had a new king – Edward I. Edward I had grown up hearing stories about King Arthur, a legendary, sixth-century ruler of Britain. Edward wanted to be like Arthur. Edward wanted to rule the British Isles.

A defiant Welsh prince

But in north Wales, Prince Llywelyn ap Gruffydd was planning rebellion. Edward was furious. Llywelyn was supposed to be one of Edward's tenants-in-chief, not a rebel! Edward's father, Henry III, had recognised Llywelyn as Prince of Wales. In return, Llywelyn had agreed to support the English king.

Then, in 1275 Llywelyn made Edward I even more furious. Llywelyn married the daughter of Simon de Montfort! Do you remember how de Montfort had challenged Henry III by insisting on a proper parliament? It seemed to Edward that his enemies were joining forces against him.

Edward I now sent messengers to Llywelyn commanding him to travel to Westminster to pay **homage** to Edward. Paying homage was a way of showing loyalty. Llywelyn refused.

In December 1276, Edward declared Llywelyn a rebel. In his border stronghold of Chester, Edward prepared his soldiers for war.

Your enquiry

English expansion into Wales and Scotland in the twelfth and thirteenth centuries could easily just be the story of rulers clashing. But that would not be the full story. Battles won and lost could change who controlled the land, but they also changed how people lived, worked and thought. Ordinary people also made their own changes, as they reacted to rulers' actions, or built their own worlds despite them. You are going to think about who was affected by English expansion and how, and for how long.

Control by castle

The Welsh were experts at ambushing the English and then disappearing into the mountains. But Edward had a solution – castles.

Edward now gathered another army, but not of soldiers. He brought stonemasons, carpenters, diggers and woodsmen from England. Their first stop was Flint. Find Flint on the map on page 91. Boats on the River Dee or the sea could easily bring Edward supplies. Flint was also just a few days' march from Chester. 970 diggers, 300 carpenters and 200 stonemasons began to build.

From his castles, Edward could control the surrounding land. As he moved across Wales, Edward also used his workers to clear woodland where Llywelyn's men could hide before an ambush. Burning woodland and farms, Edward's troops created wide spaces on each side of roads.

Homage and humiliation

In the autumn of 1277, Edward sent 2000 soldiers to capture the island of Anglesey. The farmers of Anglesey watched Edward's men seize their rich, flat, fertile farmlands, full of crops. Now Edward could feed his army. Llywelyn and his men retreated into the mountains of Snowdonia.

Soon, Llywelyn had no choice but to surrender. He was forced to sign the Treaty of Aberconwy. This treaty allowed Edward to control parts of north Wales. Then, on Christmas Day, 1277, Llywelyn's humiliation was complete. Llywelyn had to kneel before Edward at Westminster and promise loyalty. This was called paying homage. Edward wanted everyone to see Llywelyn's humiliation.

The peace of Aberconwy did not last. Between 1277 and 1283, Llywelyn and his brothers rebelled again. They did not succeed. This time, Edward's revenge was even worse. Llywelyn's successor Dafydd met a terrible fate. He was captured and condemned to death by hanging, drawing and quartering.

Symbols of English power

In 1284, in the ancient Welsh palace at Nefyn, Edward celebrated his conquest. He built a round table for feasting, just like the famous round table in the legends of Arthur.

In May 1285, a holy relic that was precious to the Welsh people was paraded through London. The solemn procession was led by King Edward, Queen Eleanor, the Archbishop of Canterbury, fourteen bishops and many great nobles. Called the Cross of Neith, it was believed to be a fragment of Jesus's cross. Some said a ninth-century saint had brought it from Jerusalem. By parading the Cross of Neith through London, Edward was saying that Llywelyn's dynasty was dead. A Welsh chronicler wrote, 'and then all Wales was cast to the ground'.

To show his power over Wales, Edward I now built castles. Castles could house soldiers, act as watchtowers and scare people into obeying the English.

Another symbol of English power was the walled towns, known as boroughs, that Edward built around the castles. The English controlled who could live and trade in the towns. On this page you can see a reconstruction of Flint Castle as it would have looked at the end of the thirteenth century. Notice the walled town set out in a grid pattern, behind the castle.

Notice, too, the thickness of the castle walls. Some castles had walls which were even thicker. Caernarfon Castle had walls five metres thick. Its octagonal towers copied those far away in Constantinople. Find Caernarfon on the map on page 91. How were Edward I's castle building tactics similar to William I's that you read about in Chapter 4? What else do you notice about the position of Edward I's major castles?

Welsh land in English hands

Across Wales, rich farmlands were given to English nobles from Yorkshire and Lancashire. In Chapter 4 you learned how quickly English land changed hands after the Norman Conquest, and how this affected peasants. The conquest of Wales, two centuries later, was similar. More and more Welsh people lost control over trade and farming.

Symbols of Welsh identity

Edward's actions made many Welsh people want to protect and celebrate their own symbols – whether stories, traditions or culture – all the more.

Do you remember the poetry in the caliphs' court at Baghdad? Do you remember the troubadours of Aquitaine? In a similar way, Welsh princes had given encouragement, training and status to Welsh poets and musicians.

This ruin is near Tregaron in the county of Ceredigion. Founded in 1164, it is called Abaty Ystrad Fflur (often known as Strata Florida), which means Abbey of the Valley of Flowers. Here, from Llywelyn's death in 1282 until around 1350, the monks fought the English in a different way. The monks at Strata Florida now gathered all the Welsh poetry they could find. This collection of Welsh poems drew together the traditions of Welsh court poets. To this day, Welsh poetry is celebrated in Eisteddfods.

The tradition of support for Welsh culture and independence continued in Strata Florida Abbey. In 1401, when the Abbey was taken by the English King Henry IV, the monks were evicted for their loyalty to the Welsh rebels.

Step 1

Copy the table below. Use pages 91–94 to find effects of English expansion and decide which heading to put them under. We have started you off.

Cultural (ideas, traditions and values)	Economic (land, life and work)
Welsh monks made sure that traditions of Welsh poetry were preserved.	The English seize rich farmland.

Scotland and England: warfare and resistance

High on a rock sits Edinburgh Castle. Alexander III, King of Scotland enjoys its roaring fires. The markets and houses of Edinburgh sprawl below. It is spring. Food is short for many Scots at this time of year, but in his banqueting hall, Alexander dines on fine venison, caught in his forests.

Since he was seven, Alexander has worked to maintain Scotland's strength. His people are pleased to see Alexander continue the proud tradition of Scottish kings. Alexander is friendly with his English neighbour, Edward. To Alexander, the two kings are equals. They are fellow kings, both anointed by God.

This map shows the kingdom of Scotland in the thirteenth century.

Scotland's growing wealth gave Alexander power. In the thirteenth century, the people of Berwick-upon-Tweed had grown rich by trading fish, grain, wool and animal skins. Scottish kings often stopped at Berwick to visit the royal mint where the kingdom's coins were made. Across Scotland, Alexander had fortresses, such as his castles at Stirling and Edinburgh.

Study the table about medieval Scotland. What similarities/differences did it have with Wales?

But Alexander and Scotland were in for some very bad luck...

	Medieval Scotland
Population	c. 500,000 people
Type of land	Lowlands with rich, fertile land for crops Highlands used for grazing sheep and cattle
Ways of making a living	Farming the land (crops and animals) Weaving wool Trading wool and other goods from the ports on large rivers, such as the Forth and the Clyde, and towns such as Berwick
Large towns	Stirling – population of about 1000 Edinburgh and Berwick – populations of over 6000
Change in the 12th and 13th centuries	Increased foreign trade and growing wealth

Disaster 1: In 1275 King Alexander's wife, Margaret, sister of Edward I, died.

Disaster 2: Between 1281 and 1284 all three of Alexander's children died.

Alexander named his granddaughter Margaret 'the Maid of Norway' as his **heir**. Meanwhile, his new wife, Yolande, waited for him in Fife. Alexander set off from Edinburgh Castle, riding along the coast, to see Yolande for her birthday.

Disaster 3: Alexander never made it to Fife. In March 1286, he was found dead at the bottom of a cliff.

Without monarch or heir, Scotland's future was in peril. Perhaps seven-year-old Margaret in Norway could come and save them? Margaret was sent for. There was even talk of her marrying Edward I's son Edward in a new alliance.

Disaster 4: Margaret never made it to Scotland. In 1290, she died from food poisoning on the way.

Edward I as judge

No-one could decide who should become the next ruler of Scotland. Some said John Balliol. Others said Robert Bruce. To avoid civil war, some church leaders urged Edward I to help the Scots decide who should be king.

Edward I seized the opportunity, but many Scottish nobles resisted his interference. After much argument, and many threats by Edward, Edward got his way. In 1292 John Balliol was crowned King of Scotland.

John Balliol was under the control of Edward...

...or so Edward thought.

John Balliol: a disobedient king

As King of Scotland, John Balliol became less and less willing to do what Edward wanted, so Edward decided to take back control.

In late March 1296, Edward approached Berwick with a vast army of English and Irish soldiers. Edward demanded the surrender of the town, but the citizens refused. The people of Berwick were used to warfare. They didn't scare easily. They jeered, swore and bared their buttocks at Edward's army.

Edward's revenge was brutal. Scottish sources from two centuries later reveal how the memory stayed with the people of Berwick:

> When the town had been taken Edward spared no one, whatever the age or sex, and for two days streams of blood flowed from the bodies of the slain...he ordered 7500 souls of both sexes to be massacred...So that mills could be turned by the flow of their blood.

'Massacre of Berwick' from Bower's *Scotichronicon* written in the fifteenth century.

Soon Edward had captured John Balliol and was in control of Scotland. He even confiscated the Stone of Scone – the traditional seat on which Scottish kings were crowned. He fitted it underneath his own coronation chair in Westminster Abbey. Edward was determined to remove the idea that Scotland was an independent kingdom.

1297: Scottish victory at Stirling Bridge

Just as he had in Wales, Edward built castles across lowland Scotland and granted land to English nobles. This disrupted Scottish trade and made travel dangerous for ordinary people. People in Scotland resented this disruption. They also resented English laws. They resented unjust and brutal treatment.

Can you see the Stone of Scone tucked underneath the coronation chair? Why do you think Edward put it there? The Stone of Scone was not returned to Scotland until 1996. It is now kept in Edinburgh Castle.

Many felt that their once-powerful kingdom was being destroyed.

It did not take long for a new rebellion to begin. In the north of Scotland, the rebellion's new, young leaders – Robert Bruce and William Wallace – gained much support. Wallace united Scottish people around the dream of freedom from English control.

To reach Wallace's army, Edward needed to cross the Firth of Forth, and the place to do that was Stirling Bridge. In September 1297, the English army reached Stirling. They lined up on one side of the bridge, ready to cross.

Across the Firth of Forth, Wallace's army taunted the English. As the English struggled across the narrow bridge, they slowed down and broke ranks. By the time the straggling English troops reached the other side, they were easy to slaughter. Many English soldiers fled.

A nineteenth-century Scottish painting of the Battle of Stirling Bridge.

1297–1298: Terror in the borders

Seeing the English flee Stirling Bridge, Wallace took the opportunity to spread devastation and fear in the borders and the north of England. He raided land, castles and monasteries from Carlisle to Newcastle. Monks and priests fled.

Then in 1298, it was the turn of the English army to roam the Scottish countryside. They were looking for Wallace. Wherever they went, English soldiers terrorised people, burned houses, destroyed farmland and threatened trade.

Edward eventually found where Wallace was hiding. In July 1298, they met in battle near Falkirk, in the Scottish borders. The Scots had no chance against the power of the English army.

After their defeat, Wallace, Bruce and many Scottish nobles escaped. Edward's forces hunted for Bruce. They never found him.

1304: English victory at Stirling Castle

In 1304 Edward was back in Scotland. Inside Stirling Castle, twenty Scottish soldiers prepared for a siege. In nearby woodland, the English prepared arrows and siege engines. In the local quarry, English masons carved stones into missiles. Local people, seeing such preparation, fled in fear.

The siege of Stirling Castle began.

After three months, exhausted and starving, the Scottish defenders sent a message of surrender to Edward. Yet Edward refused the surrender because he wanted to try out his new giant catapult. Edward's new catapult was known by its French name, trebuchet, but the English nicknamed it 'Warwolf'. Only when Warwolf had destroyed the castle walls did Edward let the exhausted Scots leave.

This time, securing control of Scotland was easy. Divided and quarrelling, the Scots could be chased through the countryside. Ordinary people, their lands destroyed by both sides, scarcely knew whom to support.

1305: Wallace's capture and execution

Scottish nobles agreed to hunt Wallace down. After capture, Wallace remained defiant. He said, 'I could not be a traitor to Edward, for I was never his subject.' Wallace was hanged, drawn and quartered in London. Parts of his body were displayed in Newcastle, Berwick and Stirling; his head on a spike above London Bridge.

1314: Scottish victory at Bannockburn

Scotland was to win back control in a battle that became legendary.

Edward I had died in 1307. On a night in 1314, his son Edward II's troops crossed a stream called Bannockburn, just south of Stirling. At daybreak, Edward II saw Scottish pikemen advancing. They paused and knelt in prayer. Edward is said to have cried in delight, 'They pray for mercy!'

'For mercy, yes,' his attendant replied, 'but from God, not you. These men will conquer or die.'

The English forces were massacred.

Even after Bannockburn, English kings did not give up. In 1333, Edward III occupied the borderlands and tried to impose yet another king on Scotland. He failed. At the Treaty of Berwick in 1357, Edward III finally accepted Scottish independence.

Stories of Scottish pasts

Scottish people wrote their histories of resistance. In 1370, Robert II of Scotland asked a poet to write about his grandfather Robert Bruce. The poem showed Bruce as romantic hero and the English as enemies of freedom. The poem shaped stories for centuries and nurtured the idea of Scotland as an independent nation.

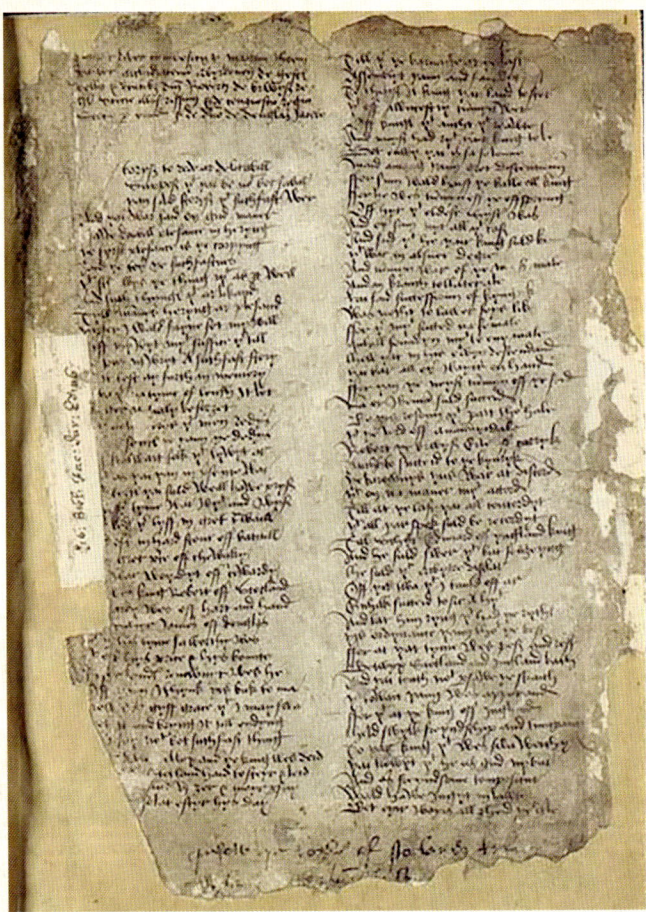

A 1489 copy of the poem The Brus.

The Anglo-Scottish borders

The border lands were known as the marches. The landscape, which you saw on the previous two pages, was wild and remote. The Anglo-Scottish wars had long-lasting effects here. Edward I created the role of Warden of the Marches to control border people and keep them prepared for battle.

Now notice something else on the map – all the surnames. This is what they were called: not 'clans' or 'tribes', but 'surnames'. These strong family groups developed when Scotland and England were frequently at war. Families banded together for protection against raids.

The Anglo-Scottish marches and the surname groups by the sixteenth century.

When England and Scotland were not at war, the raiding continued. This verse from a Scottish riding ballad shows how the borderers used their warring history as an excuse for raiding:

> Then Johnie Armstrong to Willie can say,
> 'Billie a riding then will we
> England and us has long been at **feud**.
> Perhaps we may hit off some booty.'

From Dick o' the Cow, *a sixteenth-century riding ballad.*

The Scottish riding ballads were long poems or songs, often shared and sung by the surnames. These ballads reveal fascinating detail about the borderers' ways of life. They have become useful sources for historians studying how these communities evolved in the medieval period and later. What questions might this extract prompt a historian to ask?

Scottish and English monarchs often encouraged the surnames in violent, warlike behaviour. Sometimes a monarch would plot with the surname groups on the opposite side of the border. Loyal neither to Scotland nor to England, the surname groups switched sides constantly.

The borderers gained a reputation for lawlessness, but they had plenty of rules and customs of their own. Study the purple box to learn about one of their local rules, the 'hot trod'. To the surnames, these local ways were sometimes more important than Scottish or English laws. Wardens of the marches on both sides could rarely control the borderers' violence, and were sometimes part of it themselves.

Step 2

Using pages 94–99, complete your table.

How did the hot trod work?

Imagine the Armstrongs in England are raided by the Elliots from Scotland. The Elliots steal the Armstrongs' cattle. To get justice, the Armstrongs:

- are not allowed to get the warden of the English west march to lead a raid on the Elliots
- are not allowed to wait a week, gather more support and then raid the Elliots
- *are* allowed to set out immediately, chase the Elliots and take back the stolen cattle by force. This is called a hot trod.

Think carefully about this special local custom of the 'hot trod'. Why do you think that the borderers might have developed these rules? Why do you think that they did not want anyone to wait before taking revenge, or to ask for the warden's help?

Shaping your answer

You will now use the two columns in your table to annotate a map of Britain with the effects of English expansion. Use two colours for information from the two columns. Include plenty of dates and names so that you can be as precise as possible.

For both Wales and Scotland, try to find examples of different kinds of people's experience. Look for examples of both rulers and ruled, and think about different types of effects, such as ways of life or changing culture.

Finally, decide which events were likely to have had the most long-lasting effects, and underline them.

We have started you off with two examples.

15 Order and disorder in Walsham

How did one village respond to the Black Death?

It is the week before Christmas 1347. In the small Suffolk village of Walsham, the parish church is bustling with people. The villagers are preparing for the Christmas feast and the Midnight Mass. They have decorated the church with holly and ivy. The church seems alive. A little choir practises a carol. In front of the altar, a huddle of villagers is absorbed in moving brightly painted pieces of wood. They are assembling a tiny wooden stable.

But Master John, the priest, notices none of this. He hurries past his busy parishioners. In his hands he holds a letter. It is from his friend Richard, a monk at the nearby abbey in Bury St Edmunds. Richard's letter is brief, and terrifying.

A terrible disease, believed to have begun in the far east, in the lands of the Great Khan, is moving swiftly westwards across Europe. The letter says that it has crossed the Mediterranean Sea. The **pestilence** rages in the Italian and French seaports. Nothing, it seems, can halt its progress towards England … and Walsham.

Your enquiry

During the 1340s much of Europe, west Asia and north Africa was devastated by a terrible disease. It became known as the Black Death. One historian who has studied the Black Death is John Hatcher. He has written a book about the Black Death in one English village in Suffolk – Walsham. Hatcher based his book on sources but used his imagination to turn those sources into the story of what is likely to have happened. In this enquiry, you will use Hatcher's story to explore how ordinary people responded to disaster.

The world of Walsham

Today Walsham is a small village in the county of Suffolk. In the fourteenth century, this part of East Anglia was one of the richest in England. This is what the village looked like in the mid-fourteenth century. What similarities with the village of Bourn (on pages 34–37) do you notice?

Let's take a walk around, to see what Walsham was like…

Our journey starts on the village's eastern edge, on Finningham Road. All around us are fields of wheat, barley, oats and peas, neatly separated into strips. Tidy hedgerows, wooden fences and earthen banks line the road. The villagers' lives are marked by the passing of the seasons. Older, experienced hands decide what to plant, when to sow seed, how to plan the harvest, and on which pasture-lands each family can graze their animals. Everyone needs a good harvest, so the villagers work together.

But the harvest also depends on the weather. In recent years terrible rains caused the harvests of 1346 and 1347 to fail. The price of bread rose so high that the poorest nearly starved. Some took to eating roots and berries. Older folk remember the three years of Great Famines of 1315 to 1317, when in some villages one in ten died. Villagers ate their cats and dogs.

This picture from a German prayer book shows medieval peasants hard at work during the harvest. On the left you can see crops being threshed to separate the grain from the stalk. On the right, you can see crops being cut with a sickle and bound into sheaves.

Life at home

As we approach the edge of the village and High Hall Wood we see some scattered cottages. They are the home to the village's poorest families.

Here is an artist's impression of what the inside of the cottage might have looked like:

For 200 years, England's population has been growing fast. Parents have many children to help work the land and to take care of them when they get old or sick. But now there is not enough land for everyone. When William I ordered the Domesday survey in 1086, only about 300 people lived in Walsham, making it roughly the same size as the village of Bourn in the same year. But now, in the 1340s, over a thousand people live in Walsham. Only a few families have enough land to feed themselves. 300 families have little or no land at all. They rent small garden plots from their lord or from richer neighbours, or they try to find work on the land of richer farmers. With so many people looking for work, wages are very low. For these families, life is hard and uncertain.

Let us meet the Chapman family: John, Agnes and little three-year-old Agnes. The Chapmans own little: a few cooking pots, bed covers, some rough furniture. In the small garden behind their cottage, they grow vegetables and graze their cow. In order to earn a little money, Agnes works as a house servant for John Wodebite, a richer villager. Some villagers work as shepherds and cowherds. Some are blacksmiths, carpenters, thatchers, tilers, weavers, tailors, cobblers or leatherworkers. Many women brew ale, bake bread or make pies to sell.

Step 1

At the end of this enquiry, you will answer this question:

How did one village respond to the Black Death?

First, you need to find out about life in the village *before* the Black Death arrived. John Hatcher says that village life was **hard and uncertain**, but **familiar and well-ordered**. Use pages 100–102 to find examples of each. We have included some examples to start you off.

	Hard and uncertain	Well ordered by familiar routines
Food and work		Work was organised by the farming year.
Home and village life		At the manor court disagreements were sorted out.
Religious beliefs and practices	Life expectancy was short.	Church rituals marked important stages in life.

The manor

A little further along the road, a fine manor house comes into view. High Hall has many rooms and a great hall, a dovecote, a sheepcote and barn. The house, wood and most of the surrounding farmland belong to the local lord, Edmund de Welles. High Hall has not survived, but it might have looked like this manor house in Kent.

Each village in England has a lord of the manor, just as it did 300 years earlier when the Normans arrived. But Walsham is unusual. Walsham has two manors. Lady Rose de Valognes is the lady of the other, larger, manor. She does not live in the village because she owns many other manors, but Walsham is her richest.

Other things have changed. At the time of Domesday, nearly half of Suffolk's peasants were free. This was unusual but Walsham was even more unusual, because most of its villagers were free. But now, in the 1340s, most Walsham villagers are unfree. They are villeins. As you know from studying the village of Bourn, all villeins rent their homes and land from their lord. They work for free on the manor farm. They ask permission and pay fines if they want to leave the village, to marry or to inherit land. When they die, the lord takes their best animal.

While lords have rights, they also have responsibilities. Taxes must be collected for the king. Law-breakers must be punished. Careful records are kept of duties and fines owed, of who has moved into or left the village, of who has married or died, and of when land changes hands. These records are made at the manor court, held every few months. The court also sorts out disagreements between neighbours. With land scarce, squabbles are frequent. At one manor court in Walsham in 1345 Edmund de Welles had to deal with over a hundred cases!

Lords of the manor have great power over villeins' lives. But villages have customs and traditions as well as laws. Like all villages, Walsham has its own traditions. These traditions give the villagers rights. The manor court helps to protect these rights.

This is Ightham Mote, in Kent. High Hall has not survived. It might have looked something like this.

The common lands and market

Find Cranmer Green on the map on page 101. On this wide stretch of rough grass, the villagers' animals graze. It is called 'common land' because it belongs to everyone. Richer villagers might own a cow, horse or a few sheep. Poorer villagers raise pigs and chickens, which wander in nearby woods or in the neat garden plots.

Around Cranmer Green is a cluster of larger, well-built houses. One belongs to the Cranmer family. The Cranmers have lived in the village longer than anyone can remember. One of the few richer families in the village, the Cranmers own over twenty acres of land.

Just to the west of Cranmer Green is the site of the weekly market.

Villagers come here to buy and sell bread and ale, fruit and vegetables, cheap woollen or linen cloth and leather. For anything more unusual or expensive, such as wine, spices or fine cloth, they must travel to one of the nearby market towns, around half a day's journey away. For something really special they might even travel to a port city such as Ipswich or London.

The market attracts many visitors to the village. They bring with them news of the wider world. In a world of hunger and hardship, tales of far-off lands at the edge of the world, with their terrifying sea-monsters and dragons, strange peoples and cities made of gold, are always popular in the tavern. But in 1347 it is news of King Edward III's recent successes in his wars against the French and Scots that is enthralling the village. Rich and poor alike tell and re-tell the story of Edward's famous victory in the Battle of Crécy, and of the famed English longbow-men. It is said that peasants just like them have shot their arrows with such force and speed that it seemed as if it were snowing.

We are not sure what the market at Walsham looked like, but this painting of a market made in France in the fourteenth century gives us some idea. What goods can you see being sold?

The church

We have come to the middle of the village. Just before we get to the cross-roads, we pass Alice Pye's alehouse, a popular village tavern. A little further on lies High Hall, Lady Rose's manor house. On the other side of the road is St Mary's church.

St Mary's church in Walsham is still standing today.

The church lies at the heart of village life. Each village must keep its church in good repair, and provide the objects needed for worship. To help pay for it all, everyone pays a special church tax called the tithe. They also give their second-best animal to the church when they die.

The village priest keeps a careful watch over his parishioners. It is his job to make sure that they live moral lives. Anyone accused of serious sins (such as having a child outside of marriage) can be punished by a church court. But for most people, most of the time, the church is not really about taxes, laws or punishments. It is about devotion, community and hope. And the church is part of everyone's lives. The church shapes the year. Alongside the changing jobs of the farming seasons, it is feast days and holy days such as All Saints Day, Christmas, Easter and Midsummer that give structure to the year.

Everyone looks forward to feast days: they are a welcome break from work. Everyone dresses up in their best clothes, and there is singing, dancing and games.

Church rituals mark the stages of life: birth, marriage and death. Dying a 'good death' is especially important. Dying well will allow the soul to escape purgatory and get to heaven quickly. The Church's role is vital. It is the priest who hears the dying confess their sins, sprinkles holy water over their body and anoints them with oil. It is the priest who gives the last sacraments: bread and wine. And the holy ground of the churchyard is the resting place of the dead.

Step 2
Add more examples to your table.

This painting of a village feast day is from two centuries later, but it gives us a feel for the atmosphere of fun and merriment. It is by Pieter Brueghel the Younger. It is called 'A Village Festival in Honour of St Hubert and St Anthony'. Notice the procession taking place on the right of the painting. Some people are carrying an image of the saints. The artist is suggesting that most merry-makers are not very interested in the religious part of the feast day!

The plague approaches

While the villagers of Walsham worried about their harvests and amused themselves with tavern tales, thousands of miles away a terrible disease raged. Historians disagree about where exactly the Black Death began. Some say it spread among rats on the steppes of central Asia, in the lands of the Mongols. Some say the spread gained momentum from natural disasters including earthquakes, floods and famines. Rumours certainly reached Walsham of disaster and disease at the far ends of the earth, but few worried about such fantastical tales.

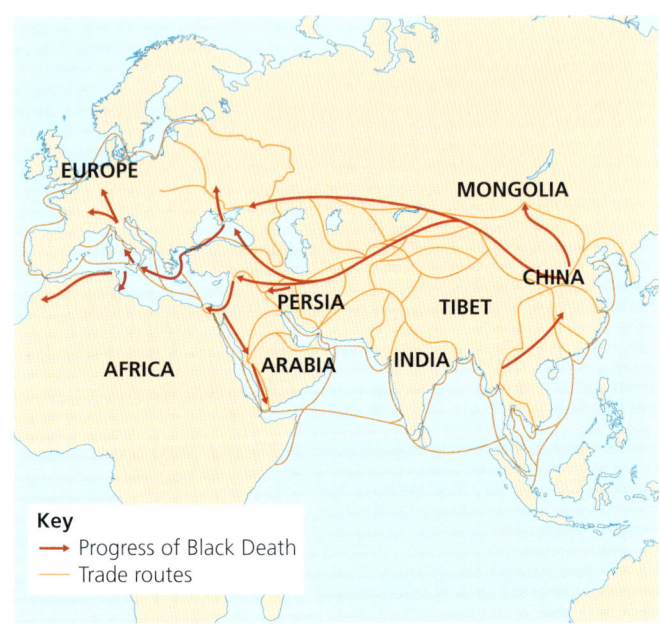

This map shows how the Black Death spread between 1346 and early 1348.

Winter 1347

By Christmas 1347, when Master John received his letter, the stories reaching Walsham were more troubling. Merchants and sailors, travellers and traders all told the same terrifying tale: the many thousands dead, the ill left to die alone, the rotting bodies with no churchyard space nor people to bury them, and the cities lying ruined.

We now know from sources such as this one, written by an Italian lawyer, which stories were likely to have reached Walsham.

> First, out of the blue, a kind of chilly stiffness troubled their bodies. They felt a tingling sensation, as if they were being pricked by the points of arrows. The next stage was a fearsome attack which took the form of an extremely hard, solid boil… as it grew more solid, its burning heat caused the patients to fall into an acute and putrid fever, with severe headaches. As it intensified, its extreme bitterness could have various effects. In some cases, it gave rise to an intolerable stench. In others, it brought spitting of blood, for others, swellings… Some people lay as if in a drunken stupor and could not be roused. Some died on the very day the illness took possession of them, others on the next day, others – the majority – between the third and fifth day.

An extract from History of the Disease OR the Great Dying of the Year of our Lord 1348, a book by Gabriele de' Mussis, an Italian lawyer, about the Black Death reaching Italy.

This image, from the south-eastern corner of France, shows a doctor trying to cut a boil from the neck of a terrified woman. She is being held upright by a man who looks on with pity and wonder. Two more frightened patients wait for help. They have raised their arms to ease the pain of the boils in their armpits.

There was no known cure. Death was coming to England. It could not be slowed or stopped.

A wall painting in the Chapel of St Sebastian in Savoy.

Spring 1348

For medieval Christians, the way to avoid disaster was to turn away God's anger. Priests urged people to confess their sins. St Mary's church was packed. Many rushed to perform penance and good works, giving money or food to the poor.

Others went further afield. Thirty miles away, in the little Norfolk village of Walsingham, lay one of England's holiest shrines. Its statue of the Virgin Mary was known as Our Lady of Walsingham. So remarkable were her miracles, that kings gave land, rents and even entire churches to Walsingham's priests. In May, pilgrims from Walsham made the week-long journey to the shrine, walking the last mile barefoot. They passed along a track through these fields, where pilgrims still walk today. Once inside, the Walsham pilgrims prayed, lit candles and left wax figures of their loved ones.

Returning home, they clutched tiny lead flasks containing droplets of the Virgin Mary's milk.

Summer and autumn 1348

By summer, the plague had reached England's southern seaports. Life in Walsham continued as normal. Peasants travelled to market. Manor court fines were paid. Young couples gained permission to marry. That year, the harvest was good. But there was growing unease. Wandering preachers warned of doom and sold holy relics. Peasants made wax charms and sprinkled holy water on food and doorways.

Eleven villeins shocked everyone by refusing to harvest Lady Rose's crops. Why bother to work when the end of the world was coming?

Winter 1348

By November 1348 plague had reached London, just 80 miles away. Strangers were watched with suspicion. A man found sleeping in the church was chased away. A guard looked for outsiders on local roads.

Spring 1349

The charms and relics, the prayers and precautions all failed. As winter turned to spring, a strange calm fell. At Easter, the first villagers fell ill.

Step 3

You will now consider how life in Walsham changed as the Black Death approached, and how it stayed the same. Copy this table. Using this page, collect points for the first row only. Use two colours: one for what changed, one for what stayed the same.

	farming and work	community life	religious beliefs
Spring 1348 to Spring 1349: the Black Death approaches Walsham			
April to June 1349: the Black Death arrives in Walsham			
Summer 1349 to 1355: the aftermath			

The plague arrives

By early June, more than half of Walsham was dead.

In his book, the historian John Hatcher uses his knowledge from fourteenth-century sources to imagine how one family, the Chapmans, responded to the Black Death. Here is a simplified version of John Hatcher's account.

When their neighbours fell ill, the Chapman family retreated to their cottage. They left the cottage only to tend to their animals and crops. Soon John complained of tiredness and a strange tingling. When he developed a fever, Agnes went for help. She found the local midwife, Julia. Julia was also a healer. For a penny or two, Julia would give advice, make up herbal potions and give out charms to ward off evil. But Julia refused to visit John. Instead, she passed Agnes a potion through her cottage window. At home, Agnes rubbed it into John's skin. She tucked a little wooden carving of St Katherine under John's bedcovers.

That night, John's skin blackened. Now afraid, Agnes took her sleeping daughter and walked to her brother's cottage. Finding her brother also sick, Agnes ran to John Wodebite's home. Agnes had often worked for him, cleaning and cooking. John Wodebite opened the door but would not let her in. Agnes pleaded with him to take care of her child whilst she nursed her husband. Reluctantly, John Wodebite let little Agnes into a small barn, telling Agnes a servant would care for her daughter.

By the fourth day, John's fever had worsened. Agnes begged passers-by to send for the midwife and priest. When neither came, Agnes set out for the church herself. She found it empty.

The next day, Agnes tried again. On the way, she bumped into the priest. He was returning home, exhausted from visiting the dying. The priest agreed to return with Agnes to see John. Inside the cottage, the priest unpacked his candles, a crucifix and a cup. He tried to get John to confess his sins, but John did not reply. He asked John to kiss the cross, but John pushed it away. He tried to anoint John's body with oil, but John screamed in agony. Agnes was desperate. If her husband did not confess his sins before he died, his soul would be damned. But the priest could do no more, and he had other dying villagers to see.

Next morning, John died at sunrise. Now alone, Agnes lit a candle, washed the body and wrapped it in a clean sheet.

Later that morning Agnes walked to her brother's cottage. She sat with him until he died that evening. As darkness fell, Agnes stumbled home. As she approached, she could hear the distressed bellowing of her un-milked cow and the cries of her elderly neighbour, begging for her help. Ashamed, Agnes mumbled excuses and hurried on.

The cart that arrived the next day to take John's body to the church was not the clean, polished wagon normally used for funerals. Few friends and neighbours joined the funeral procession and the poor folk who arrived to act as mourners were strangers. They even demanded to be paid three halfpence each, rather than the usual two. Returning home from the churchyard Agnes found her neighbour's cottage silent and her cow lying dead. As death raged around her, Agnes tended her animals.

Yet John's death was better than others. Few had family and friends with them. Many died before a priest could hear their confession. Former graves were reopened to make space for new bodies, while old bones piled up against the church walls. Desperate people buried their dead in fields or ditches.

Step 4

Now complete the second row of your table: 'April to June 1349: the Black Death arrives in Walsham'. Remember to use different colours for what changed and what stayed the same.

Walsham recovers

By the summer, a terrible stench hung over the hastily dug graves in Walsham's churchyard. Weeds grew high in the fields. Animals strayed across neglected gardens. By the time the plague left Walsham, more than half of the villagers had died. It was the same in other villages.

The only people on the roads were the poor. They had no choice but to continue working if they were to feed themselves.

Struggles to impose order

Yet as the pestilence faded away, Edmund de Welles, the lord of the manor at High Hall, had other worries. In June, houses and land lay empty. Rent was uncollected, the manor farm neglected. Hardly any of Edmund's surviving villeins did their labour services, and few workers could be hired cheaply anymore. Instead, they demanded good meals, including meat! Some were demanding nearly twice as much money. If Edmund refused, workers simply looked for work elsewhere.

Edmund feared that if order were not quickly restored, he would lose his authority altogether.

So, on 15 June 1349 Edmund held a manor court. The first job was to record all those who had died: 109 villeins. But for Edmund, there were more important questions to answer:

- Who has died?
- Have they paid for inheriting the land?
- Has the surviving family paid a death tax?
- Which children have been orphaned?
- Who is the heir to each empty piece of land?
- Who should be each child's guardian?

Edmund was worried about how he would restore order to the village. Whole families had died and it was not always clear who the heir should be. If no adult male heir survived, distant relatives or even women or children would inherit instead. Little Agnes Chapman inherited her father John's two acres of land.

Do you remember the Cranmers who we met on page 104? Hilary and Olivia Cranmer now found themselves well off after the deaths of their husbands, grandfather, father, two brothers and two sisters. The two sisters were pleased to inherit so much land.

But others who inherited land were reluctant to take up the duties that came with that land, especially if they had better inheritances elsewhere. Some land around Walsham fell into neglect.

Lords like Edmund de Welles were not the only ones worried about order breaking down. Three days after Edmund held his manor court, King Edward III issued a law called the Statute of Labourers. He ordered it be read out in every church. This new law said that free as well as unfree peasants had to work for whoever wanted to hire them, not just for their lords. They had to accept pay and conditions no better than those which they had received before the pestilence arrived. In the taverns, peasants grumbled.

1349–1355: finding a new normal

But despite the efforts of the lords and king to restore the old order, life in Walsham did not quickly return to normal.

Familiar faces were replaced by newcomers. These newcomers did not know the customs that governed village life. Villagers began to quarrel about how to organise shared tasks such as setting up sheep folds on the commons, selecting crops to sow and planning the harvest. Many disputes between new neighbours now came before Edmund de Welles's manor court.

Yet some villagers did not want things to go back to how they had been before. Some peasants now realised that their labour was worth more money. Many questioned the old ways of doing things. The manor rolls from Walsham show many disputes between villagers and their lords during the 1350s. Some refused to perform labour services. Others moved away from the village without permission. They refused to return.

Yet life did move on. Seeking companionship or practical help, some remarried quickly. Agnes Chapman's sister-in-law, Alice, found a new husband quickly (although Agnes feared that Alice's new husband was more interested in Alice's newly-inherited land!). Agnes herself did not remarry. Instead, she joined a band of travelling harvest workers, where she was able to earn more money than ever before. Her friend Hillary, who used to work as a servant, got work as a thatcher's assistant. To Agnes's amazement, Hillary told her that she was being paid twice as much as a man had been paid before the plague, and with a meal and ale on top!

The Cranmer sisters also thrived. With the cost of hiring farm labour so high, they decided to invest their money in expanding their herds of cows and flocks of sheep instead. So did

In the years after the Black Death many women took up jobs normally done by men. Historians have found evidence that blacksmith guilds began inviting widowed wives of craftsmen to continue running the family business in their husbands' place. This picture from a fourteenth-century Bible shows a woman working as a blacksmith. By the mid-sixteenth century, when populations began to rise, these jobs reverted to men only.

Alice Pye, the tavern owner. It was a clever choice. Many villagers spent their higher wages on milk, cheese and meat. The Cranmer sisters and Alice Pye were soon much better off.

Step 5

Complete the final row of your table: 'Summer 1349 to 1355: the aftermath'.

Shaping your argument

In many ways, the disaster of the Black Death *disordered* village life. But in other, important ways, life remained *ordered*. Go back through your table. Colour-code your notes to show:

- The ways in which the Black Death brought **disorder** to Walsham. Make sure you look for ways in which disorder brought both suffering and new opportunities.
- The ways in which **order** was kept or restored. Make sure you look for all kinds of order. This includes familiar customs, beliefs and routines, as well as ways of controlling the peasants.

You are now ready to write a story which answers the enquiry question, 'How did one village respond to the Black Death? Your story will have four sections:

1. life before the Black Death
2. life as the Black Death approached
3. life when the Black Death arrived
4. life after the Black Death

In each section of your story, make sure you show how life **both** became more disordered **and** stayed very ordered.

16 The consequences of the Black Death

A story of changing histories

The Dance of Death, a picture made in 1493. It comes from the Nuremberg Chronicle.

Ask your teacher to find an old history textbook on the Middle Ages. Blow off the dust. Look up 'consequences of the Black Death'. You are likely to find:

- devastating death tolls
- new opportunities for survivors
- the 1381 Great Revolt (or Peasants' Revolt as it used to be known).

School textbooks focused on these things because historians did too. Let's now learn what historians have said more recently, about each one.

Devastating death tolls

The Black Death was a human tragedy. It killed between 40 per cent and 60 per cent of the population of Europe, the Middle East and north Africa. The immediate effects were devastating. This is why historians have studied people's emotional experience. You've seen in Chapter 15 how historian John Hatcher tried to capture this.

Wharram Percy church.

To research human experience and emotion, historians have used accounts by people who had lost loved ones. Historians have also used art. The picture above of dancing skeletons shows medieval people's fascination with death. From such sources, historians have built arguments about the effects on survivors of losing many family members and fellow villagers.

Historians have also used the changing landscape. Look at the photograph of Wharram Percy church. It seems so normal. You can almost hear the bell ringing on a Sunday morning. It was the centre of the community. But look more closely. The windows have gone. If you were to visit the church today, you would see that, in the landscape around it, there are no houses. Within 150 years of the Black Death, Wharram Percy was deserted. So many people died between 1347 and 1352 that some villages disappeared. To this day, that high death rate scars the landscape.

New opportunities for the survivors

Some historians have studied how life changed for the survivors. Fewer people meant more land. Without enough workers to go around, employers had to raise wages to persuade people to work for them. The government passed laws to stop workers being paid more. But most employers did not obey these new laws. They were too desperate for workers.

The 1381 Great Revolt

In this painting, armed protesters, on the banks of the River Thames, are shouting. This was the Great Revolt of 1381.

The protesters had come from all walks of life. The young King Richard II was forced to meet with them. He tried to calm them but protests continued for weeks across all parts of England.

Some historians have linked the Black Death and the Great Revolt. These historians argue that survivors of the Black Death gained new confidence. When the government tried to restrict them, some people were ready to rebel.

This painting of Richard II meeting the rebels in June 1381 is from a 1470s version of a fourteenth-century chronicle by Jean Froissart.

Changing histories of the Black Death

These three arguments are a starting point. But history never stands still. Historians are always making new arguments.

'Look at this evidence I've found', one historian will say. They then write a book about it. 'That's great but look what I dug up over here!', cries another. They publish an article in a history journal. 'That's all very well but no one has considered these people over here', declares a third historian at a history conference. Each re-shapes our understanding of the past.

Recently, historians have asked fresh questions about the consequences of the Black Death. Here are three such questions:

1 Questions about continuity: Did change really happen straight away?

Increasingly historians are arguing that the big changes in the economy (such as higher wages) and society (such as peasants gaining higher status) didn't happen until the early 1370s. This is about 30 years after the Black Death arrived in England!

One historian, Mark Bailey, focuses on the factors that slowed change down. In a book published in 2021, Mark Bailey does these things:

- He uses data which show that poverty remained severe for many ordinary people for two decades after the Black Death.
- He points out that, in the 1360s, plague returned twice and the weather was extreme.
- He argues that, in the 1350s, the government's attempts to keep the peasants in their place were successful.

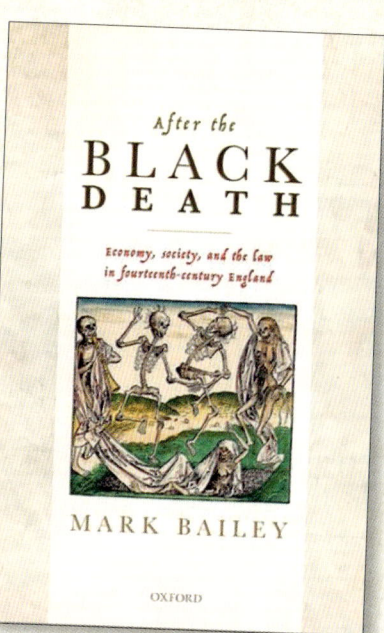

Putting all this together, Bailey concludes that change took longer to work through than previously thought.

2 Questions about change: How was life in towns transformed?

Sometimes a different story emerges when historians look at particular places. Historian Claire Kennan has focused on towns. Kennan found evidence to show that by the 1370s, more people were working in towns and fewer people were farming. More were working in urban industries, such as weaving. More worked in services, such as bakeries (like the women bakers shown here).

Also, with more money to spend, even ordinary people began to buy luxury items, such as silk clothes or shoes of fine leather.

3 Questions about similarity and difference: How did the Black Death affect women?

Historians are now using new sources to show how the Black Death changed opportunities for women. Historian Caroline Barron has found evidence of women running workshops and employing male servants. Many women were hired as apprentices.

Questioning more, revealing more

So, what were the consequences of the Black Death? Well, that depends. It depends which historian you ask. Their answers depend on the questions that they asked and the sources that they used. This is why histories are always changing.

New histories rarely replace the arguments that came before; they just reveal more. This can make things more complicated! The more we ask fresh questions about the diversity of the past, the more we must take care when summing things up.

(Top-to-bottom) Mark Bailey, Claire Kennan and Caroline Barron have each revealed more about the consequences of the Black Death.

17 Meanwhile, somewhere in northern France

The story of the Hundred Years War

It is 1415. Dawn is breaking on a special saint's day – the feast of St Crispin.

Across a field near the small town of Agincourt, Henry V of England can just see the French army gathering. The torrential rain of the last few days has left the ploughed field boggy. But today, at last, the weather is clear and bright.

Henry's men are tired. For weeks they have battled their way through northern France. Taking control of the port of Harfleur sapped their energy. Many soldiers have been lost to illness. Watching the French army gather, the English know that they are outnumbered.

Yet Henry has positioned his best soldiers well. His archers are trained and professional. Rows of sharp wooden stakes, driven into the ground, protect them.

At 11 o'clock, the French charge begins. The English archers flex their bows. Under waves of arrows, the French begin to fall. Some drown in the mud. Others are impaled on the stakes. The English climb onto piles of struggling French soldiers, killing them with hammers, axes and daggers.

Realising there is no hope, the French army flees.

Henry V: king of the battlefield

Henry V had done what was expected of him. He had led his men to victory in battle. Returning to London in triumph, Henry's subjects put on huge celebrations for him. His people believed that Henry had God's support. In Westminster Abbey, they saw Henry giving thanks to God. Henry V was everything an English king was expected to be.

150 years later, the English playwright Shakespeare wrote a play called *Henry V*. The play captured this view of Henry V as a great king and hero. In this extract, King Henry addresses his men before the Battle of Agincourt.

Shakespeare uses St Crispin's feast day to encourage people to remember. Carefully read this extract from the play *Henry V*, or listen to it spoken aloud by an actor. In what ways does Shakespeare say that Agincourt will be remembered?

> This story shall the good man teach his son;
> And Crispin Crispian shall ne'er go by,
> From this day to the ending of the world,
> But we in it shall be remember'd;
> We few, we happy few, we band of brothers;
> For he to-day that sheds his blood with me
> Shall be my brother; be he ne'er so vile,
> This day shall gentle his condition:
> And gentlemen in England now a-bed
> Shall think themselves accursed they were not here,
> And hold their manhoods cheap whiles any speaks
> That fought with us upon Saint Crispin's day.

The Battle of Agincourt was indeed remembered in England. This engraving was made four centuries later. In what ways does this nineteenth-century artist present Henry V as a great hero? To this day, films, art and music continue to remember Henry V's victory at Agincourt.

A long war

By 1415, the English and French had been fighting almost non-stop for 70 years. The Battle of Agincourt was part of what is known as the Hundred Years War. It lasted from 1337 to 1453.

Why had the English and French been fighting for so long? You will remember that the English monarchs had controlled large parts of France since the time of Eleanor of Aquitaine. In the 1330s, Edward III had declared that he was the rightful heir to the French throne. The war began because Edward III and his son, the Black Prince, went to France to claim the throne.

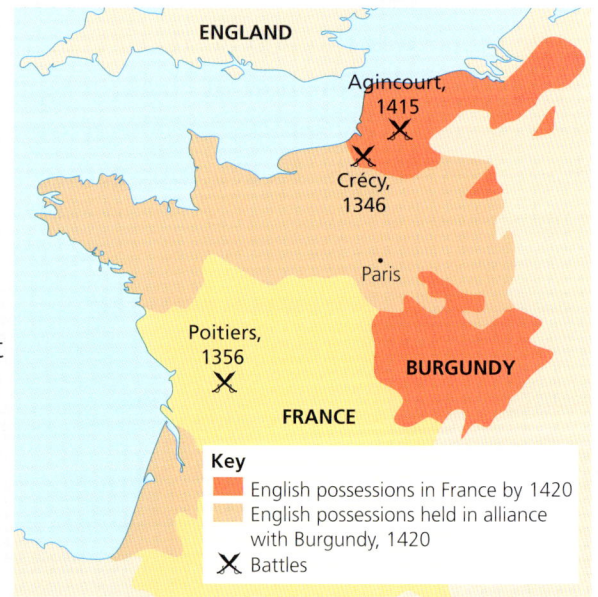

This map shows English territory in 1420, five years after the Battle of Agincourt. It also shows the major battles of the Hundred Years War.

The war lasted so long because it was difficult for English kings to keep land in France and, at the same time, to rule in England. They were always dealing with challenges from English noblemen. They were always trying to control the Welsh and the Scots too.

The English also wanted to repeat their victories of the past. At Crécy in 1346, they had brilliantly outwitted the French cavalry. At Poitiers in 1356, they had captured the French king and taken him prisoner. Memories of a past which felt glorious kept driving them on.

Look at this picture from an illuminated manuscript made in the fourteenth century. It shows the English victory at the Battle of Crécy. Find the English archers, with their longbows, attacking the French. The English had tricked the French into attacking uphill. Find the French knights fleeing on horseback.

The price of the war

The struggles between England and France did not just affect soldiers. Between battles, the English army roamed through the French countryside. They attacked villages and destroyed crops. They raped women, ransacked towns and killed townspeople randomly. These attacks were meant to scare people and to weaken their morale.

Over time, ordinary people in both England and France became sick of war. In France, people's lives and livelihoods were destroyed by the roaming armies. In England, people tired of paying for expensive wars. Kings both in England and in France faced rebellions.

By the end of the fourteenth century many in England wanted peace. The economy of

This painting of the Battle of Crécy is in a fourteenth-century chronicle of the Hundred Years War written by Jean Froissart.

England was suffering, worsened by some of the effects of the Black Death. The Hundred Years War…

   …was bad for trade

   …led to heavy taxes

   …destroyed crops and livelihoods.

The end of the war

After Agincourt, the English and French continued to fight and make peace, to fight and make peace again, until 1453.

The Hundred Years War changed both countries. The English would never control vast regions of France again. Kings in France slowly became more powerful as they tried to regain control. Kings in England learned that they needed to keep people safe and content if they were to keep control of the throne.

Not all English kings, however, learned this lesson. Not all were even in control of the kingdom. More instability was on its way.

18 Challengers and defenders of the late medieval crown

What do the Wars of the Roses reveal about power and instability in fifteenth-century England?

Do you remember Henry V's victories in the Hundred Years War? Henry crushed men into the mud at Agincourt in 1415. Henry V conquered Paris. Henry V claimed the French throne. Henry V strode about his court telling noble families what to do. Henry V settled arguments decisively. In the minds of English people, the battle-scarred Henry V deserved his crown.

When Henry V died unexpectedly in 1422, many began to write about him. Writing about Henry V was easy: Henry V was a success story.

Enter: Henry VI, King of England

While Englishmen wrote tales of Henry V's brave victories, a baby wailed in a cot at Windsor Castle. This baby was Henry V's son. This baby was now King Henry VI of England.

The baby grew into a boy. The nobles at court watched and waited. They gave him a tutor. They gave him a sword. They ruled for him, settling disagreements over land and waging war in France. At eight years old, the crown was placed on his head.

The boy-king became a teenager. The nobles watched and waited. Henry VI sat beneath tapestries of gold. He prayed in chapel. He visited monasteries.

The young king was encouraged to rule. In 1438, aged 16, Henry asked two noblemen to manage some land. But he gave them both the same land! The nobles had watched, but now they whispered: was he just not ready to govern? Or was something wrong with him?

In 1445, the king married. Margaret of Anjou, his 15-year-old French noble bride, found her husband quiet, gentle and showing no interest in government. His favourite nobles still ruled on his behalf. But he was 23! The nobles had whispered, but now they worried: why wasn't Henry taking charge?

Land ruled by Henry V in 1422

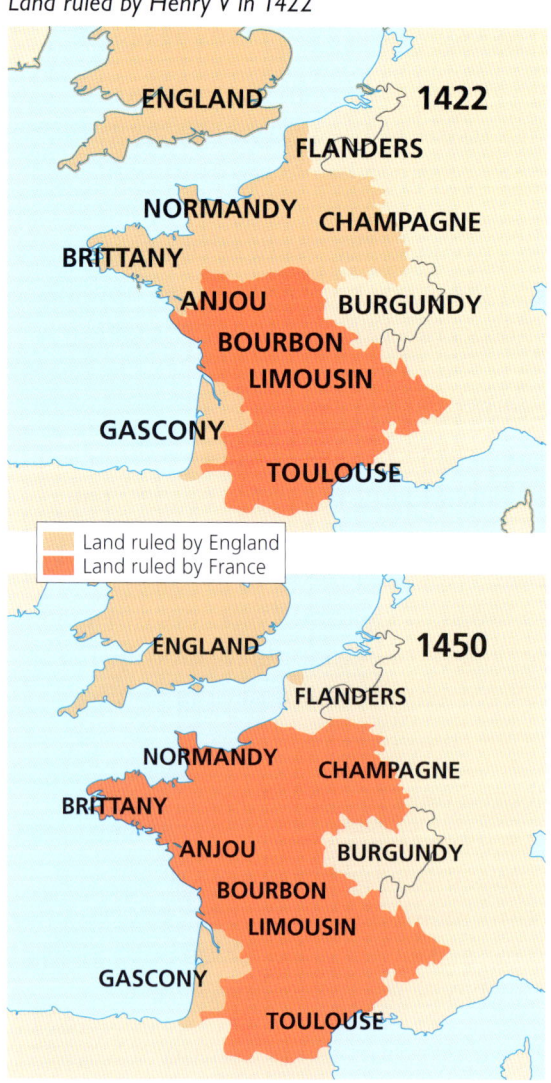

Land ruled by Henry VI in 1450.

Across the channel, the French clawed back land. English forts fell like dominoes. Yet Henry VI showed no sign of wanting to lead armies into France. How could a king lack battle scars? The nobles worried, and now they schemed. If this king would not lead, where should power lie?

Then, in 1450, disaster: Normandy was lost.

A rebellion against the king swept through southern England. London was sacked. The nobles were aghast.

Enter: Richard of York, of royal blood

A great nobleman, Richard, the Duke of York, had watched in horror as Normandy fell. Who was this man? Look at the family tree. As great-grandson of Edward III, royal blood flowed through Richard's veins. Richard wanted a leading position in government, but Henry VI would not give him one. Richard watched as order broke down. Without a strong king to settle disagreements, noblemen began to raid each other's lands.

Then, at the beginning of August 1453, disaster: another part of France was lost. Gascony, held by the English for 300 years, was gone. This was all too much for Henry: he collapsed. Falling into a strange trance, he could neither move nor talk. Even when they showed Henry his newborn son, he continued to stare blankly, and did not react.

A great council of nobles now took control, and Richard, Duke of York seized his chance. By March of 1454, Richard had taken charge of government.

But then, on Christmas Day in 1454, sixteen months after his collapse, Henry VI woke from his trance! He recalled his favourite noble lords. Richard, Duke of York was left out in the cold. Richard needed a more radical plan. He now gathered 3,000 soldiers from his lands in the north. At this time, kings did not have standing armies; kings relied on noblemen to gather

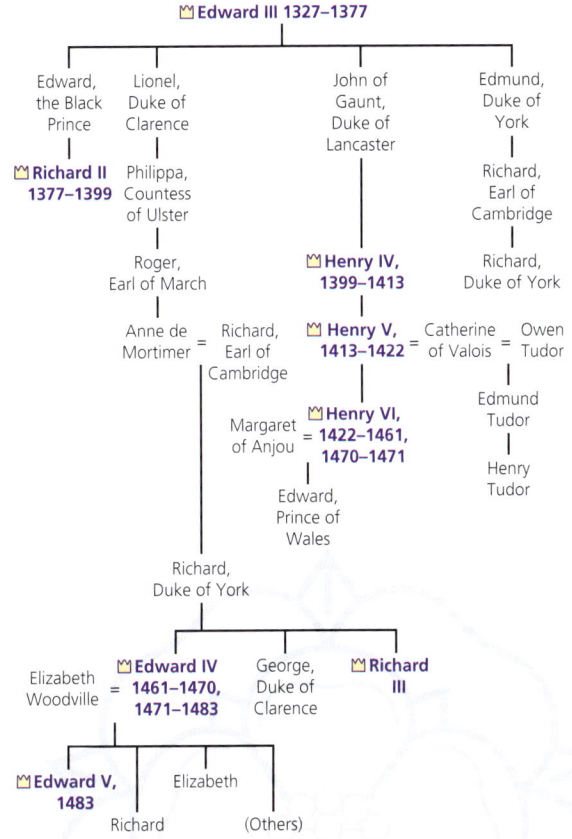

Royal family tree of England, 1327–1483.

soldiers for them. This made Richard's action shocking. Rather than provide soldiers for King Henry, Richard was asking soldiers to fight for *him*!

The battlelines of two great houses had been drawn.

Look again at the family tree. Henry VI and his supporters were called Lancastrians because they were descended from Edward III's third son, the Duke of Lancaster. The Lancastrian badge was a red rose.

Now find Richard of York. His claim to the throne was strong. Richard was descended from *both* Edward III's second son *and* Edward III's fourth son, the Duke of York. The Yorkist badge was a white rose.

In May 1455, Richard, Duke of York led his huge army southwards. In St Albans, a town just north of London, Richard's Yorkist army attacked the king's Lancastrian forces. Battle raged through the streets. The town bell rang in urgent alarm. Meanwhile, under his royal banner in the market square, Henry VI sat peacefully, watching the fighting and doing nothing.

The Yorkists won the battle, but Henry VI, the Lancastrian king, was still alive. The Wars of the Roses had begun.

Signs of unstable government

The Wars of the Roses of 1455–1485 were a time of great instability in England. A medieval government could become unstable if:

- a ruler was not supported by enough other powerful people;
- a ruler could not keep order in the country;
- a ruler could not keep lands safe abroad;
- people argued about who should be in charge of the country.

Your enquiry

During wars, decisions were made in the moment and records were rarely left. Few written sources tell us what leading characters thought or why they took action. Historians studying the motivations of these characters must work out what might have gone on behind the scenes. 'It's like piecing together a jigsaw with half of the pieces missing', said the historian Helen Castor in an interview in 2014.

Yet we catch glimpses of key characters in chronicles, letters and government records. Helen Castor uses such sources to find out how power worked in the fifteenth century and how England's government became so unstable. In this enquiry, you will decide what the stories and sources reveal about power and instability.

The historian Helen Castor.

Step 1

During the Wars of the Roses, kings, queens and nobles were often disappointed when people didn't do what was expected of them. These disappointments sometimes led to war.

Draw a table like this. Re-read pages 118–20 to find examples for the first and third columns. We have started you off.

	Kings	Queens	Nobles
What did they want?	Henry expected his nobles to support him.		The nobles wanted a strong and capable king. One noble, Richard of York, wanted a say in how the government was run, so he gathered an army of soldiers to force King Henry VI to include him.
How did others disappoint them or stop them getting what they wanted?	A powerful nobleman Richard of York gathered an army against the king.		

Look back at the signs of unstable government. Write one sentence answering this question: So far in our story, what seems to have been the *main* thing making England unstable?

Let's now learn more about Henry VI's wife, Margaret of Anjou.

🌹 ENTER: MARGARET OF ANJOU, QUEEN CONSORT

Helen Castor has worked hard to piece together Queen Margaret's story. The sources show that Richard of York was determined to be the most important man in England, but Queen Margaret's personality is harder to find. Although she was the power behind the Lancastrians, we only catch glimpses of her.

Helen Castor used a vast collection of fifteenth-century letters by one family, the Pastons. Here is an extract from one letter. What evidence can you find that Margaret was determined to rule following her husband's collapse?

> …the queen has made a bill of five articles, desiring them to be granted, the first of which is that she desires the whole rule of this land; the second is that she may appoint the chancellor, treasurer, privy seal and all other officers of this land…

Letter written by John Stodeley to the Duke of Norfolk, 19 January 1454.

Queen Margaret's desire to rule on behalf of her husband shocked noblemen in England. 'Medieval queens were meant to have babies', explained Helen Castor in an interview in 2011. 'Queens were wives and peacemakers; they were not meant to rule.'

Yet Margaret knew that women could lead. Margaret's own grandmother had been a strong ruler in France. In 1457, Margaret travelled around England building Lancastrian support for King Henry. She then removed Yorkist supporters from court.

Richard Duke of York would never bow before this queen, but Queen Margaret was ready for him, with several Lancastrian armies. The Yorkists were forced to flee. Once again, Margaret had restored Henry VI to power.

Or *had* she?

 ENTER: THE EARL OF WARWICK, KINGMAKER

In 1459, most people thought that the Yorkists were over.

But in 1460: the Yorkists were coming *again*.

This time, however, the Yorkists were led by a powerful ally – a nobleman called the Earl of Warwick. The Earl of Warwick had grown tired with Henry VI's weak leadership. He wanted a strong king who could protect his lands. On the map, find the lands owned by the Earl of Warwick's family. What does this map reveal about the power of nobles in England?

This map shows the areas controlled by noble families in late fifteenth-century England. The Earl of Warwick's family were the Nevilles.

The Earl of Warwick marched to London with 30,000 soldiers to support Richard of York. Support for the Yorkists grew.

But then, in yet another battle, Richard of York was killed! Richard's head, topped with a paper crown, was stuck on a pole outside the gates of York. Despite all the Earl of Warwick's support, the Yorkists looked doomed.

But they were not doomed. A leader stronger, cleverer and more skilful than any since Henry V was about to emerge.

Enter: Edward, the new Duke of York

Richard Duke of York's son, Edward, was 18 when he was told about the death of his father. Edward was already an impressive-looking nobleman: strong, unusually tall and strikingly handsome. A diplomat from Burgundy remarked that he had never seen a finer-looking man.

Edward had no time to mourn his father's death: the Lancastrians were coming.

Shortly after dawn, on a freezing February day in 1461, on the border of England and Wales, the Battle of Mortimer's Cross was about to begin. With icy fingers, knights buckled on their armour, swords and daggers. Archers put on padded jackets and strung their **longbows**. Then, a blinding light lit up the sky. Edward's soldiers looked up and saw three suns. It was a trick of the light on freezing ice crystals, but Edward saw it as God's blessing.

On that cold February day in 1461, Edward inspired his men with his courage. He won the battle. It was the first of many Yorkist victories. Less than two months after this battle, in London, Edward was proclaimed king.

But the biggest Yorkist victory yet, the one that defeated Queen Margaret and her Lancastrian army, took place on 29 March 1461. With his growing armies, every soldier displaying the white rose, Edward had marched northwards. He took up position in Yorkshire, near the village of Towton.

Towton was the bloodiest battle of the war. It was fought in driving snow. The blizzard blew straight into the Lancastrians' faces, blinding them. Their arrows fell short of the Yorkist line. The massive steel-armoured figure of Edward held this line. The Lancastrians buckled and ran. But the Yorkists came for them. We do not know how many were killed, but some claimed as many as 20,000. The river ran with blood.

This is an extract from a letter, written by the Chancellor of England on 7 April 1461, describing the Battle of Towton. He was writing to Franscesco Coppini, an Italian churchman who the Pope had sent to England to try to stop the fighting.

> There was a great conflict, which began with the rising of the sun, and lasted until the tenth hour of the night, so great was the boldness of the men…Of the enemy who fled, great numbers were drowned in the river…a great part of the rest who got away were slain and so many dead bodies were seen as to cover an area six miles long.

ENTER: KING EDWARD IV, THE NEW KING OF ENGLAND

While Margaret and Henry fled to Scotland, Edward marched to London in triumph. Walking beneath a golden canopy, he arrived at his coronation on 28 June 1461. At six foot, four inches, the new Edward IV was a giant. The crown had never sat so high.

Edward IV would not have an easy start. Many nobles still saw Henry VI as the rightful king. Edward IV would have to work hard to keep his new crown. Look at the thought bubbles to see Edward's main challenges.

I've got to put down the rebellions in **Wales** and the **West country**.

I need to ask Warwick to use his men to put down rebellions in the **North**.

I need to show noblemen in my court in **London** that I am the rightful king, not Henry VI.

We know from images of Edward IV that he was young, tall and considered very handsome. This is a modern actor dressed as a young nobleman. Perhaps Edward IV would have appeared something like this?

The new young king was successful. By 1464, Edward could claim to be the ruler of all England and Wales.

By restoring law and order and by improving the crown's finances, Edward IV won the support of many noblemen.

Step 2

Add more details to your table using pages 121–23

	Kings	Queens	Nobles
What did they want?	Edward IV wanted to keep his new crown.	Margaret of Anjou wanted to protect Henry VI's throne when Henry was too weak to rule.	The Earl of Warwick wanted a strong king to protect his lands. He chose to support … Other nobles …
How did others disappoint them or stop them getting what they wanted?			

Write your thoughts so far in response to this question:
What seems to have been the main thing making England unstable?

ENTER: ELIZABETH WOODVILLE, IN THE WOODS

One story is often told of how the young King Edward IV met his wife. Galloping through a forest, Edward was stopped by a beautiful widow called Elizabeth Woodville. Dazzled by her beauty, he dismounted to press a kiss into Elizabeth's palm. At the age of 22, Edward had fallen in love. Whether that story is true or not, we do know that Edward secretly married Elizabeth in May 1464.

But there was a problem. Edward's new queen did not have royal blood. Edward's supporter, the Earl of Warwick, became very angry. Marrying for love was not kingly behaviour.

There was another problem, too. Warwick had been arranging for Edward to do his royal duty and marry a French princess. Marrying a foreign princess gave England allies abroad. Do you remember how Henry II's marriage to Eleanor of Aquitaine made England more prosperous? But now Warwick had to tell the French that Edward was already married! The Earl of Warwick was now even angrier with Edward.

This miniature painting decorates a fifteenth-century chronicle. It shows the marriage of Edward IV and Elizabeth Woodville.

Elizabeth was crowned queen in May 1465. Her family, the Woodvilles, now created more problems. Elizabeth wanted her uncles and brothers to be given land and titles by the king. Elizabeth's younger brother became Master of the Horse. Before long, a new group of noble favourites had been created. Warwick was left out in the cold.

When Warwick left England for France in April 1470, he was so furious with Edward that he decided to turn on him.

Re-enter: Margaret of Anjou... with the Earl of Warwick!

In France, on 24 July 1470, Queen Margaret did a deal with Warwick. Warwick would invade England and restore Henry VI to the throne. Margaret's son would marry Warwick's daughter. The nobles were astonished: Warwick was a Yorkist! He was the kingmaker who had helped make Edward IV king! Now he had changed sides and supported the Lancastrians?

So Warwick invaded England, this time in support of the Lancastrians. Edward had to flee abroad. Do you remember the marshy fens where Hereward the Wake rebelled against William the Conqueror? In mounting darkness, Edward now crossed those treacherous Norfolk marshes. Finally reaching the coast, Edward slipped out of the shallows and into the North Sea. It was 30 September 1470. Was Edward's nine-year reign over? It certainly looked like it: Warwick, the 'Kingmaker', had returned the crown to Henry VI.

Penniless and desperate, Edward sailed to Holland. But Edward had always been good in a crisis. He was determined to win back his crown. We have pictured Edward, here, on the waterfront in Holland, thinking about his plans.

Meanwhile, where was Edward's wife and queen, Elizabeth Woodville?

To avoid being caught by Lancastrian soldiers, Elizabeth Woodville, now heavily pregnant, fled across London and into **sanctuary** in Westminster Abbey. There she could not be harmed by the Lancastrians. Elizabeth stayed in sanctuary for six months while her husband Edward tried to win back his crown.

On 11 March 1471, after just five months in exile, Edward set sail for England with 2,000 men. The journey wasn't easy: gale-force winds drove his boats towards the Lancastrian armies waiting for him on the Norfolk coast. A ship full of warhorses was lost. Other boats were scattered.

Edward and his men finally made landfall on the Yorkshire coast, at Ravenspur.

King Edward IV was back.

Edward now needed to gather supporters to bolster his army. Reuniting with his brothers, he marched to London. On 11 April 1471, Edward rode, unopposed, into the city. In Westminster Abbey, he was crowned all over again. Edward IV was reunited with Elizabeth and his baby son.

But he still needed to defeat Warwick. He soon had his chance.

Just three days after his triumphant return to London, Edward was in the saddle again. Edward knew that Lancastrian forces were approaching London from the north. Now he led his Yorkist army to meet them. At a place called Barnet, just north of London, on 14 April 1471, the two armies, Lancastrians and Yorkists, met. Edward was determined to destroy Warwick on the battlefield.

Edward IV's journey to reclaim the English crown, 1471.

Edward was ready for the Battle of Barnet. Hours of practice with swords and lances, weeks spent in full-plate armour, years spent learning military strategy: all had prepared him for this moment. Like a glove around his body, Edward's servants fitted layers of polished plate. Advancing in the dark of night, Edward carefully organised his troops. No fires were lit to give away his position. Silently, the soldiers waited for daybreak.

When daybreak came, Edward advanced on an invisible enemy, hidden by thick fog. Leading from the front, Edward fought in a crazed fury. Warwick was finally killed.

Edward now knew that the only way he would secure the throne for good would be to remove Henry VI altogether. Historians are not sure how Henry VI was murdered. Perhaps Edward's soldiers did it. Perhaps, at dead of night, they went into his room, and smothered him.

Queen Margaret did not try to run. There was no one left to fight for. As Edward made his triumphant entry into London, the queen sat, straight-backed and blank-faced, staring at nothing.

Step 3

Continue your table using pages 124–26. Remember to answer the summary question: What seems to be the main thing making England unstable?

Re-enter: Edward IV, King of England...again

When King Edward had been reunited with Queen Elizabeth, he had met his new-born son for the first time. Not only had Edward IV overcome his biggest challenges, he could now proudly boast an heir to carry on the Yorkist dynasty.

Edward's second reign was more peaceful and prosperous. Edward tackled lawlessness. He helped the wool trade grow. In 1476, the first English printing press was set up, enabling many more books to be produced. New schools were built.

Edward cut an impressive figure at court. With a nod here, a smile there, he was confident and charming. When men kneeled before him, King Edward lifted them up with a handshake.

As for Elizabeth Woodville, she was now accepted as queen. Historian Helen Castor has used sources to show that Elizabeth was now admired for having weathered so many changes of fortune. This source describes a discussion in Parliament's House of Commons about the queen:

> The desire of the commons was to commend the womanly behaviour and the great constancy of our Sovereign Lady, the Queen, the king being beyond the sea.

An account of a discussion held in Parliament, written by a royal herald, 1471.

Elizabeth often impressed visitors with the majesty of King Edward's court. Regally dressed in silks and velvet, Elizabeth entertained visitors with dancing and feasting. She hung golden tapestries in visitors' rooms. She spoke with dignity and grace. Elizabeth also gave birth to ten children. The nobles at court were delighted: Edward and Elizabeth's children could continue the Yorkist dynasty when Edward died.

But on 9 April 1483, Edward died suddenly and too early. He was just 40 years old.

Enter: Edward V... the boy who would not be king

In 1483, Edward's sons were only 9 and 12 – too young to rule. A race to control the two princes began. Powerful men swirled around the boys. The young princes were vulnerable. And so was the kingdom.

Enter: Edward IV's brother Richard, Duke of Gloucester

A powerful family member had to take charge. Without delay, Edward IV's younger brother, Richard, stepped into this role. Find this Richard on the family tree on page 119. Richard made himself Protector. He would rule until his nephew, Edward V, was old enough to do so himself.

Richard travelled quickly to find the young prince. He found his young nephew Edward in royal lodgings near Northampton. Richard dismissed all the young prince's servants and took the boy into his own care. On 4 May 1483, Richard rode into London with 12-year-old Prince Edward by his side. Edward was then taken to a strong, safe place – the Tower of London. On the bustling street of Cheapside, people watched the prince being escorted to the Tower.

Ever since 1483, historians have tried to work out what happened next. This is what we know. Prince Edward's coronation was abandoned. The prince stayed in the Tower. A month later, Richard declared that he would be king. Shocked that Richard should steal the crown from his nephew, many nobles rose in rebellion. Richard III then snatched Elizabeth's other son too. Now both the young princes were in the Tower.

The princes were never seen again. Who killed the princes? Many historians say it must have been King Richard III, but we cannot be certain. Richard's reign, however, did not last long.

Portrait of King Richard III.

Step 4

Use pages 126–28 to complete your table. Don't forget the summary question.

You now know a lot about Kings Henry VI and Edward IV. You know about their queen consorts, Margaret of Anjou and Elizabeth Woodville. You have met powerful noblemen such as the Earl of Warwick, and you know a little about Edward IV's younger brother, Richard. These characters reveal much about power and instability in fifteenth-century England.

In December 1484, Richard's royal agents seized a letter. This letter was from someone who wanted to restore his 'rightful claim' to the crown. The letter was signed with an 'H'. Go back to the family tree on page 119 one more time. Can you find an 'H' who might try and take the throne from King Richard III?

> Once you start getting to know the people and hear them talk, and they start living in your head, that's when it starts to get really fun.

Shaping your argument

You are the scriptwriter of a TV documentary about power in medieval England. The director wants the documentary to end in 1415. The director says that the rest of the fifteenth century 'was just lots of fighting'!

But you know that the Wars of the Roses of 1455–1485 show us how things became so unstable. You know that all this instability reveals how power worked in medieval times. We can use the stories and sources to understand noble rivalry, links between land and power, behaviour of kings and queens and what nobles expected of them. Write to the director explaining that the period 1455–1485 must be included in the documentary because it reveals much about power and instability.

You could begin your letter like this:

> Dear Director
>
> We must keep the years 1455 to 1485 in the documentary. They reveal so much about how power worked in medieval times! Powerful people were trapped in a struggle to regain or increase their power. The Wars of the Roses show how fragile this system was. Our documentary could show…

In the rest of your letter, show how things became unstable when:

- kings and queens did not live up to nobles' expectations
- nobles took action which kept the wars alive.

Be sure to mention the work of historian Helen Castor.

19 Meanwhile, in Norfolk
Changing family fortunes

The North Norfolk Coast, 1378

It is a land of little rivers and big skies. A man rides bareback across his fields, kicking his horse into a wild gallop that sends seagulls flying. The rider, Clement, sees his little watermill. He knows that he is nearly home. A woman waits outside his cottage. Clement urges his horse faster.

At last, Clement hears the news. He slows his horse and smiles: it's a healthy baby boy. When Clement takes his son into his arms, he whispers a promise into his tiny ear: 'You will not be a plain farmer like me.'

A few days later, the baby is baptised. The baby is called William. In church, Clement studies the bright new painting of Saint Christopher. This saint brings good luck. Clement promises to give baby William a lucky life. Clement, a peasant farmer, promises to make baby William into a scholar.

The promise of Clement Paston, c.1355–1419

Clement's promise was not a wild hope. His world had changed. In Chapter 16 you saw that the Black Death of 1348 led to new opportunities for peasant farmers. Clement was determined to take advantage of these opportunities. He was even willing to fight for them.

Three years after William was born, Clement became a local leader in the Great Revolt. Afterwards, Clement was charged with disturbing the peace.

Clement disturbed the peace because he wanted a better life for his family, the Pastons.

Clement had taken his surname, Paston, from the place where he lived on the Norfolk coast. Find Paston on the map on page 131.

How do we know about Clement Paston?

Most peasant farmers would have left no trace in written records. But we know about Clement and William because of the Paston letters, a large collection of letters sent between members of the Paston family.

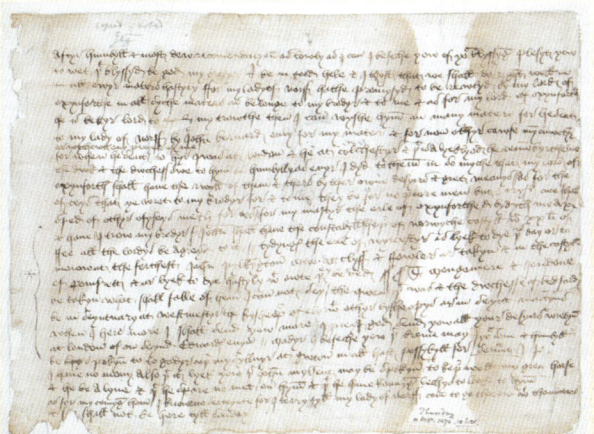

A letter from John Paston to his mother, Margaret Paston, 11 October 1470.

Clement's son, William, did become a scholar. This meant that William, along with his children and grandchildren, could read and write. The Pastons became great letter-writers. We saw in Chapter 18 how historians such as Helen Castor use the Paston letters to find out about late-medieval England.

The rise of William Paston, 1378–1444

William goes to school

Clement schemed and saved and borrowed money to send William to school. William learned to read and write in English and Latin. Knowledge of Latin opened doors. It was the language of priests and lawyers.

William was now a scholar, and his world had changed.

Clement kept turning the soil on his farmlands, scaring gulls away from his seeds. But William bent his head and scratched his quill over mounting pieces of parchment.

William studies law

After school, William travelled to London to study law. Now his world changed again. Four important law courts sat in this Great Hall at Westminster. Here, William watched lawyers argue in court. He recorded judges' decisions. He practised arguing cases in mock-trials.

Clement continued to grind corn in his little watermill, bending his back to stuff sacks with flour. But William sat on a wooden bench, hearing the great hum of lawyers' voices as they rose up to the hammer-beam roof of the vast Westminster Hall.

William becomes a lawyer

After his training, William returned to Norfolk to begin his career as a lawyer. William became such a good lawyer that by 1415 he was working for the two most powerful people in

the county: the Bishop of Norwich and the Duke of Norfolk. William was now a senior lawyer. His world had changed beyond his father's dreams.

Clement carried on farming his land and selling his produce, patching-up his plough every new season, until he died in 1419. But William spent his days at a desk, squinting in the glow of a beeswax candle, penning letters to dukes and noblemen.

William becomes a landowner

In 1429, William became a judge. This was a great honour. William was now wealthy and highly respected.

But this *still* wasn't enough. William was not yet recognised as a member of the powerful upper-class. Remember that land was power in medieval England. In order to become a gentleman, William needed to be a landowner, and so he used his money to buy several manors in Norfolk. One of these manors was Gresham. Find Gresham on the map.

The **manor** purchase included the manor house, but also the surrounding fields.

A reconstruction of the manor of Gresham, bought by William Paston in 1427. The tower walls are shown half-built.

Free peasants living in the village of Gresham rented land from William. Collecting rents from peasants gave William a steady income.

Buying the manor meant buying people as well as land. The manor purchase included ownership of **villeins**, who farmed the land for the lord.

William Paston, now lord of the manor, would stay in the manor house when visiting Gresham. Other members of the Paston family might also stay here. Servants would attend to William, and they managed manor activities, including farming, when William was away.

William makes some marriages

William then secured more land for himself by marrying well. Coming from a wealthy family, his wife expected to inherit three manors, including Marlingford. Find Marlingford on the map.

William later arranged another useful marriage – for his son John. In 1441, William arranged for John to marry a woman called Margaret. Margaret would inherit many lands, including Mautby Manor. Find Mautby on the map.

During their 25-year marriage, William's son John and his daughter-in-law Margaret sent hundreds of letters to each other. This remarkable collection of letters reveals rich detail about everyday life as well as wider effects of the Wars of the Roses. The letters show Margaret as a clever, practical and assertive woman. Here Margaret is writing to her husband, John. What does Margaret want and why?

> As for cloth for my gown, I can get none here in Norwich. It is too simple. I pray you that you will buy for me three yards and a quarter in whatever colour pleases you from London. Also I pray you that you will buy good sugar and half a pound of whole cinnamon, for there is none good in this town.

Adapted from a letter by Margaret to John Paston, November 1450.

The Pastons in danger

William died in 1444. This was a dangerous moment. The Pastons were not yet accepted among the upper classes. Just months after William's death, Margaret was threatened in the street and insulted as a 'peasant'.

John was only 22. He lacked his father's strong reputation. He hadn't had time to ally with noblemen who could protect him. Moreover, as you know from Chapter 18, King Henry VI was so weak that noblemen were raiding each other's lands. John and Margaret were vulnerable. It wasn't long before they were attacked.

Manors bought or inherited by William, or passed to the Paston family through marriage, in 1419–1444.

A nobleman claimed that because his family had previously owned the manor at East Beckham, it was rightfully his. Three years later, the Pastons were attacked again. This time, their manor was taken by force.

The strength of Margaret Paston, c.1422–1484

Margaret holds the fort

While Henry VI sat vaguely on his throne, 25-year-old Margaret Paston hatched a battle plan. It was February 1448. A nobleman called Lord Moleyns had sent a gang of men to seize Gresham manor.

John was in London for work, so Margaret had to act. She took their two children, aged six and four, to live in a house on the doorstep of Gresham manor.

When she arrived, Margaret found Gresham's doors barred against her. Holes had been made in the walls of her home for shooting crossbows. Handguns were propped in all directions.

Margaret wasn't one to panic. She took a good look at her enemy and wrote a shopping list. Read Margaret's letter. What did Margaret ask John for and why?

> I ask you to get some crossbows... two or three pole-axes, and leather jackets with metal plates. Please also be so kind as to buy me a pound of almonds, a pound of sugar, and buy some cloth to make gowns for your children.

Adapted from a letter by Margaret to John Paston, October 1448.

A few months later, Moleyns's men attacked Margaret's household, forcing her to flee. There was nothing John Paston could do. King Henry VI was not interested in governing. England now erupted into civil war.

The Pastons and the Wars of the Roses

The Wars of the Roses brought both challenges and opportunities to the Pastons. Margaret and John's children fought on both sides of the conflict. Find out more from the information boxes next to the family tree, below.

Margaret was a survivor. She remained strong in a violent and unstable time. Her family won and lost their estates many times. Two children died in an outbreak of the Black Death in 1479. Margaret died in 1484, aged 61, one year before the Wars of the Roses ended.

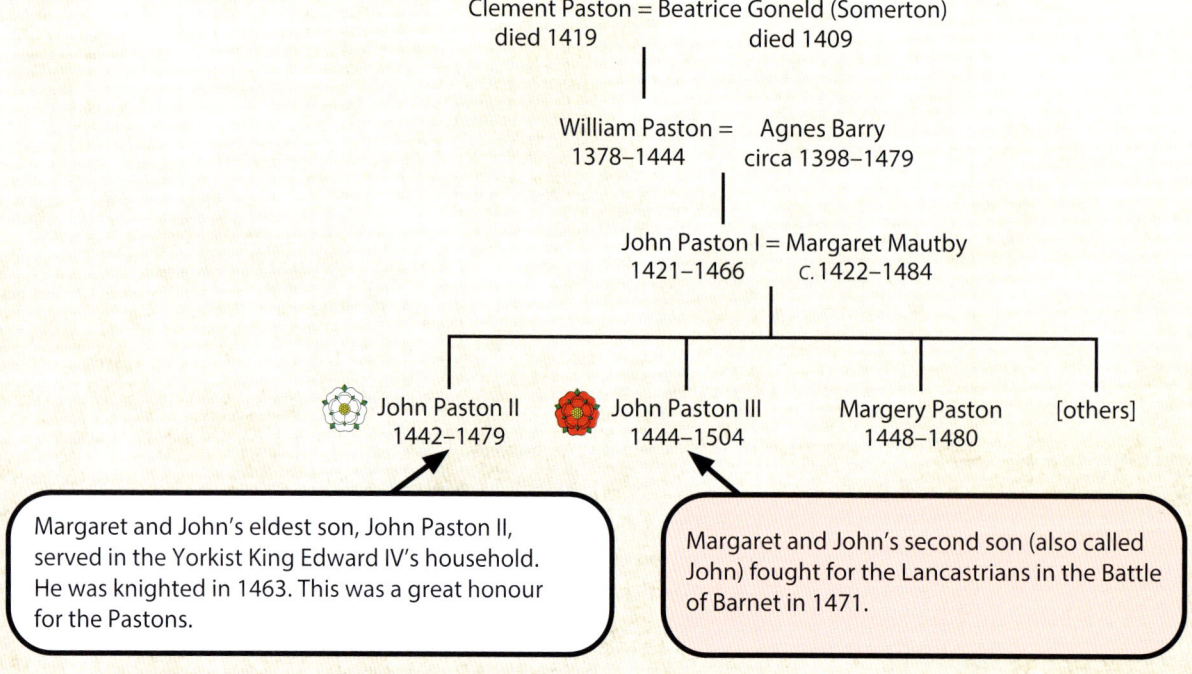

Clement Paston = Beatrice Goneld (Somerton)
died 1419 — died 1409

William Paston = Agnes Barry
1378–1444 — circa 1398–1479

John Paston I = Margaret Mautby
1421–1466 — c.1422–1484

John Paston II 1442–1479 | John Paston III 1444–1504 | Margery Paston 1448–1480 | [others]

Margaret and John's eldest son, John Paston II, served in the Yorkist King Edward IV's household. He was knighted in 1463. This was a great honour for the Pastons.

Margaret and John's second son (also called John) fought for the Lancastrians in the Battle of Barnet in 1471.

20 Meanwhile, in Henry VII's court

A story of strong monarchy returned

Behind the dank walls of a castle tower, in an airless room, Margaret Beaufort lay in agony. A slight girl of just thirteen, her labour was long and terrifying. The birth of her son damaged her young body. She never bore another child.

It was January 1457, and Margaret's child was the mysterious 'H' whom you met at the end of Chapter 18 – Henry Tudor. The Wars of the Roses were well under way. It was this child's destiny to end them.

Margaret and baby Henry were almost alone in the world. Henry's father, Edmund Tudor, had died two months earlier. A Lancastrian, he had been imprisoned by the Yorkists. Margaret had fled to her brother-in-law's Welsh castle at Pembroke – a brave journey for a heavily pregnant girl.

Henry Tudor did not have a king's upbringing. He spent his youth as a refugee. Dodging Yorkist plots to capture him, he moved between safe houses in Brittany and France. This was not a normal king's upbringing, but it proved an excellent training in survival.

Henry Tudor's claim to the throne came only through his mother, Margaret Beaufort. Nonetheless, Henry was the last hope of the Lancastrians. In 1485, against the odds, that hope was fulfilled: Henry Tudor defeated King Richard III at the Battle of Bosworth.

To survive as king, Henry needed to be clever...

A clever marriage

Henry's first clever move was to marry Elizabeth of York, daughter of the Yorkist Edward IV. By marrying her, Henry united the houses of Lancaster and York, ending their fighting.

This double portrait of Elizabeth of York and Henry VII was painted by Sarah, Countess of Essex in the eighteenth century. Notice how she has used roses in the portrait.

Henry VII now made this Tudor rose his family's symbol. It symbolises the union of Henry VII (the red rose of Lancaster) and Elizabeth of York (the white rose of York).

Henry also cleverly timed his marriage so that no one could claim that his power came only from Elizabeth. Henry had himself crowned quickly, in October 1485. He then married Elizabeth afterwards, in January 1486.

The marriage turned out to be happy. Henry and Elizabeth came to love each other deeply. Four of their children would survive childhood – Arthur, Henry, Margaret and Mary.

Clever with the nobles

Henry's next clever action was to deal with the power of the English nobility. Throughout his reign, Henry blended rewards, fear and punishment to keep the nobles in check.

First, using heavy fines, he stopped nobles from keeping retainers (their own private armies). He fined one noble £70,000. Henry also used bonds to force powerful noblemen into loyalty. Bonds were like contracts for good behaviour. These were created by a shady group of lawyers called the Council Learned in the Law.

Henry increasingly came to rely on two members of the Council Learned – Empson and Dudley – to control England. They met in Henry's private chambers, away from the prying eyes of the court. The Council Learned became hated.

Clever with money

In his private rooms, Henry pored over his account books. Taxation meant money. Bonds meant money. Money meant security. Money bought soldiers and weapons. Henry recorded money in and money out in his own hand. He wanted each coin accounted for. The king showed off his wealth to visitors by handing out golden coins featuring an image of himself – the **sovereign**. Henry VII would be given the nickname the 'dark prince' for his methods of controlling money and nobles.

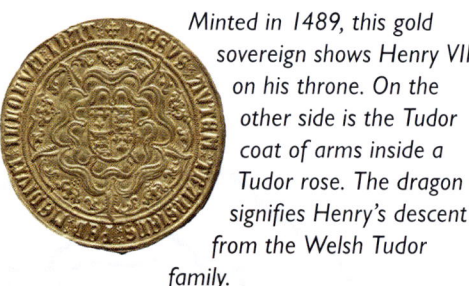

Minted in 1489, this gold sovereign shows Henry VII on his throne. On the other side is the Tudor coat of arms inside a Tudor rose. The dragon signifies Henry's descent from the Welsh Tudor family.

Clever abroad

Henry faced many rebellions. The most dangerous occurred in 1491. Some Yorkists spotted a 17-year-old with a striking Yorkist family resemblance. The young man was called Perkin Warbeck. The Yorkists hatched a plan to portray Warbeck as one of the lost princes in the tower, and to seize Henry's crown.

To deal with this, Henry needed to be clever abroad. One of his greatest threats was the powerful Margaret of Burgundy, a Yorkist supporter. Margaret began to supply Warbeck with troops. Then in 1496, James IV, King of Scotland invaded England on Warbeck's behalf! This then triggered a Yorkist rebellion in Cornwall. Henry VII's reign was in real danger.

But Henry's well-paid forces defeated the Yorkists in Kent in 1497. Warbeck was finally captured, and then executed in 1499. The Wars of the Roses were truly over.

In 1503, Henry cemented peace with Scotland by marrying his eldest daughter to the Scottish king, James IV.

A clever wedding

Clever marriages for his children did not stop there. Henry's cleverest move abroad was to wed his eldest son, Arthur, to Catherine of Aragon, a princess of Europe's most powerful kingdom – Spain.

The wedding, in 1501, was a royal event like none seen before. For days, it was one, big, endless carnival across London. Pageants, plays and processions told stories about the greatness of England's ancient royal line, about bible stories, about the learning of scholars, about connections with art and science in Europe.

Then there was the beauty of the young Spanish princess. Catherine of Aragon stunned the London crowds. Her gleaming white satin gown and a jewelled gold headdress sang out against the blue carpet that led her to the doors of St Paul's Cathedral.

By Catherine's side, trusted with the important role of walking her down the aisle, stood Arthur's younger brother, a charming and excitable 10-year-old prince, called Henry.

Catherine found England's court a place of luxury and learning. Built in the fashionable Renaissance style, Henry's palace at Richmond even had running water. In its halls, scholars mixed with ambassadors and Italian merchants.

A lonely death

Within months of his wedding, Prince Arthur died. Henry and Elizabeth wept in each other's arms. The next year, 1503, Elizabeth would die in childbirth. Witnesses at the time describe Henry's grief. He retreated to a small suite of rooms. He would allow no one near him for days. The marriage had been a cleverly political one, but it had become a marriage of love.

King Henry lived on for six years after Elizabeth's death, but his court fell into fear and darkness. He closed himself away in Richmond palace, stress and sickness having destroyed his health.

21 The Reformation begins in Germany

How did Luther's protest become so big, so fast?

As storm clouds tore across the sky, huge drops of rain began to fall. The young man quickened his step. He was walking back to the university where he was studying law. As he neared the town, thunder cracked and rolled. Suddenly, a bolt of lightning narrowly missed him. Terrified, the man cried out, 'Saint Anne! Saint Anne! Help me now, and I promise to become a monk!'

The young man was true to his vow. He exchanged his law books for a long, black, woollen robe and a tiny monastic cell.

As he prepared to take the vows of a monk, Martin Luther wondered if he would make a good one. The priest at the altar lifted the cup of wine. Martin looked up. The priest spoke the words of Jesus that priests had spoken for centuries when they offered up the sacrifice that they called the Mass:

'Take this cup and drink from it. This is my blood which is poured out for you, for the forgiveness of sins.'

Martin Luther thought about his many sins. He hoped that God would forgive him.

Surprised by a Bible verse

In the town of Wittenberg in the German state of Saxony, Luther lived the life of a monk. He taught students, read the Bible and attended Mass. He rose early to pray. At night, however, Luther was different from other monks. He stayed awake all night, begging God to forgive his sins. Sometimes he lay on the stone floor of his monk's cell rather than in his bed. Sometimes, to show God how sorry he was, he even slept out in the snow. Luther was desperate for forgiveness.

Luther studied hard. He learned the ancient languages of the Bible – Hebrew and Greek. He became a professor. His students loved his lessons. But Luther still worried about forgiveness.

One night, as usual, Luther was reading the Bible. Reaching a familiar verse, he suddenly stopped. His heart raced. 'The just shall live by faith', he read. 'Just' meant justified – to be forgiven for sins. So all that was necessary for God's forgiveness was to have faith! Not striving to please God. Not performing religious rituals. Just faith.

Angered by a priest

One day in 1517, the marketplace in Wittenberg was busy as usual. A fancy carriage full of monks rolled past. A priest stepped out. This was John Tetzel. Tetzel announced something special for the town. 'Look!' he said, 'Look at these wonderful **indulgences**!'

On a banner hung many little envelopes, each sealed with the Pope's symbol. The townspeople crowded around, while Tetzel explained. Each envelope contained an indulgence, a special blessing that could forgive sins. Did they need to say extra prayers or go on a pilgrimage? No! They just had to buy the indulgence! People eagerly dropped coins into Tetzel's casket.

For hundreds of years, the Catholic Church had taught that there were things you could do to show that you were sorry for your sins. You could:

- say extra prayers
- go to Mass more often
- go on a pilgrimage
- give money to the poor
- help pay for a church building.

But John Tetzel was **selling** forgiveness.

Tetzel travelled around selling his indulgences on behalf of the Church. He was raising money for rebuilding St Peter's Church in Rome.

A fifteenth-century woodcut showing John Tetzel selling indulgences.

A little rhyme became linked with Tetzel:

'As the gold in the casket rings

The rescued soul to heaven springs!'

Listening to Tetzel, Luther grew angry. Faith was all God asked for! In October 1517, in his monk's cell, Luther began to write. He wrote 95 theses (reasons) why indulgences were wrong. Here are some of them:

(32) Indulgences do not make God forgive you.

(36) You need to be truly sorry for your sins.

(66) Indulgences are really just about money.

(76) Indulgences cannot remove your sins.

Luther sent his 95 theses to the archbishop. At first, nothing happened, but within weeks, Luther's protest was being discussed by professors in other German universities. Within months, Luther's 95 theses were being discussed all over Europe.

A protest by one monk in a small German town would lead to a religious revolution called the **Reformation**. It would divide the Church, divide Europe, cause wars and affect ordinary lives for centuries.

Your enquiry

Martin Luther wanted to start a debate. He did not plan to divide the Catholic Church. So how did the German Reformation happen? At the end of this enquiry, you will explain why Luther's protest spread so far, so fast.

Luther's ideas spread

The printing press

Luther had written his 95 theses by dipping his pen in ink. It was the printing press that allowed Luther's theses to reach thousands.

Look carefully at this image and you will see the processes at work in a printer's workshop.

In 1439, in the German city of Mainz, Johannes Gutenberg had become the first European to mass-produce printed pages. Movable type had been used in Korea over a century before, but it was unknown in Europe.

This engraving, made around 1600 in Antwerp, shows a printer's workshop in the sixteenth century. On the left, workers are choosing little tiles with letters carved onto them. They arranged the tiles until they had a full page to print. In the centre background, we see workers rolling ink over the tiles. On the right, you can see a heavy lever pressing a blank page onto the inked letters. The paper was then hung up to dry. Find the master printer, in a fur-lined gown, supervising the work.

A century earlier, no one in Europe could have imagined such a thing.

Luther is protected

The Pope in Rome told Luther's **monastery** to silence him. The monastery, however, voted to support Luther. The Pope then ordered Saxony's ruler to send Luther to Rome. But the ruler of Saxony, Frederick the Wise, who was proud of his new university at Wittenberg, refused.

This map shows the Holy Roman Empire. It was made up of over 300 separate German-speaking states and cities. There was no country called Germany. The Holy Roman Emperor was elected by seven men. Frederick the Wise was the Elector of Saxony.

The Pope tried again. He sent a representative to meet with Luther in the town of Augsburg. The two men had heated arguments in which Luther refused to back down. After the debate, Luther's supporters were now afraid for him because he was likely to be arrested for the crime of **heresy**. Acting quickly, they smuggled him back to the safety of Wittenberg.

The debate at Leipzig

In 1517, Luther was ordered to debate with a very important Catholic professor in the town of Leipzig. When he arrived in Leipzig, cheering crowds lined the street. During the debate, Luther protested about the Pope's authority. Luther protested that *the Bible* had authority. Luther protested that all that was needed was faith *alone*. The crowds outside cheered even more. Some started calling themselves 'Lutherans'.

Luther publishes pamphlets

In 1520, Luther wrote three pamphlets. Each was printed and spread throughout Germany. Luther now wrote about much more than indulgences…

Luther addressed this pamphlet to the nobles who governed the states and cities of Germany. He argued that bishops, priests and monks were no different from other Christians and that the Pope should not decide what the Bible meant. He wrote that priests should be allowed to marry and that all children should go to school.

Here Luther said that the Church's seven sacraments – **baptism**, penance, holy communion, confirmation, priests' ordination, marriage and the last rites – had become too complicated. Luther wanted just two: baptism and holy communion.

Here Luther explained the view that he had reached from reading the Bible: that Christians gained God's forgiveness by faith alone.

Step 1

Looking back over pages 135–38, make some notes on why Luther's protest grew and spread. Now choose a colour for each of the five themes below. Go through your notes. Look for points that match these themes and colour code them.

- Luther's personality (for example, his determination)
- Luther's beliefs and ideas
- the problems in the Church
- the politics and geography of German lands (how they were organised and ruled)
- the printing press

The burning of the papal bull

In 1520, the Pope sent Luther a special letter called a papal bull. The papal bull gave Luther 60 days to recant (take back) his views. Instead of recanting, Luther and his supporters went to one of Wittenberg's town gates and lit a bonfire. A crowd of students, professors and townspeople watched as Luther walked to the fire and threw the papal bull into the flames.

The Diet of Worms

In April 1521, in the German city of Worms, the Holy Roman Emperor, Charles V, called a diet (a meeting) of the rulers in the Holy Roman Empire. As Luther stepped out of his carriage, crowds chanted his name. Some shouted, 'Death to Rome!'

This 1871 painting by Anton van Werner shows Luther facing the Emperor at the Diet of Worms.

The room was packed. Everyone talked excitedly about the German monk. The room then fell silent as the Emperor appeared and ascended his throne.

On the one side was a clever scholar called Johann Eck. Eck represented the Pope. On the other side was Martin Luther. A large table was stacked with books by Luther. 'Are these books yours?' asked Eck. 'Will you recant what you have written?'

Everyone stared at Luther. Luther thought for a moment. He said he needed a day to consider. The Emperor agreed.

The next day, Luther answered.

Yes, the books were his. No, he would not recant what he had written.

Straight after the Diet of Worms, the Emperor declared Luther an outlaw. This meant that no one could protect him. Luther could be arrested and imprisoned at any moment. Frederick the Wise and Luther's friends came up with a plan. They arranged for Luther to be kidnapped and then protected in Frederick's fortress – Wartburg Castle.

Luther in Wartburg Castle

For one year, Luther hid in Wartburg and wrote. He wrote about faith. He translated the Bible into German. On some nights, Luther crept out of the castle and visited taverns so that he could listen to ordinary people talking. Instead of wearing monk's clothes, he disguised himself as a knight. He called himself Knight George ('Junker Jörg' in German).

Back in Wittenberg

Luther's sermons

After a year, Luther thought it safe to return to Wittenberg. Now he preached every Sunday in church. He preached that all believers were priests. He preached that the Bible, not the Mass, should be the centre of people's lives. He told ordinary people to read the Bible, in German. Luther's sermons were printed and sent to other towns for priests to preach.

New ways of worship

Anyone attending a church led by Luther's supporters would have been struck by changes from the past. Prayers were said in German, not in Latin. The priest wore simple robes only. The sermon, when the Bible was explained, was longer and more important.

One startling change was the singing. Luther knew that ordinary people liked to sing folk songs in their homes, out in the fields and in the taverns. To teach them about their faith, Luther wrote hymns, often using familiar folk tunes.

This is one of Luther's hymns. It begins, 'A mighty fortress is our God'.

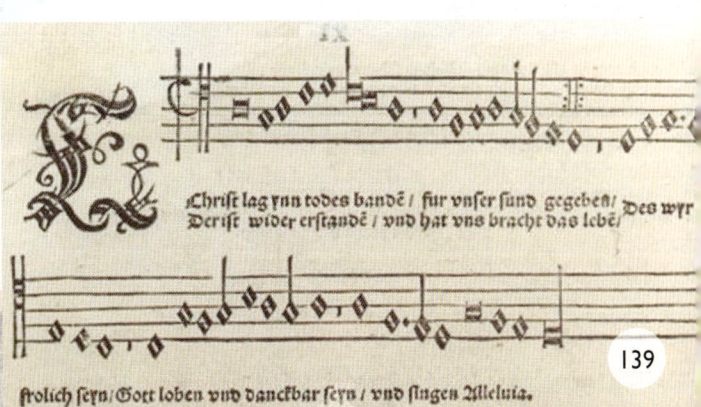

The Peasants' War 1524–1525

Luther had much support from the German peasantry. But many peasants interpreted Luther's message as a call to freedom from not just the clergy, but from their landlords! In 1524, peasant demands for better conditions became uprisings. Peasants gathered armies, stormed castles and burned crops.

Luther was horrified. He said that peasants should obey their lords. Luther likened the rebels to mad, dangerous dogs. He called on the nobles to fight and kill them.

Luther marries

By 1525, many monks and nuns who supported Luther were leaving their monasteries. Some were even marrying. In 1525, Luther himself married a former nun, Katherine von Bora. They had five children.

Protestants and Catholics

The Diet of Augsburg

In 1530, alarmed by spreading Lutheranism, Charles V called a diet in Augsburg. The previous year, the Empire's Catholic princes had nicknamed the Lutheran princes '**Protestants**'. Both Charles V and the Catholic princes now hoped that the Diet of Augsburg would see the Protestants crushed.

The Protestant rulers hoped for something quite different! They wanted the meeting to grant them freedom to worship in Lutheran ways.

Across a huge room in Augsburg, Catholic and Protestant rulers stared at each other. 170 years later, an artist imagined the scene in the engraving that you see at the bottom of this page. Find the man reading a large document. That document was the Augsburg Confession. It set out the Protestant case.

The Augsburg Confession was not written by Luther. It was written by his friend, Melanchthon – a much gentler personality than Luther. Luther knew that his strong feelings would make it hard to write a calm argument! Yet Luther liked what Melanchthon wrote: 'It pleases me right well and I do not know how to improve it; neither would it be proper, for I cannot tread so gently and quietly.'

Much of the Augsburg Confession summarised where Catholics and Protestants agreed. Only in the final section did it criticise the Catholic Church and explain Lutheran beliefs.

The Augsburg Confession took two hours to read aloud. Afterwards, Johann Eck, Luther's old opponent from the Leipzig debate, read aloud the Catholic reply.

No agreement was reached. From now on, the states and cities of the Holy Roman Empire were divided. It was clear that neither side could crush the other.

Europe divides

Soon the whole of Europe divided. Rulers decided which side their country was on. England, Scotland, the Netherlands, Denmark and Sweden became Protestant. Rulers in France, Spain, Italy and Poland chose to remain Catholic.

But as you will see in Chapter 25, things were often more complicated. Even where a ruler made a country Protestant, ordinary people found ways to resist.

Step 2
Using pages 138–41, make more notes on why Luther's protest grew and spread. Then colour-code your notes to show the themes listed on page 138.

Shaping your argument
Christians had often challenged the Church before, but no protest had grown this big or led to such a lasting change. You will write an essay to explain how this happened.

In your notes, you have found five themes. These are your factors that explain why Luther's protest grew so big so fast. Write a paragraph explaining the role of each one.

For your conclusion, try to decide which factors were most crucial in splitting the Church.

Protestantism divides

Towards the end of his life, Luther wrote, 'I am an old, tired, chilled, frozen man.' He often argued with his supporters. Luther had hoped that Wittenberg would become a kind, loving Christian community. Yet many disagreed with each other and with Luther. Luther's influence over his followers was weakening. He often felt a failure.

As Protestantism spread, it quickly became extremely diverse. Here are two examples that have had a lasting, world-wide influence.

The Anabaptists
Anabaptists horrified Luther. Anabaptists believed that Christians should only baptise adults. They also believed that Jesus himself was not present in the bread and wine. Sharing bread and wine was just a way of remembering Jesus's last meal. By 1550, Anabaptist communities were flourishing in Netherlands, Germany and Switzerland.

Calvinism
In 1536, a French Protestant called John Calvin fled France to avoid persecution. A friend then begged Calvin to help reform Geneva's church. From 1541, Calvin had a big influence on how the Genevans worshipped, lived and governed themselves. Calvinism was adopted by more extreme Protestants in England and Scotland.

22 Meanwhile, in England

Henry VIII breaks with Rome

Portrait of Henry VIII painted in 1509 by a Dutch artist employed in the Tudor court.

The young Henry: academic and athletic

When the exhausted, grief-stricken Henry VII died in 1509, a lively, handsome 17-year-old came to the throne. This was Henry VIII. He was a great linguist and an enthusiastic scholar. He had read many works of science, literature, philosophy and theology in Latin. An impressive sportsman, he enjoyed wrestling and double-axe fighting, became a dab hand at archery and fencing, and excelled at jousting. Great things were expected of Henry. His energy, his fearlessness on horseback and his great learning all boded well for a glorious reign by a dynamic king.

Henry's marriage, too, boded well. Just weeks before coming to the throne, Henry had married his dead brother's wife. This was the Spanish princess, Catherine of Aragon, whose first wedding featured in Chapter 20. Everyone, especially Catherine and Henry, assumed that children would follow, including a son and heir. Catherine had even chosen a symbol of fertility – the pomegranate – as her personal badge.

To the Tudor dynasty, marriage to Catherine of Aragon brought prestige. A princess from mighty Spain was a great prize. And Henry adored her. She was charming, intelligent and well-read. Described by sources as very pretty, with copper-gold hair tumbling to her knees, she seems to have entranced her new husband, who often invited guests to admire her beauty.

By 1 November 1509, Henry had news for Catherine's father, the King of Spain:

> Your daughter, our Serene Highness the Queen, our dearest consort, has conceived in her womb a living child, and is right heavy therewith, which we signify to your Majesty for the great joy thereof that we take, and the exultation of our whole realm.

But the child was stillborn.

During her first nine years as queen, Catherine had five more pregnancies. Only two babies were born alive. Only one lived – a daughter, Mary.

The young Catherine: clever and courageous

Catherine was popular. Admired early for adapting well to English royal life, she was admired even more for her dignity and courage during so many miscarriages and stillbirths. Catherine was admired, too, for deep religious devotion and great learning. A lively communicator, her energy shines through in her letters.

Catherine was also busy. She ran her own estates and was involved in great affairs of state. For five years, she acted as England's Spanish ambassador. Growing up in Spain, she had learned from watching her parents manage war and diplomacy.

A portrait of Catherine of Aragon as a young girl when she was still in Spain, painted by a Flemish artist.

In 1513, aged 27, Catherine took command of England while Henry waged war in France. When Scotland declared war on England, Catherine relished the chance to take charge. In a letter in August 1513, she remarked, 'We are all very glad to be busy with the Scots. My heart is very good to it.' As well as adopting a woman's more traditional role in warfare ('I am horribly busy with making standards, banners and badges', she wrote), she now led the war against Scotland. She organised troops, weapons, ships and supplies. On horseback, she led the troops north, as far as Warwick.

Desperate for a son

By 1525, nearing 40, Catherine was past normal childbearing age. In Tudor England, stillbirths and babies' deaths were usually blamed on women. So Catherine bore the sense of failure.

Meanwhile, Henry began to wonder if God was blaming him. He found a Bible verse saying that it was wrong to take your brother's wife. Had the Pope been wrong to allow the marriage? In 1527, Henry asked leading churchmen to investigate.

But there was more to Henry questioning his marriage than a worry about sin. For Henry had fallen in love with one of Catherine's ladies-in-waiting, Anne Boleyn. Glamorous and lively, Anne captivated the king. At only 26, she was probably fertile. Marrying Anne could give Henry an heir.

Henry asked his Chancellor, Thomas Wolsey, to persuade the Pope to annul his marriage to Catherine.

The king's Great Matter

But it was not so simple. This is why:

- Catherine stood up for herself. She refused to be pushed aside. She publicly embarrassed Henry by kneeling before him and exclaiming, 'I have been your true, humble and obedient wife. Grant me pity and compassion!'
- Catherine had powerful connections. She was aunt to Charles V, the Holy Roman Emperor and Spain's king.
- Leading English churchmen did not support Henry's case.
- The Pope was unwilling to admit that an earlier Pope had made an error.
- In 1529 (just when Wolsey was trying to change the Pope's mind) Catherine's nephew, the Emperor Charles V, invaded Rome and took the Pope prisoner.

Henry's 'Great Matter' seemed impossible to solve.

Copying the German princes

Do you remember what was happening in Germany? Some rulers had cast off the Pope and were leading the Church themselves. Anne Boleyn admired such ideas. She lent Henry a book by William Tyndale (who had also translated the Bible into English). Tyndale had written that the king, not the Pope, was true head of England's Church.

Henry now listened to more criticisms of the Catholic Church. Dismissing Wolsey, he appointed these two men to his Council:

Thomas Cranmer, a priest who had started to listen to Lutheran ideas. Cranmer became Archbishop of Canterbury in 1532.

Thomas Cromwell, a skilful lawyer. Cromwell became Henry's chief **minister** in 1534.

The Reformation begins

Cromwell and Cranmer now shaped their solution to Henry's Great Matter. Late in 1532, they had no time to lose, for Anne Boleyn was pregnant. First, Henry married Anne in secret. Archbishop Cranmer then acted quickly. In a special court, in May 1533, he declared Catherine and Henry's marriage unlawful in the sight of God. Despite being married to Henry for 24 years, Catherine was now told that she had never been Henry's wife.

In June 1533, Catherine had to endure seeing Anne, six months pregnant, crowned Queen of England. Catherine's daughter Mary was declared illegitimate.

Now it was Thomas Cromwell's turn to act. In 1534, using his lawyer's skill, Cromwell persuaded Parliament to pass two new laws. These laws were the first steps in the English Reformation.

The Act of Supremacy	The Act of Succession
Henry became Supreme Head of the Church of England, instead of the Pope.	Nobles and churchmen had to agree to Anne's children being heirs.

Once Henry controlled the Church, he could claim its property. Some German Lutheran princes had closed all monasteries and confiscated their land. Henry had his eye on the great wealth of the monasteries.

The end of a way of life: the dissolution of the monasteries

Copying the German princes was easy for Henry to defend. Since the fifteenth century, many had criticised the monasteries for becoming too wealthy and comfortable.

In 1536, Thomas Cromwell began to disband the monasteries of England and Wales. At first, it looked as though he would just close the smaller ones and reform the rest. But by 1540, Cromwell had closed all monasteries and convents, about 850 in total, in England and Wales. Their lands and buildings were seized. Tens of thousands of monks and nuns were scattered. Many were left destitute.

It was not just monks and nuns who suffered. Monasteries and convents had provided care and shelter to the poor and education to thousands. Their religious services and holy places were of deep importance to ordinary Christian people. You have read in Chapters 3, 4 and 15 about devotion to saints' shrines. In 1538, Henry even forbade pilgrimages to monastic shrines.

The dissolution of the monasteries therefore disrupted people's social, economic and religious lives. It was a major cause of a huge uprising in northern England in 1536 called the Pilgrimage of Grace. Henry VIII suppressed this rebellion brutally, executing over 200 leaders.

We can still visit the ruins of these monasteries. This is Neath Abbey, in Carmarthenshire, in Wales.

23 Meanwhile, in Poland
Nicolas Copernicus studies the beauty of the heavens

It is 1484. We are in Royal Prussia, part of the Kingdom of Poland. In a tall brick house on a narrow street in the town of Torun, a merchant has just died. He leaves four orphans. Ten-year-old Niklas Koppernigk, his brother and his sisters await their fate. The children's uncle, a powerful churchman, will decide it.

Niklas expects to become a merchant, like his father. The wharves and warehouses by the wide River Vistula are Niklas's world. Niklas knows the barrels of Baltic Sea herring, the spices from the east, the corn from Poland's fields and the sheets of burnished copper. It was the copper trade that once gave Niklas's family its name: Koppernigk.

Now the powerful uncle shatters the orphans' worlds. He finds a husband for one sister, a convent for the other. The boys will go to a Cathedral school, far away.

Three years later, in 1487, Niklas lives in a new world. Boots clatter on floorboards, masters bellow across noisy rooms, classmates recite Latin verbs. Up at five for prayers, lessons begin at seven. Niklas learns arithmetic, and Euclid's geometry. He studies astronomy. From his teachers, he hears how thirteen centuries ago, Ptolemy described the dance of Sun, Moon, planets and stars around an immoveable Earth.

On bright days, Niklas watches shadows shift across a sundial. By night, he tracks planets in their strange paths.

Niklas's future is set. Niklas must obey his uncle, who pays for his education. Niklas must prepare to serve the Church. In 1491, Niklas begins university in Krakow. He studies humanities, theology, logic, poetry, **rhetoric**, philosophy and mathematical astronomy.

Niklas buys star tables for calculating the position of the stars. He binds them with 16 blank pages for his calculations and notes. 'What could be more beautiful than the heavens?', he writes.

A scholar now, Niklas uses a Latin name: Nicolas Copernicus.

In 1496, 22-year-old Nicolas heads for Italy. At the University of Bologna, he will learn church law, known as canon law. This will prepare him to be a canon. A canon is a senior church official. It is his uncle's wish that Nicolas becomes one of the 16 cathedral canons who govern the diocese of Varmia in Poland. His uncle, now Bishop of Varmia, is well-connected. He will fix it for his nephew.

In Bologna, Nicolas lodges with Novara, a famous astronomy professor. Other astronomers whisper. Novara has shocking views. Novara thinks that **Ptolemy might have been wrong**.

By night, Nicolas and Novara observe planets and stars. Together, they watch the Moon conceal a bright star.

In 1501, Nicolas is allowed to stay in Italy, provided he trains as a doctor. Once trained, he must return to Varmia as doctor to his uncle and the canons. At the University of Padua, Nicolas learns to let blood with leeches. He watches the dissection of corpses, his perfume-soaked handkerchief masking the stench.

Nicolas falls in love with Padua's streets and piazzas, its bridges and barges, the brightness of a burning midday, the moon-soaked nights, the banter with friends about stars. He learns Greek so that he can read Ptolemy's *Almagest*. An artist teaches him to paint.

In the sky, the planets seem to advance and then retreat. Ptolemy said they moved in little 'epicycles'. But in Nicolas's mind, a better explanation is starting to form. Here, in Padua, a daring idea gains shape. What if the Earth circles the Sun? What if the Earth also turns on its own axis? Yes! It now seems so obvious! Why hasn't he thought of it before?

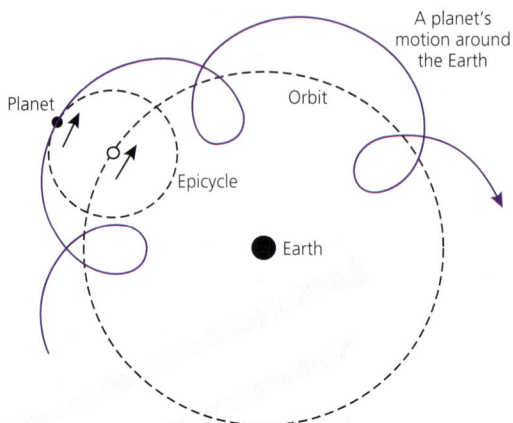

This is how Ptolemy explained planetary movement in his book known as the Almagest.

Nicolas also grasps something else. The stars are much, much further away than anyone realises. The distance between Earth and Sun is tiny by comparison.

But proving his theory will take Nicolas years. Years of mathematical calculations lie ahead.

Nicolas's uncle won't make this easy. In 1503, Nicolas is summoned to the dark stairways and damp rooms of the Bishop of Varmia's palace in Heilsberg. He must serve his uncle, as doctor and secretary. By day, he writes letters and doctor's prescriptions. By night, he works to prove his theory.

In 1503, the bishop needs yet more help from his nephew, for Varmia is threatened by the Teutonic Knights. These knights were once crusaders. Back in the thirteenth century, Polish rulers invited the knights into Prussia to help fight pagan raiders. But when the knights became too powerful, the Poles forced them out of western Prussia. Western Prussia became Royal Prussia, controlled by the King of Poland. The knights retreated to east Prussia.

The knights long to regain their land. They especially resent Varmia. (Find it on the map.) The knights constantly raid Varmia. The bishop, and his over-worked secretary Nicolas, constantly write to Poland's king for help.

By night, Nicolas records positions of Jupiter, Saturn and Mars. In 1509, he watches Earth's shadow creep across the Moon.

In 1510, his uncle dying, Nicolas leaves Heilsburg. From now on, he will work with the cathedral canons in Frauenburg Cathedral. The cathedral spires and turrets overlook the Vistula bay. Buildings huddle round the cathedral. Here, Nicolas gains a little house. He also gains a friend. A canon called Giese shares his love of astronomy. Giese urges Nicolas to publish a short pamphlet. Nicolas agrees.

In 1511, Nicolas's daytime work becomes more challenging. The cathedral canons give him a huge new job – Chancellor of Varmia. Nicolas must now manage the finances of all Varmia.

In 1513, Nicolas builds a platform by his house. He calls it his pavimentum. At night, he stands on it for hours. He maps the stars. He traces the planets' paths. Sometimes, the mists above the Vistula frustrate him. How lucky were the ancient Greeks, he writes in his notes, with their clear skies!

In 1515, a Latin translation of Ptolemy's *Almagest* appears. Until now, Nicolas has read only a shortened version. Now he has the whole book! Nicolas plans to write a similar book, but showing that Ptolemy was wrong.

But time to write is snatched away. In November 1516, the canons choose Nicolas for another huge task: sorting out Varmia's peasant landholdings. Living in dreadful poverty and in terror of the knights, Varmia's peasants pay the canons for the right to farm their land. When peasants flee in search of better lives, Nicolas must find others to farm the land. For three years, Nicolas must live in Allenstein Castle. By day, he rides out on horseback. He has 120 villages to visit. Soon, he discovers problems with the currency. No one agrees what coins are worth! By night, he writes plans for currency reform. He is exhausted.

Still, on Allenstein's castle walls, he leaves his mark. He paints a sundial. Charting the Sun's changing position, he calculates the length of a year, to the second.

In 1519, he can return, at last, to Frauenburg. At last, he can stand on his pavimentum again, stealing hours of sleep with the stars. But not for long. The Teutonic Knights' ambitious young ruler, Albrecht von Hohenzollern, declares war. The canons must flee! Where? Back to Allenstein.

Copernicus had no telescope. He just measured.

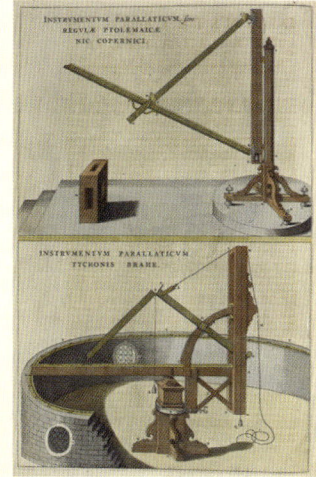

His **triquetrum** measured a star's height.

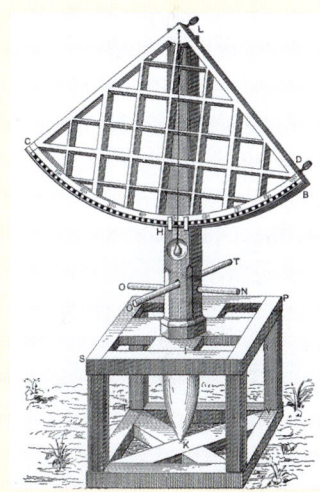

His **quadrant** measured the Sun's height throughout the year.

His **armillary sphere** modelled the solar system.

At last, in 1521, a truce is signed. Nicolas can return to Frauenburg.

In August 1521, he watches the Moon dip into Earth's shadow and, bit by bit, immerse itself entirely. He notes the time precisely – 2.48 am. The Moon, soaking up the Sun's colour, glows fire-pink and rose-gold, reflecting all the light from the evening before and the dawn ahead.

This is an eclipse of the Moon. More than any other drama in the sky, an eclipse of the Moon helps accurate measurement. Nicolas can measure distances of stars and planets from the Sun and Moon. He is up all night.

Soon, Nicolas's days are more exhausting than ever, for in January 1523, another bishop of Varmia dies. Nicolas must now lead Varmia until a new one is appointed in April.

A year later, in 1524, many more eyes are on the sky. It is the Great Conjunction of Jupiter and Saturn! Astrologers predict catastrophe, as bad as Noah's flood. Coast dwellers flee to the mountains. Some consult the Bible on how to build an ark. But Nicolas does not believe in astrology. He studies the heavens for their order and beauty, not to predict the future.

Spring 1525 sees a lasting peace between Albrecht and Poland. Remarkably, Albrecht has dissolved the Teutonic Knights! Albrecht hands his territory to the King of Poland, who hands it back as the Duchy of Prussia. From now on, east Prussia will be called Ducal Prussia.

Meanwhile, some rulers imagine that they do see the horror foretold by Jupiter and Saturn.

The Pope watches in horror as Luther's heresy spills over German borders. In east Prussia, the knights' territory, one bishop publicly supports Luther. Duke Albrecht, now a Lutheran, turns Ducal Prussia into a Protestant state.

The Bishop of Varmia watches in horror. 'Prussia teems with Lutherans!' he writes. In 1526, he banishes Lutherans from Varmia.

The King of Poland watches in horror. He tolerates Jewish people, but he will not tolerate Lutherans. In Spring 1526, he orders Protestants' homes to be set on fire.

Years pass. By day, Nicolas manages money and land. By night, he watches and records, calculates and writes. In 1529, he makes the last observation to go in his book – the Moon hiding Venus. His book will be called *On the Revolutions of the Heavenly Spheres*.

In 1532, Varmia's new bishop issues harsh laws against Lutherans. Nicolas's friend, Giese, is troubled by this. 'Have we estranged ourselves entirely from love?' he writes.

In 1535, Nicolas's book is nearly complete. His supporters urge him to publish. His friend Giese insists, 'Publish!'. The Pope's secretary writes, 'Publish!' Nicolas refuses to publish.

In 1536, a Cardinal writes from Rome:

> …with utmost earnestness, I entreat you, most learned Sir… to communicate this discovery of yours to scholars, together with tables and whatever else is relevant to this subject.

Nicolas does not reply.

If the story had ended there, there might have been no *On the Revolutions*, the foundation of modern astronomy. There might have been no book for another great astronomer, Galileo, to confirm as correct with his telescope in 1609.

Galileo would be arrested for contradicting what the Bible seemed to say – that the Sun moved and Earth stood still. Back in the sixteenth century, however, the Catholic Church did not criticise Copernicus; it mostly urged him on! So why was Copernicus reluctant to publish? Perhaps he sensed that the Church could turn against him. Perhaps he feared that his calculations were incomplete. Perhaps he was just exhausted.

On the Revolutions was only published thanks to a 25-year-old man who walked into Frauenburg in May 1539. The young man was a mathematics professor from the University of Wittenberg. He called himself Rheticus. Determined to meet Copernicus, he was risking his life. For Rheticus was a Lutheran.

We do not know how Rheticus persuaded Copernicus to publish, nor do we know why the bishop chose to overlook this Lutheran in Varmia. We only know that Rheticus succeeded. First, he published his own summary, which prepared readers slowly for Copernicus's shocking conclusions. Rheticus did not mention the Earth's movement until page 19.

The summary was sent everywhere. (Copernicus's friend Giese even sent it to Duke Albrecht!) It did the trick: new calls for Copernicus to publish his book poured in. Meanwhile, Rheticus helped Copernicus to tidy up the manuscript.

Rheticus did not leave until September 1541. 'Upon my departure', Rheticus later recalled, 'the grand old man solemnly charged me to finish what he, prevented by old age and impending death, was unable to complete himself.'

In May 1542, Rheticus took the manuscript to a printer in Germany. Skilled carvers had to cut woodblocks for 142 diagrams. A metal plate was inked and pressed down on the blocks. Each double page then took two days to print. Each page was hung up to dry. It took months.

In May 1543, 69-year-old Copernicus was dying. A friend took the final printed pages to Copernicus's bedside, placed them in his hands, then watched the life go out of him.

What became of Rheticus? A highly-respected mathematics professor, his scholarly career soared. Then, in 1551, he was accused of a sexual act with another man. The punishment was death by fire.

Yet Rheticus survived. He fled to Prague, where he began a new career as a doctor.

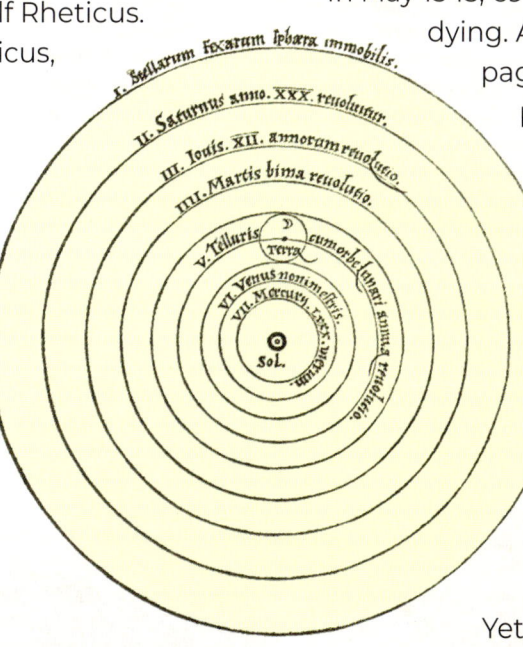

This is how Copernicus drew the solar system. The outer ring ('stellarum') is the stars. Earth is 'terra'.

Copernicus loved to gaze and observe. Perhaps this is why he also liked to paint. Do you remember Copernicus learning to paint in Padua? This sixteenth-century portrait, by an unknown artist, is based on Copernicus's own self-portrait.

24 Sofonisba Anguissola studies the beauty of the Earth

What shaped the art of a Renaissance painter?

Sofonisba puts down her paintbrush. She is pleased. She has painted her three sisters, all delighting in their game of chess, and in one another. The family servant looks on.

Yet something isn't right. What will bring out the play of light on her sister's face? Sofonisba thinks about paintings she has seen. She needs darker tones. She will add another tree behind her sister's head.

It is just what is needed to complete her painting.

> **Your enquiry**
>
> Sofonisba did not paint alone. What she painted and how she painted were affected by changes in art before her, by mathematics and astronomy, and by her own experience as a woman at this time. At the end of this enquiry, you will build a visual collage to show the worlds that shaped Sofonisba's art.

Sofonisba Anguissola was an Italian noblewoman. She was born during the **Renaissance**. The Renaissance is a label that historians give to developments in art and ideas in the fifteenth and sixteenth centuries. Artists and scholars looked afresh at the achievements of the ancient world and tried to go beyond them.

Like other Renaissance artists, Sofonisba was adventurous. She drew on others' work, but she did so in order to do something new. By studying a great artist such as Sofonisba, we can learn about how ideas moved and connected during the Renaissance.

Cremona: small town, big ideas

Sofonisba was born in Cremona in northern Italy, in 1532. (Find Cremona on the map.) She was educated in the Renaissance tradition, studying music, science, Latin and Greek. At the age of 14, Sofonisba's father asked the artist Barnadino Campi to teach Sofonisba to paint. For three years, Sofonisba experimented with pencils and paints, learning from Master Campi.

No longer were artists painting flat pictures such as you saw on page 124. Fifteenth-century artists had begun to portray people and plants as real, rounded and lifelike. In the city of Florence (find it on the map) Renaissance artists delighted in new techniques. Studying anatomy, they recreated muscles and veins in sculpture and on paper. Influenced by these artists, Master Campi would have sketched naked men from different angles, or even dissected corpses.

Master Campi encouraged Sofonisba to study the human body. Women and girls were not allowed to study nudes, nor to dissect corpses, but Sofonisba drew her family. Notice how in her painting, *The Chess Game*, she made her sisters lifelike.

The Laocoön was a marble sculpture made between 42 and 20 BCE. Laocoön was a priest for a Greek god.

But Sofonisba was also experimenting with something new. Artists usually painted formal portraits, or scenes from the Bible. But here Sofonisba painted an everyday situation.

Venice: experiments with colour

In the fifteenth century, Venetian painters such as Titian experimented with colour. Whether in portraits or landscapes, scenes from the Bible or legends, Titian built up layers of colour to create realistic paintings. He captured light and shadow, such as a darkening sky.

Master Campi encouraged Sofonisba to study Titian's art and to experiment with colour. Using her new knowledge, Sofonisba brought people alive on paper. She began making money by selling her paintings. She became known as Cremona's bright star.

Step 1

What people, places and traditions influenced Sofonisba's art? Copy and complete the table.

People	Places	Traditions
Master Campi...	In Florence...	The study of anatomy...
Titian...	In Venice....	

Rome: an ancient city of new ideas

In 1554, aged 22, Sofonisba travelled to Rome. What might have inspired Sofonisba as she wandered around with her sketchbook? Rome was a city old and new. Architects and artists came here to draw ancient buildings such as the Colosseum, and ancient sculptures such as The Laocoön.

By studying works like The Laocoön, Renaissance artists learnt how to sculpt in the magnificent style of ancient Rome. Renewed interest in ancient Rome changed what artists were painting. Artists like Botticelli became interested in classical themes. Here is the image of the Roman goddess Venus from Botticelli's famous painting of her.

In this golden age of Italian art, nobles, merchants and even the Pope became patrons of the arts. They paid artists such as Botticelli to beautify their buildings.

One building in Rome was particularly exciting: the Sistine Chapel – a chapel used by the Pope himself. Sofonisba would have admired Botticelli's frescos. Frescos are murals painted onto freshly-laid plaster. The Pope had invited Botticelli and other artists to paint biblical scenes on the chapel walls.

But it was not the walls that would have made Sofonisba gasp. It was the ceiling. In 1512, about forty years before Sofonisba's visit in 1554, the artist Michelangelo painted the finishing touches to the chapel ceiling. It had taken him four lonely years to complete his masterpiece.

Michelangelo used the laws of perspective to make these figures seem real. Some figures are painted smaller, or are shrouded in shadow, so that they appear further away. Muscles twist and turn in every direction.

In Rome Sofonisba met the 79-year-old Michelangelo. He gave Sofonisba sketches from his notebooks.

In 1554, Michelangelo challenged Sofonisba to draw a difficult subject: a crying boy.

A small part of Michelangelo's fresco, on the ceiling of the Sistine Chapel, painted for Pope Julius II between 1508 and 1512.

This is how Sofonisba responded to Michelangelo's challenge. Under his guidance, Sofonisba began using new techniques to create a sense of depth.

Cities connecting new worlds

Milan

In 1558, now established as a painter, Sofonisba travelled to Milan. Like Florence, Venice and Rome, Milan was strewn with scaffolding. New marble statues dazzled everywhere. While there, Sofonisba probably saw the painting below, *The Last Supper*, painted by Leonardo da Vinci, at the request of the Duke of Milan, in the 1490s. Notice how all the lines meet in one place, known as the vanishing point. Which figure is Jesus? How does da Vinci's use of perspective emphasise Jesus's importance?

In Milan, Sofonisba was invited to paint a portrait of the Duke of Alba, advisor to King Philip II of Spain. The duke was so impressed that Sofonisba was invited to join the Spanish court in Madrid.

Madrid

After her arrival in Spain in 1559, Sofonisba began teaching Philip II's new wife, Elisabeth of Valois, to paint. She and Sofonisba became good friends.

At the Spanish court, Sofonisba would have heard stories of peoples and lands lying across the ocean. She would have seen the gold and silver flooding into Spain on treasure ships that sailed from the Inka empire. Sofonisba showed Spain's riches in her portraits of the royal family: a Spanish princess is covered head-to-toe with silver, jewels and pearls.

Sofonisba called this painting Asdrubale bitten by a crayfish. *Can you feel the distance between the crying boy and the girl, the roundness of their bodies and the contrast in their expressions?*

In 1571, Sofonisba married a Sicilian nobleman, but he died just a few years later. She later fell in love with a sea captain and married him in 1584.

Sofonisba died in 1625, aged 93. She had seen great change, and she had pioneered new ways of studying and presenting the world.

Step 2

Continue your table using pages 152–53.

People	Places	Traditions
Leonardo da Vinci,...	In Milan... In Madrid,...	Experiments with colour,... The new laws of perspective...

Shaping your answer

On a large piece of paper, or on a computer, make a collage showing the worlds that shaped Sofonisba's art. Decide how you will show the three themes of people, places and traditions, and how you will show their connections.

25 Reformation and rebellion in an English village

What changed in the village of Morebath between 1520 and 1574?

The sun is setting in the little Devon village of Morebath. Inside Morebath's stone church, the only light comes from candles. Candles burn at the front, near the altar. Candles light the crucifix showing Jesus hanging on the cross. Candles catch the colours in the images of St George and the other Christian saints. Mary, the mother of Jesus, dressed in blue, has a crown of flowers on her head.

Staring up at the beautiful image of Mary is a villager called Margery Lake. Margery is on her knees, praying. She counts each prayer using her rosary beads. The beads help Margery to concentrate. She can forget her troubles for a while.

Margery often comes to the church to ask Mary for help. She calls Mary, 'Our Lady'. Margery says her prayer in Latin. She does not speak Latin, but she knows many Latin prayers. She knows the *Pater Noster* (Our Father) and *Ave Maria* (Hail, Mary).

Meanwhile, men are returning to Morebath from their work in the fields. They pass the noisy workshop of Thomas Glasse. Thomas is carving a splendid new image of St George.

This image is even bigger and better than the one in the church! St George, like the other saints, has his own special side altar and his own special altar cloth. The church bursts with colour.

Outside the church, an older woman speaks with a girl. The older woman is called Joan. The girl is Elenor Nichol. Elenor hopes to marry one day. Old Joan is giving her advice.

Many in Morebath listen to Joan's advice, even Sir Christopher. Sir Christopher is the new priest. When he arrived in Morebath last year, in 1520, Sir Christopher gave something special to the village. It was an image of a female saint. All the parish were delighted, but especially the girls and young women. The saint is St Sidwell. They placed her near Our Lady. Elenor Nichol often places new candles in front of St Sidwell.

As its priest, Sir Christopher Trychay is at the heart of this village's life. He baptises them, marries them, buries them. When they are troubled, he advises and, with stories of heaven, gives them hope.

A special source: Sir Christopher's book

The story that you have just read is about real historical people, places and events. The way in which we have told you the story makes it sound as though we are there. It is possible to do this because the story is built from a source found in the village of Morebath between 1520 and 1574.

For those 54 years, Morebath had the same priest, Sir Christopher Trychay. He wrote down what happened in his village in this big book where he kept the church accounts.

But Sir Christopher wrote far more than priests normally wrote in such accounts. He wrote about the people in the village, what they did, how much money was spent, and how the village reacted to things that the kings and queens, a long way away in London, commanded them to do.

Look at this extract, for instance. It is one of the first things that Sir Christopher wrote in his book, when he arrived in August 1520:

> Sir Christopher Trychay, one time priest of this church, the first year that he was made priest here, he gave St Sidwell and paid for her making.

A curious historian

In the 1990s, a historian called Eamon Duffy found Sir Christopher's book of church accounts. Professor Duffy spent years studying this extraordinary source. He used it to learn how Morebath adapted to the bewildering changes that Tudor monarchs imposed on the country. Using Sir Christopher's church accounts, Professor Duffy wrote a history book about Morebath's people.

These are the first sentences in Duffy's book.

> This is a book about a sixteenth-century country priest, and the extraordinary records he kept. It deals with ordinary people in an unimportant place, whose claim to fame is that they lived through the most decisive revolution in English history, and whose priest wrote everything down.

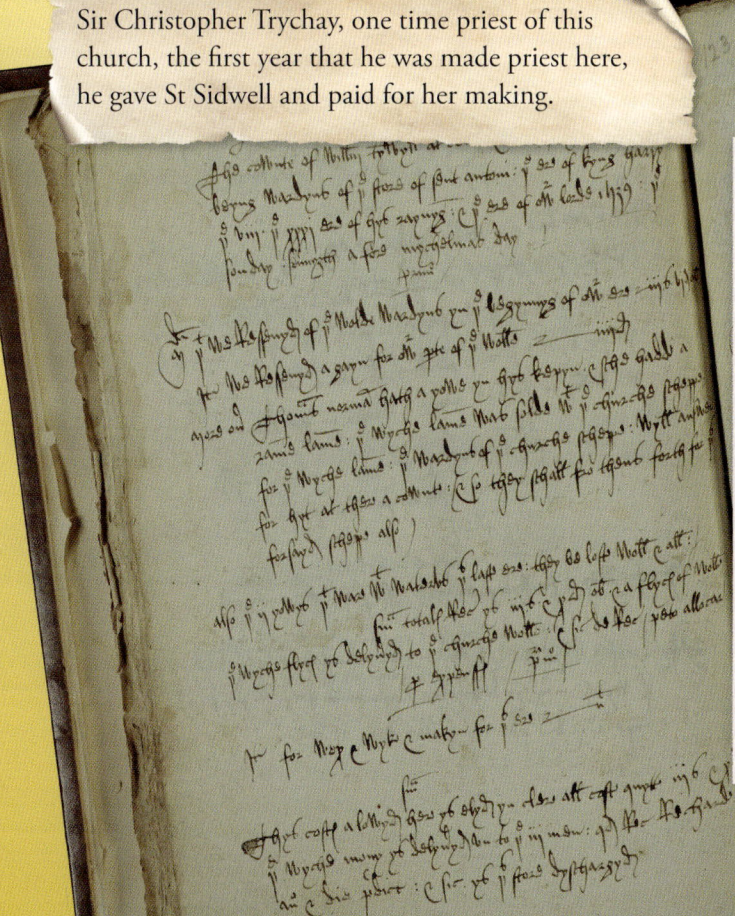

Your enquiry

You are going to read a re-telling of the story of Morebath in this extraordinary century of change. The people and events are all from those original pages written by Morebath's priest, Sir Christopher Trychay. Because of this exceptional source and Professor Duffy's remarkable work on it, we can tell stories of real lives in colourful detail.

As you read, you will think about how much changed, capturing the changes in spider diagrams. You will then re-tell the story yourself, commenting on what changed at each stage.

A remote Devon village

Morebath is a tiny village in Devon in south-west England. In the early sixteenth century, about 300 people lived there, farming the land. Morebath was a sheep-farming village. Sheep grazed on the surrounding hills. This map shows the sixteenth-century parish of Morebath with its many farms.

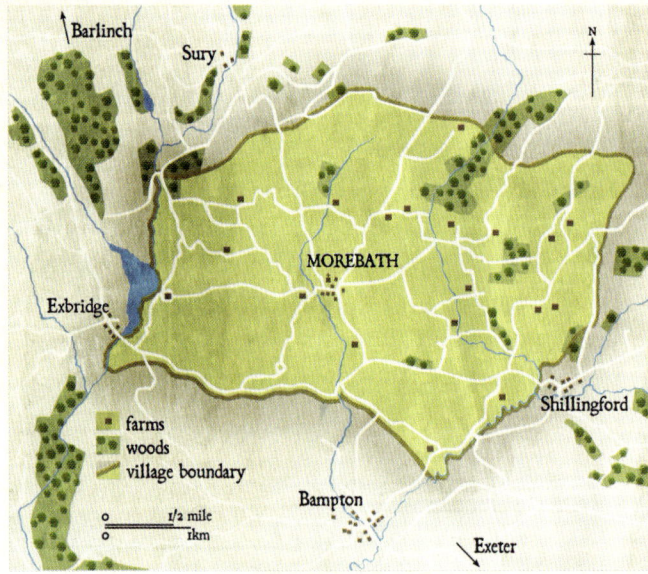

Thirty-three families lived in Morebath, but all the land was owned by a monastery in nearby Barlinch. The Prior of Barlinch was therefore the lord of Morebath, although the villagers hardly ever saw him. As long as they paid their taxes to the Prior, he left the villagers alone.

Although poor, the villagers spent time and money making their church look beautiful. They paid for each candle. Everyone in the village was a member of a store. A store collected money to spend on caring for an image. For example, Our Lady's store looked after the image of Mary. Many young women were members of Mary's store. Some stores had their own small flock of sheep. The sheep's wool was sold to buy candles to place in front of a saint's image in Morebath's church.

The stores held holy feast days for various saints. These feast days were called ales. Money from selling ale went towards buying more candles. Young unmarried men in the Young Men's store cared for the image of St George. Craftsmen, such as Thomas Glasse, were in St Anthony's store. Sometimes, when a member of a store died, he or she left money in a will to buy even more candles.

A death, and a new idea for the village

In 1529, Sir Christopher wrote in his book that old Joan had died. At Joan's funeral, the priest wore the black vestments used at special services.

Sir Christopher also recorded something else. He recorded the money that Joan's will had gifted to Morebath's church. Joan left money for a new image of Mary. Sir Christopher wrote in his book:

> We received by the death of Joan Rumbelow [...] a new image of Our Lady...

An extract from Sir Christopher Trychay's book.

The new image of Mary replaced the old image. Everyone in Morebath was pleased. Each time the villagers looked at Mary's statue, they could think of Joan.

Soon afterwards, a villager called Harry Hurley made a suggestion. He said that the priest's old black vestments were looking shabby and should be replaced. New vestments would be expensive so the village would need to save up for them. Everyone agreed and a black vestments fund began. Sir Christopher recorded this in his book:

> Thus resteth in Harry's hande from my tithes 2/8d (2 shillings and 8 pence)... this money shall go to buy a pair of black vestments. As for the vestments of black, we be full agreed that these tithes shall pay for it altogether though it shall never be more than 20/= (20 shillings).

An extract from Sir Christopher Trychay's book.

Step 1

Between 1520 and 1532, new people and new objects had come to Morebath. Make a spider diagram to show these changes. At the centre of your diagram, list some things that stayed the same, for example, the villagers' devotion to the saints.

King Henry VIII makes some changes

In 1533, Sir Christopher received a shocking message. King Henry VIII had divorced his wife, Catherine of Aragon! Even more shocking for the villagers, was a new law stating that the Pope no longer had power over England's churches! The king was now the head of the English Church.

What would this mean for Morebath? No one was yet sure.

In 1534, all priests in England had to travel to their nearest town to swear an oath to the king. Visiting the church as usual, Margery Lake probably said a prayer for the priest. It was an unsettling time. But the villagers, and especially the young women, continued to find joy in their saints, and especially the beautiful statue of St Sidwell that Sir Christopher Trychay had given them.

One day in 1534, the young women staring at St Sidwell would have noticed something new and remarkable – a little silver shoe for one of St Sidwell's feet. The shoe was made from Elenor Nichol's wedding ring. Elenor had it melted down and used the silver to make a little shoe, as a gift for her favourite saint.

Meanwhile, Sir Christopher travelled to the nearest town to swear the oath to the king. Some priests refused to swear the oath and were imprisoned. In the city of Exeter, a radical Protestant preached. Some priests listened and agreed. Others disagreed. Some called the Protestant preacher a heretic.

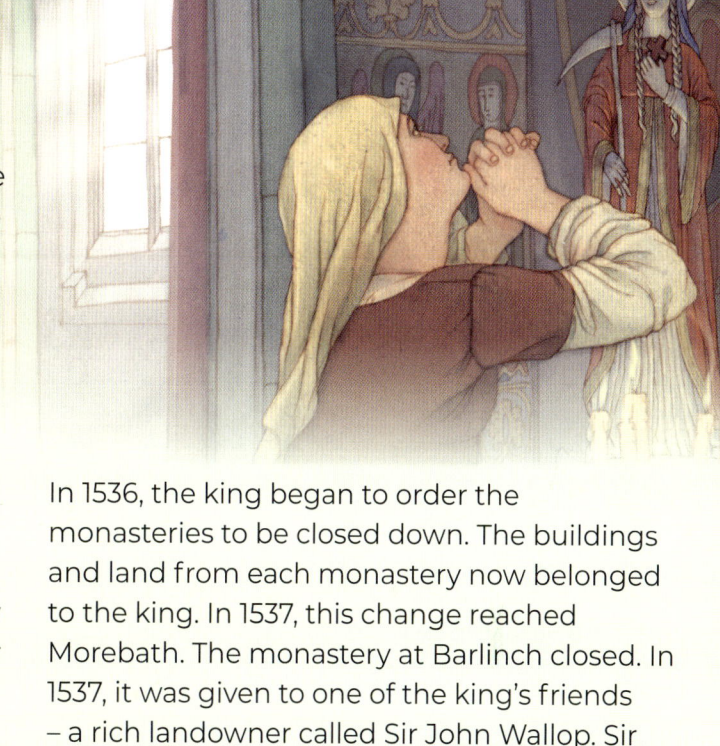

In 1536, the king began to order the monasteries to be closed down. The buildings and land from each monastery now belonged to the king. In 1537, this change reached Morebath. The monastery at Barlinch closed. In 1537, it was given to one of the king's friends – a rich landowner called Sir John Wallop. Sir John lived miles away but he was now the lord of Morebath! The monks were homeless.

In other ways, however, life in Morebath changed little. Neither the king's divorce, nor breaking away from the Pope, had much effect on village life. Morebath carried on much as it had for hundreds of years.

Around the same time, Thomas Glasse finished carving his new image of St George. What an exciting day. The image was placed at the front of the church, near where the people would walk up to the altar to receive the bread and wine from the priest. The villagers were overjoyed. They crept into the church to wonder at Thomas Glasse's work. St George was magnificent.

Then, in 1538, King Henry VIII issued special instructions, called injunctions. Sir Christopher read the injunctions out to the village. This is a summary of the injunctions:

> King Henry VIII's injunctions
> 1. No candles are permitted in front of images.
> 2. All holy feast days for saints, organised by the stores, are abolished.
> 3. The Pater Noster (Our Father) prayer must be in English.
> 4. Every church must have a copy of the Bible in English.

Morebath responds to Henry's changes

The people of Morebath had no choice but to obey the king. But they could not bear to take the lights away from the images. They did not want to stop celebrating feast days with ales. The villagers had to think hard about how to obey King Henry's instructions.

The villagers of Morebath soon came up with crafty plans. Sir Christopher's book tells us what the villagers did.

Crafty Plan 1
The villagers moved the candles from in front of the images to beside the images.

Crafty Plan 2
They decided to keep the feast days, too, but they craftily gave different reasons for them: the king's birthday or collecting the harvest.

Crafty Plan 3
The village did not have enough money to buy a Bible. The money that they did have, they wanted to keep spending on candles and saving for new black vestments. So, the villagers agreed that they would *say* they would buy an English Bible, in future. They would *say* that a Bible would come when they had enough money. That promise, they hoped, would keep the king's officers happy if they were to visit.

Margery would have said a prayer on her rosary beads, thanking Our Lady for keeping Morebath safe.

Nonetheless Morebath was changing. There was not quite the same need for all the stores. So, gradually the stores collected less money.

The black vestments arrive

On a July day in 1547, Harry Hurley could not contain his excitement. For nearly twenty years, the village had been saving hard for new black vestments. For nearly twenty years, they had dreamed of these new vestments. Finally, they had arrived! Sir Christopher tried them on. The villagers were proud to have saved up for so long.

Step 2
Make a spider diagram listing changes in Morebath between 1532 and 1547. In the centre of the diagram, list some things that stayed the same.

King Edward VI makes big changes...

Just a few weeks after the arrival of the black vestments, more news arrived. King Henry had died. His son, nine-year-old Edward, was king.

In 1547, aged only nine, the young Edward VI needed advisers to help him rule. These advisers included Archbishop Cranmer, a committed Protestant. Edward VI himself was a serious Protestant too. Henry VIII had made some changes to the Church, but he had never been a Protestant.

Archbishop Cranmer had been waiting for a Protestant king. Now he could advise young Edward to remove every last trace of the Catholic religion.

In the first year of his reign, King Edward VI issued some injunctions. They arrived in Morebath early in 1548. Use your knowledge to suggest what the villagers would have thought of each one. Which treasured objects and ways of life would they have to give up?

The king's instructions went even further! The villagers now had to hand in a list of all their images, vestments, coloured altar cloths, and much more. Everything on the list would be taken or destroyed.

This later sixteenth-century painting shows Henry VIII on his deathbed, pointing to his heir Edward. Underneath, the Pope is being crushed.

Edward VI's injunctions
1. No praying with rosary beads.
2. No candles in churches except for two on the altar.
3. All images of saints to be destroyed.
4. No ales to be held.
5. Every church must have a locked box for collecting money for the poor.
6. When people die, they can leave money only to the poor, not to anything else.
7. Every church must have a prayer book with prayers in English, not Latin.

Morebath responds to Edward's changes

Sir Christopher had to be careful. The Morebath villagers did not want to lose their treasured possessions, but they could not hand in an empty list – no one would believe them! Then someone – Sir Christopher's book does not tell us who – came up with another crafty plan.

The crafty plan was to make a list which included only some items but not all of them. The list would keep the king's officials happy, and no one would know that not everything was on it. It was an excellent plan. The list was handed to the king's officials.

We expect you can guess what the villagers chose to keep off the list...

- The list did not include old Joan's image of Our Lady.
- The list did not include Thomas Glasse's new image of St George.
- **The list did not include the black vestments!**

Meanwhile, the villagers quietly hid these most treasured possessions in their houses. Then they moved them from house to house so that word could not spread about where they were. The villagers were sad not to have their beautiful objects in their church, but at least they were safe, hidden in the villagers' homes.

By 1549, the church in Morebath was stripped to the bone. The images on the list were gone. The special vestments were hidden away. The life of the stores was no more.

During the reign of Henry VIII, the village had raised a huge sum of money each year – around £10. By 1549, no money was being raised because there were no more images in Morebath church.

This is how much money was raised by the stores between 1539 and 1549. Notice what happened to the stores. Look at the dates. Why do you think these changes occurred at these times? (The currency at this time consisted of pounds (£), shillings (s) and pence (d). There were 20 shillings in a pound and 12 pence in a shilling.)

YEAR	Other ale receipts	Ale receipts for Young Men's store	Ale receipts for Young Maidens' store	Ale receipts for St Sunday's store and St Anthony's store
1539	£3/-/=	18/3d	X	X
1540	£2/15/6½d	£1/4/4½d	X	Stores dissolved
1541	£2/2/2½d	£1/3/9½d	Store dissolved	
1542	£2/4/4½d	X		
1543	£2/1/4	X		
1544	£2/2/1½d	£1/3/3		
1545	£2/9/8	£1/7/8½d		
1546	£2/-/=	£1/7/6		
1547	£2/10/7	£1/11/10½d		
1548	No ale	No ale		
1549	No ale	No ale		

Morebath joins the rebels

South of Morebath lay the great city of Exeter. During the long, hot summer of 1549, something strange was spotted there. Morebath villagers heard of a banner showing two wounded hands, two wounded feet and a crown made from thorns. Morebath villagers knew exactly what those symbols meant. There was no mistaking it: this was a Catholic banner. The villagers would have heard how angry men and women shouted as they held the banner high.

The banner was a sign of rebellion against King Edward's Protestant ways. The rebels who were holding up that strange banner in Exeter wanted many things. They wanted to have images during the weeks leading up to Easter. They wanted their monasteries back. They hated the king's new English Prayer Book. They missed the old Latin prayers to Our Lady and the saints.

During that sweltering summer of 1549, the king's men put down the rebellion. Edward's soldiers killed many rebels.

Step 3

Make another spider diagram to show what changed and what stayed the same in Morebath during the reign of King Edward (1547–1553).

A new queen and hope for Morebath?

In 1553, Morebath received news: 15-year-old King Edward was dead!

King Edward's sister, Mary, was now queen. Mary was daughter of Henry VIII and his first wife, Catherine of Aragon (who we met in Chapters 20 and 22). Mary was a Catholic. She hated the new Protestant faith. How do you think the news of a Catholic queen was greeted by Morebath's villagers?

Sir Christopher Trychay was hopeful. The village was hopeful. Morebath hoped that things would slowly return to how they were before. But it would not be straightforward. The stores had disappeared, as had the ales and the images. The altars to house the images of the saints had been removed. They had no candles for their saints' images.

At least the village still had some of the most precious things hidden away…

…or so they thought.

The black vestments had been passed secretly from villager to villager. Who had them now? Who had them last? 'I thought you had them?' said one villager. 'Weren't they in that house?' said another. No one was sure. No one could remember!

A portrait of Mary Tudor painted by a Dutch artist in 1554.

According to Sir Christopher's book, the vestments were never found.

The Young Men's store was set up again, but it never became as important as it had been before. Morebath did buy new vestments, however. Also, in time, the villagers had new images carved. And, of course, eventually, they bought new candles.

YEAR	Other ale receipts	Ale receipts for Young Men's store	Ale receipts for Young Maidens' store	Ale receipts for St Sunday's store and St Anthony's store
1553	–	No ale	–	–
1554	£2/13/4d	No ale	–	–
1555	£2/8/10d	No ale	–	–
1556	£3/7/11d	No ale	–	–
1557	£4/0/2½d	£3/6/8d	–	–
1558	£4/14/4d	£2/2/10d	–	–

This is how much money was raised by the stores when Mary was queen. You can see that during Mary's reign fundraising got going again. Why do you think that some stores did not recover?

Step 4

Make a spider diagram showing what changed and what stayed the same in Morebath during Mary's reign (1553–1558).

Another new queen

Morebath was to be disappointed. Mary only reigned for five years. What is more, Mary had no children. Her heir, Elizabeth, was a Protestant.

In 1558, as news reached Morebath that Elizabeth was queen, the villagers must have worried. Would it be all-change again? Mary had been unpopular in those parts of the country where Protestant beliefs had taken hold, but not everywhere, and not in Morebath. In Morebath, Mary's reign had been welcomed. But it was over. What on earth would happen now?

There was nothing the village could do. They had to show loyalty to the new monarch. And so, one Sunday late in 1558, Sir Christopher put on his best Catholic vestments and stood in the church as usual. He then said a prayer for the new Protestant queen, Elizabeth.

As the village expected, the new Protestant queen issued her own injunctions. Once again, Sir Christopher was required to hand in his vestments. Once again, the villagers hid them. So for the next three years, Sir Christopher reminded the village of the whereabouts of his vestments. He was not going to lose them again!

Morebath responds to Elizabeth's changes

Although Elizabeth was a Protestant, she was not such a strict Protestant as her brother, Edward, had been. Elizabeth introduced Protestant ways, but as you will soon see in Chapter 28, she softened them a little so as to encourage more Catholics to accept her Church.

Morebath obeyed the new queen, but only slowly. Morebath removed the images but continued to use the Catholic prayer book.

By the end of the 1560s, however, Elizabeth's government was getting tougher on villages that were slow to get rid of their Catholic ways. Morebath obeyed, but only with its usual craftiness!

This is a portrait of the young Elizabeth before she became queen. She holds a copy of the New Testament, the part of the Bible that describes Jesus's life and the early Christian church.

New Crafty Idea 1

Morebath had been told by Elizabeth's officials to get rid of its altar and to replace it with a wooden communion table. When old Joan Rumbelow's husband gave a beautiful silk altar cloth to the church, in memory of his dear wife, can you guess what the villagers did? The cloth was placed over the wooden table so as to pretend that it was still a Catholic altar.

New Crafty Idea 2

Morebath was told to get rid of its Catholic silver cup and to replace it with a simple Protestant cup. Morebath had two Catholic silver cups, a large one and small one. They sold the large one and just used the small one, hoping that no one would notice.

By the early 1570s, the church had everything it needed to look Protestant (except for that naughty little silver cup). Even Sir Christopher's book said less about religious things such as cups and vestments, and more about things such as taxes, bridges and cattle.

Sir Christopher dies

By the 1570s, Sir Christopher was old, but he was still the priest, and still writing in his book. When he died in 1574, the villagers must have been in shock. Sir Christopher had been their priest for 54 years.

Sir Christopher's body was placed where he had asked to be buried – under the communion table, or, as Sir Christopher was still calling it, under the 'altar'.

Let's read the last paragraph in Professor Eamon Duffy's history book.

> He had been their priest, Catholic and Protestant, for fifty-four years, for fifty-four years the heart and voice, above everything else the voice. …He had been the spirit of Morebath. He had baptised their children, buried their dead, married every one of them. Perhaps Morebath knew that with Sir Christopher Trychay they had lost something unique… and that there, between the altar and the table, they had buried something of themselves.

The year after they lost their priest, the village of Morebath finally bought a Protestant cup.

Step 5

Make a spider diagram to show what changed and what stayed the same in Morebath from Elizabeth becoming queen (1558) to Sir Christopher Trychay's death (1574).

Shaping your answer

You will now use your spider diagrams to shape your own answer to the enquiry question: What changed in Morebath between 1520 and 1574? You will do this by writing a story.

First, use your five spider diagrams to plan the five main paragraphs of your story. Then improve your paragraph plans by thinking about:

- how you will bring out the importance of wider events for the Morebath villagers, so that the reader is engaged by their hopes and fears;
- how you will show change (for example, how big a particular change was, what kind of change it was, how rapid the change was or how the change came about).

Then write your story. Remember, you want others to enjoy reading your story!

26 Meanwhile, in the Tudor court
The story of Mary Tudor, Queen of England

A troubled early life

Life had never been easy for Mary Tudor. Henry VIII had divorced her beloved mother, Catherine of Aragon, when Mary was just 18. Henry then took away his daughter's title of 'princess'. She was now plain Lady Mary.

Another problem with being Henry VIII's daughter was all the stepmothers. Mary was to have five of them! After her parents' divorce, Mary was not allowed to see her mother. Worse, Mary and her father's new queen, Anne Boleyn, hated each other. Anne soon demanded that Mary be sent away from court.

At least Mary's next stepmother, Henry's third wife, Jane Seymour, was kinder. Mary was devastated when Jane Seymour died. Jane Seymour died after giving birth to Edward, in October 1537. Edward was now heir to the throne, not Mary, but Mary still adored her little half-brother.

Brother trouble

In 1547, Henry VIII died and young Edward came to the throne. He was nine. Mary now watched in horror as her little brother, now King Edward VI, ripped up the Catholic traditions that she held dear. Edward VI and his advisers were committed Protestants.

It became harder and harder for Mary to resist her brother's new prayer books. In one last effort to change Edward's course of action, Mary confronted Edward at court. Both wept. They loved each other. But the gulf between their beliefs was too vast.

Mary even considered fleeing abroad. She planned to take refuge in a Catholic country. At dead of night, a ship waited on the English coast. Mary's ladies-in-waiting desperately shoved clothes into sacks and trunks. Then, at the last minute, Mary decided to stay. To stay and wait. It was to prove a good decision.

A troubled monarch

From the start, Mary asserted herself as a confident monarch. Yet beneath her outward strength, the pressures of being a woman in Tudor England were tiring. Mary needed an heir. But who could the Queen of England marry? An English noble? A foreign prince? Mary made the decision. She would marry King Philip II of Spain.

On paper, Philip was perfect: young, Catholic, powerful. Mary adored him. But Philip didn't love Mary. He wasn't even attracted to Mary. The marriage was just a way of connecting England and Spain.

When the marriage was announced, thousands rebelled. On arrival in London, Philip's advisers were pelted with snowballs. Later, Philip charmed Mary into joining a war against France. This cost England huge sums of money. It also cost England its very last piece of France: Calais.

An assertive monarch

In spite of this, Queen Mary was a trailblazer. She dressed the part, with clothes of gold and silver. She talked the part, giving an inspirational speech from London's Guildhall when people protested against her marriage. She was decisive. She stood firm against powerful Spain when negotiating Philip's rights as her husband. Mary made sure that Philip could not claim to be King of England when she died.

Mary Tudor overcame challenges posed by her family, her public and her enemies. Yet, for centuries, two words came to summarise Mary's life: Bloody Mary. She gained this nickname because of her persecution of Protestants. About 300 were burned to death.

A troubled end

In 1558, Mary was 42, childless, and dying from cancer. Mary had shown that a woman could be monarch. But she would be remembered as 'Bloody Mary'. Days after her death, Londoners danced in the streets to the news that her sister Elizabeth was queen.

Trouble from cunning Protestant nobles

In 1553, 15-year-old Edward lay dying. Edward's advisers knew that the Catholic Mary would undo all the Protestant reforms. The Duke of Northumberland convinced Edward that Mary should not become queen. So who could? Who could keep the country Protestant?

The Duke of Northumberland hatched a cunning plan. 15-year-old Lady Jane Grey was the perfect solution. Lady Jane Grey, the granddaughter of Henry VII, was a Protestant. She was also married to Northumberland's son. If Jane became queen, Northumberland's family would be the most powerful family in England.

Jane never wanted to be queen, but Mary did. Mary had no difficulty raising an army: 30,000 troops came to support her. Jane had no chance. Jane reigned for just nine days. At the age of 37, in 1553, Mary became queen.

27 The Inkas

How do historians use sources to study the Inkas?

While Yorkists and Lancastrians clashed on English battlefields, while Christians and Muslims wrestled to control land and ideas, far away another empire grew. Between 1400 and 1532, the Inkas surged through South America. Each of the conquering peoples you have met so far, whether Arabs, Normans or Mongols, would have been amazed if they had seen the speed with which this empire expanded. In 1400, the Inkas numbered around 100,000. By 1500, when Henry VII was on England's throne, the Inkas ruled over 10 million people.

Squeezed between the Pacific Ocean and the Andes mountains, the empire ran for thousands of miles. Based in what is now Peru, the Inkas' power also reached into present-day Colombia, Ecuador, Chile, Argentina and Bolivia. At the heart of the Inka empire was Qosqo (pronounced Cusco). This image shows a valley near Qosqo.

Although high in the mountains, this land is rich and fertile. Notice how the land is layered into terraces. Terraces stopped water rushing downwards. Terraces kept the water on the crops. This helped the Inkas to create a bountiful food supply.

Historians have argued about how the Inka empire grew so big, so quickly. The Inkas were clearly well-organised. They created a huge labour force and vast armies. But these things can't explain why the expansion happened *then*. Why did the Inka empire grow rapidly from around 1400? Why not earlier?

In 2009, some historians and scientists offered a new answer: climate change. Their evidence for this claim lay in the soil and the landscape. Using soil samples from a dry lakebed in the Andes, they worked out which crops the Inka started growing, and when. Clues came from seeds, pollen and charcoal found in the soil. These scientists claimed that 400 years of natural warming must have begun in about 1100, causing water to rush down from melting glaciers. The Inkas could now dig more terraces to create fertile farmland, moving further and further up the valleys towards the mountains.

Not all historians agree, however. Some historians say that climate varies far too much across South America for climate change to be the cause of Inka expansion.

Your enquiry

Many sources can tell us about the Inkas. But plentiful sources are not enough. Whether using soil or landscape, oral accounts or songs, textiles or writing, historians must keep asking better questions in order to find out new things. By the end of the enquiry, you will be able to show what different sources and methods have revealed about Inka politics, society and religion.

The oral traditions of the Inkas

Like most civilisations, the Inkas told stories about where they came from. The stories were not written down. When a community passes on their history through word of mouth, historians call it an oral tradition.

The Inka people had many traditions about how the world and their own people began. According to one story, the first Inka people emerged from three gaps in a hillside cave. In Inka oral tradition, the cave is always called the House of Three Windows. In the story, the first Inka brothers and sisters left the cave to seek fertile lands. The Inka brothers and sisters travelled around until they settled in the lush Qosqo valley.

In another story, the most important Inka brother became the first Inka king. He divided his new kingdom into four parts. He called his new kingdom Tawantinsuyu, which means 'the four parts together'. These oral stories are extremely important for historians because they make it possible to work out what the Inkas valued. If it was worth passing on to the next generation, it must have mattered. Such stories also provide clues about how Inka people gained and kept power.

This picture was drawn in 1615 by Guamán Poma, a descendant of the Inkas who captured many stories from Inka tradition. Find the hill, the cave and the house with three windows.

Some Inka nobles told stories about how their empire grew. In these stories, Inka kings raided the lands around them and created alliances by arranging marriages or exchanging gifts with other ruling families. These alliances gave the Inkas allies to help them conquer even more land.

One important Inka story is of a brave prince whose father did not choose him as the next king. The prince therefore had to prove himself worthy. When a neighbouring tribe attacked Qosqo, the prince's father fled but the young prince stayed to defend Qosqo. In the story, the stones from the Qosqo valley rose up to help the prince to defeat his enemies. The prince then successfully claimed the Inka kingdom for himself. He now became King Pachakutiq.

What were these stories for?

It is important to understand what the Inka stories were for. For example, Inka nobles told stories that celebrated the lives of the kings that they were related to. If a king were considered cowardly, the story would not mention him. Why do you think that this tradition makes the oral stories very useful for historians?

The early Spanish accounts of Inka civilisation

The Inka empire came to a brutal end in 1532. This map shows you what happened. By 1521, Spain had conquered another empire, the Mexica (sometimes called the Aztecs), in Central America. Spanish soldiers then went on to defeat the Inkas, gaining control of Qosqo by 1532.

How Spain built their empire in the Americas.

The earliest written accounts of the Inkas were made in the 1530s. These accounts were written by the Spanish soldiers who conquered the Inka people. Most are short descriptions of Spanish soldiers fighting in battle. The soldiers who wrote these first accounts of the Inkas drew on familiar things to explain what they saw. They often called Inka temples mosques!

In the 1540s and 1550s, about twenty years after the Spanish conquest of the Inka empire, some Spaniards began writing detailed descriptions of Inka peoples and places. They began interviewing some of the Inka nobles. These Spanish historians learnt Quechua, the language spoken by the Inkas, and wrote down some of the stories that the Inkas were telling about their past.

Spaniards, however, continued to look for things that resembled their own way of doing things. For example, the Spanish wanted to create histories by making family trees of Inka kings. Using interviews with Inka nobles, early Spanish historians tried to make a big chronicle of Inka kings in chronological order. One chronicle showed Pachakutiq as the ninth Inka king. Relating Pachakutiq to their own dating system, the Spanish calculated that he had ruled from 1438 to 1471.

Spanish histories show the reign of King Pachakutiq as a turning point in Inka history. These histories suggest that Pachakutiq and his father were the first Inka kings to expand the Inka empire far beyond Qosqo. This map shows how quickly Pachakutiq expanded the Inka empire. In the fifteenth century, the Inka empire grew by hundreds of miles. By conquering new lands, Pachakutiq gained control of more resources: fish from the Pacific Ocean, fertile lands for crops, forests for wood, and gold and silver from the Andes mountains.

This map shows the different stages of the expansion of the Inka empire.

The early Spanish conquerors wrote a great deal about Inka soldiers. As fortune-seeking soldiers themselves, many Spaniards were impressed that Inka soldiers could travel hundreds of miles, far from Qosqo, on foot. Spanish writers tell us, for example, about how the Inkas conscripted soldiers to serve in the Inka military, and about the weapons that the Inkas used, such as star-shaped clubs.

Pedro Sarmiento de Gamboa

In 1572, a sea-captain called Pedro Sarmiento de Gamboa became very interested in how Pachakutiq kept control of his empire. Asked to write an official history of the Inkas for the King of Spain, Sarmiento travelled widely in order to find out as much as he could. He asked 42 Inka leaders to listen to a reading of what he had written and to tell him if it was correct. Many Inka leaders then approved Sarmiento's history by marking or signing the last page.

The last page of Sarmiento's history with the marks of the Inka leaders.

We learn from Sarmiento that after conquering a new province, Pachakutiq would move about a quarter of its people to a different place. This made it hard for conquered peoples to gain support for rebellion.

Here is part of what Sarmiento wrote about how Pachakutiq gained control:

> All the conquests that this Inka made were done with much violence and cruelties, force and robberies…. Pachakutiq moved people from the plains to the highlands, so far removed from one another and from their native land that they could not return to it…. Besides this, the Inka placed garrisons of Qosqo natives in all the important fortresses.

An extract from History of the Incas, *by Pedro Sarmiento de Gamboa, 29 February 1572.*

Sarmiento's history contains much information about the Inkas, but it was written for a particular purpose. That purpose was to make the Inkas seem like bullies, so that the Spanish could present themselves as liberators, freeing people from Inka control. Sarmiento described the Inkas as 'terrible **tyrants**'. He did this to help the King of Spain, Philip II, to argue that the Spanish conquest of the Inkas was lawful.

Step 1

Make a table like this one. Use Column 2 to write about the opportunities that each source gives to historians. In Column 3, write about any challenges that these sources might pose for historians. We have started you off.

Sources	What kinds of things can historians learn from these sources?	What challenges might historians face in using these sources?
The soil and landscape		
The Inkas' oral tradition	What the Inkas valued in their rulers.	
The early Spanish written accounts of the Inkas		The Spanish were interested in things that were familiar to them. They would have missed or misunderstood many other things.

The drawings and writings of an Inka nobleman, Guamán Poma

During the period of Spanish rule, one Inka nobleman began to keep a rich record of Inka history, recording many stories and illustrating them himself. Guamán Poma spoke the Inka language, Quechua, but learnt to read and write in Spanish in his youth. In the 1560s and 1570s, Guamán Poma worked as an interpreter for the Spanish rulers.

Poma was a Christian. He tried to work with the Spanish rulers. But the Spaniards treated Poma badly, even taking away his lands. Soon Poma became angry.

Poma decided to make a public complaint. Remember that Sarmiento had argued that the Inkas were tyrants who had not ruled lawfully. Poma wanted to challenge Sarmiento's history. He wanted to prove that he and his family deserved to be respected as long-standing members of the Inka **nobility**.

In 1615, Guamán Poma wrote a long letter of complaint to the Spanish king. By now a new king was ruling Spain, Philip III. Guamán Poma's letter to Philip III is so long that it is known as a chronicle. It covered over a thousand pages. King Philip III never received the document, but copies of Poma's chronicle have survived. The chronicle reveals a great deal about the Inka empire.

Poma and his family lived in a mountainous area to the south of Qosqo. So Poma's chronicle helps historians to understand what people living in the provinces of the Inka empire, outside of the Inka capital, thought about Inka rule.

In his chronicle, Poma argued that the old Inka rulers, such as King Pachakutiq, had treated people far better than the Spanish rulers. Look at the three pictures drawn by Poma, below. Find the picture of Pachakutiq. What do you think Poma might have been trying to say about Pachakutiq by drawing him in this way?

Poma also described women's work in Inka society. He explained that women were expected to sew and to weave in order to make clothing for Inka nobles and soldiers. Find the picture of the woman. Study her clothes and what she seems to be doing. What questions might this picture prompt a historian to ask?

Step 2

Add another row to your table. This time, write about the writing and drawing of Guamán Poma.

Physical remains

The Spanish histories from the 1500s and 1600s do not tell us much about ordinary people. In the 1800s, **archaeologists** became interested in how ordinary Inka people lived, worked and fought. The archaeologists searched for Inka buildings and physical objects (which we call artefacts) to help them understand Inka society. The archaeologists compared these buildings and artefacts with what they had read in the Spanish histories. They worked together and compared their finds, using all this new knowledge to make new claims about Inka society.

Inka artefacts

The archaeologists found artefacts such as this star-shaped weapon made of silver.

The weapon is a mace-head. The Inkas attached it to a wooden handle. Find the mace in Guamán Poma's picture of Pachakutiq on page 170. The discovery of weapons such as mace-heads and sling stones at Inka forts has helped archaeologists to understand Inka warfare. Finding out how Inkas lived and worked has been harder because the Spanish built new homes, churches and offices on top of old Inka buildings.

Now look at Guamán Poma's third picture. It shows a woman spinning thread on a spindle. The little round object at the bottom of the spindle is a spindle whorl. Its weight helped the thread to wind more quickly. In the 1960s, archaeologists excavating in the highlands of Peru found a spindle whorl and fragments of pots and jars. These artefacts helped archaeologists to make the claim that cooking and spinning took place at the same time. The site was an Inka city called Huánuco Pampa. Archaeologists found so many artefacts at Huánuco Pampa that they ran out of collection bags and had to get more!

Some artefacts tell us about peoples whom the Inka conquered. This doll was made by the Chancay people, who were conquered by the Inkas in around 1450. The doll was found in a Chancay grave on the Central Peruvian coastal plain. Hundreds of these dolls, often clothed with sophisticated textiles, have been found in Chancay burials. Some Chancay graves contain multiple dolls engaged in activities such as boat rides, dancing or playing musical instruments.

Inka roads

The Inkas built about 15,000 miles of roadway, stretching to all corners of the empire. The roads ran within deep valleys, across high mountains and through banks of snow. With suspension bridges hanging from braided cables, the roads could cross wide rivers. The roads linked the provinces with Qosqo.

Archaeologists have found two main north–south highways, neatly paved with stone. These roads were used by soldiers, by porters using llamas to carry goods and by Inka nobility. Along the roads, garrisons housed soldiers to keep watch on conquered peoples. Alongside and under the roads, water was channelled in thousands of watercourses. These roads show archaeologists how Inka leaders reached the provinces quickly whenever they heard reports of resistance.

Archaeologists estimate that the Inkas built more than 2,000 storehouses, called tampu, along the roads. (Find these storehouses in one of Poma's pictures.) Archaeologists have found remains which show the tampu stored alpaca wool, freeze-dried potatoes and dried llama meat. By preserving foods carefully, the Inkas could feed an army constantly on the move and could survive when harvests failed.

Inka cities and buildings

In the city of Qosqo, archaeologists have found physical remains of baths, aqueducts, golden fountains and grand plazas. In the outer streets of Qosqo, archaeologists have found artefacts suggesting the presence of metalsmiths, weavers, stonemasons, potters and accountants.

About 50 miles from Qosqo is the famous site of Machu Pikchu. Many archaeologists think Machu Pikchu was one of Pachakutiq's royal palaces.

On a steep hill overlooking Qosqo city is another important Inka site: a place called Saqsaywaman. Nothing holds its enormous stones together; they fit perfectly. Archaeologists think that Pachakutiq used forced labour to build Saqsaywaman, moving the stones from nearby quarries.

In the 1500s, the Spaniards thought that Saqsaywaman was a mighty fortress: the stones formed a zig-zag wall that runs for hundreds of metres across the hillside. In 1532, one of the first Spaniards to see Saqsaywaman remarked:

> here is a very beautiful fortress made of earth and stone with big windows that look over the city…There are so many rooms that one person cannot see it all in one day…many Spaniards say that they have not seen another construction like this fortress, nor a more powerful castle….

An Account of the Conquest of Peru, written by a merchant called Sancho de la Hoz in 1532–1533.

The Spaniards seeing Saqsaywaman were soldiers; so perhaps they saw what they expected to see: a big fortress. The Spanish invaders soon began to destroy Saqsaywaman, using its vast stones to build their halls and churches. Today, only those stones too large to be moved remain.

Since then, archaeologists have excavated Saqsaywaman. Gradually, they have come to challenge the conclusions of the early Spanish historians. Although they have found armour and weapons, they have also found gold and silverware of the same type used in Inka ceremonies. Archaeologists have concluded that Saqsaywaman was not a fortress at all, but a palace or temple.

Step 3

Now continue your table, adding three more rows for:

- artefacts
- roads
- cities and buildings

The khipus

Some archaeologists study artefacts known as khipus. The word khipu comes from the Quechua word for 'knot'. Knotted cotton or wool strings were dyed in many colours. The knots on each string have different shapes and positions. Find two khipus in one of Poma's pictures on page 170.

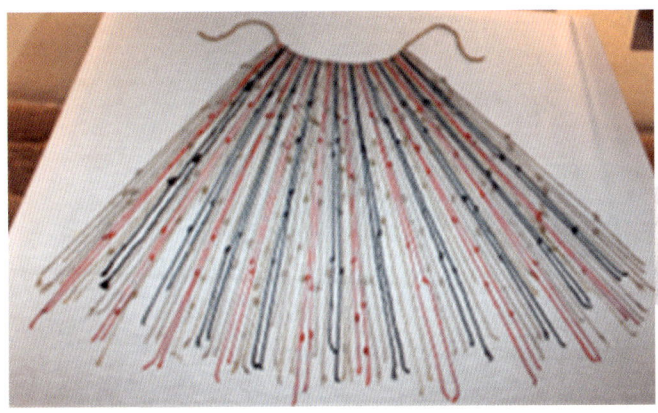

Archaeologists have found about 500 khipus across the Inka empire, mostly on the coast, where the dry climate preserves them. The first Spanish historians recorded that the Inkas used khipus to keep accounts of gifts from local rulers to the Inka royal family. The Spanish soldiers, however, decided that khipus were evil, and destroyed them.

In 1923, an American mathematician called Leland Locke made a new claim about the khipus. Locke thought that khipus recorded things such as land measurements and numbers of crops, soldiers or llamas.

Then, in 2017, a group of villagers in the mountains of Peru invited Professor Sabine Hyland to study two special khipus. These khipus have been guarded by the villagers for centuries.

Hyland is an anthropologist based in Scotland. Anthropologists are interested in how people behave and communicate. After travelling to Peru to study the newly discovered khipus, she reached an exciting conclusion. Hyland said, 'the cords have 14 colours that allow for 95 unique cord patterns. That number is within the range of symbols in writing systems.' Hyland thinks the coloured strings and knots might represent syllables or words. The village elders, who kept the khipus stored in a wooden box, said that they contain stories about wars between rival chiefs. Radiocarbon dating suggests that the khipus were made soon after the Spanish conquest, in the 1500s.

Step 4

Add another row to your table for khipus.

Combining sources to solve puzzles: the case of Inka beliefs

You have seen how different source types create opportunities and challenges. You have also seen how the ideas of people studying the past can get in the way! Let's examine this in more detail with one topic – Inka beliefs.

Many sources suggest that the most important Inka god was Inti, god of the sun, and that the most sacred place in the Inka empire was Qurikancha: Temple of the Sun. In the heart of Qosqo city, this temple was overseen by the High Priest of the Sun, the second most powerful person in the empire. But historians have long puzzled over what the priest did at this temple. How did he worship Inti?

Inka oral stories refer to Qurikancha. In these stories, the first Inka king built Qurikancha after settling in Qosqo. Look again at Poma's picture on page 167. Find symbols for Inti, god of the sun, and Mama-Quilla, goddess of the moon.

Oral traditions reveal that the high priest at Qurikancha celebrated not just Inti but other gods too, such as the goddess of the moon. But the stories don't explain what the high priest did at the temple. Archaeologists have tried to study the temple itself…

...but there is a big problem!

When the Spanish soldiers first visited Qurikancha in 1532, they estimated that over 700 square sheets of gold covered the temple. To the Inkas, gold was the sweat of the sun and silver the tears of the moon. To the Spaniards, it was riches. They melted all Qurikancha's gold and carried it all back to Spain on treasure ships.

Later, Qurikancha was converted into this monastery. The stone wall supporting the doors of the monastery is all that remains of Qurikancha.

The destruction of Qurikancha leaves little archaeological evidence of religious practices; so archaeologists began studying other holy places in Qosqo. But there are more problems! Spanish priests, thinking Inka religion wicked and sinful, set out to destroy Inka shrines. The Spaniards were horrified that the Inkas worshipped many gods.

Archaeologists have therefore had to be clever. They compared the few artefacts that they have found, often at temples and shrines far outside of Qosqo, with stories by Spanish chroniclers such as Sarmiento and Poma. Sarmiento reported that llamas, birds and children were sacrificed to honour the sun. Poma drew this llama within an Inka ceremony.

Sarmiento, drawing on Inka oral tradition, wrote that King Pachakutiq placed a statue of the sun, in the form of a small boy, inside Qurikancha. This statue was made of pure gold.

No Spanish historian recorded seeing the golden statue of Inti at Qurikancha, and no archaeologist has ever found it. But archaeologists have found small statues, like these, in shrines outside Qosqo city, along the main Inka highways. A silver female Inka figurine was found in a mountain-top shrine in Chile, near the mummy of a young boy.

By comparing the figurines with the golden statue mentioned by Sarmiento and the llamas drawn by Poma, historians can at last suggest what the high priest did at Qurikancha. Historians can't be certain, but the high priest probably used a golden statue to honour Inti. He probably sacrificed llamas to please the gods.

Step 5

Don't add a new row to your table. Use the section on Inka beliefs to add points to the existing rows.

Shaping your argument

You have decided to start a new history society for studying South American history. You plan to watch films, discuss books, invite speakers and debate the meaning of the sources. But first you need members!

Design a leaflet to fascinate people with the sources available for studying the Inkas. Your leaflet should describe and illustrate contrasting sources. Write about the kinds of questions that each source helps historians to answer.

28 Elizabethan worlds

What connected Elizabeth and the Elizabethans to wider worlds?

His rooms are dark. Candlelight flickers across books scattered on his desk. He has just read the tale of an Italian soldier born in the Muslim world of north Africa. Tonight, he starts another – Leo Africanus' *Description of Africa*. Born in Spain, Africanus had travelled to Morocco before being captured, enslaved and taken to the Pope in Italy.

The man reading is William Shakespeare, England's famous playwright.

Tales of Africa and Islam are always popular and Shakespeare likes to please an audience. He recalls the hubbub surrounding the arrival of ambassadors from Morocco in 1600. Londoners still talk of the Moroccans' deep black robes, their white turbans and their fine curved swords.

Blending these memories with books he has read, Shakespeare begins shaping a new story. A north African soldier will be trapped between the African world of his youth and his new world of Venice.

The sounds of Southwark drift up from the streets. His rooms are humble, a far cry from the rooms he had once rented among the City's merchants, and farther still from the grand home he has bought for his family in Stratford-upon-Avon. He moved here to be closer to the new theatre. Three years earlier, Shakespeare and his company of actors had transported their old theatre, timber by timber, across the river to Southwark. They were like Hercules carrying the globe on their backs, they said. They called their new theatre 'The Globe'.

Who were the Elizabethans?

Elizabeth I reigned from 1558 until 1603. The people of England, during this long reign, are now known as Elizabethans.

Elizabeth would come to be known as 'Gloriana', a queen who created a Golden Age. This portrait, known as the Rainbow Portrait, presents her as that glorious queen. White lace seems to whirl around her like clouds. Her pearls signify peace and purity. Her hand holds a rainbow, symbolising peace. The bejewelled snake suggests wisdom. The inscription, 'Non sine sole iris' ('No rainbow without the sun') means that only the queen's wisdom can ensure peace and prosperity. Find the eyes and ears in her dress. These show Elizabeth as all-seeing, all-hearing.

Yet Elizabeth's portrait tells us more than how she wanted to appear to her people. The silk of her gown had travelled along the Silk Roads from Asia. Animals, plants and patterns from lands beyond Europe are sewn with gold and silver thread. This portrait is a source from which historians can learn about ideas and goods that flowed into England.

During Elizabeth's reign, farmers expanded their lands. Merchants and sea captains made fortunes in trade and from raiding Spanish ships. They sent their sons to learn Latin and Greek in new grammar schools. They flaunted their wealth with glass windows and new-fangled chimneys.

The nobility adorned their even grander homes with glass from Venice and rugs from Turkey. They wore silks from Asia, furs from Russia, velvet from Italy. They filled libraries with authors from the ancient world. They satisfied a sweet tooth with sugar from Morocco.

Meanwhile, the lower sort lived in small, dark, overcrowded homes. As the population rose, work was increasingly hard to find. A poor harvest threatened the Elizabethan poor with starvation.

So Elizabethan England was a place of contradictions. Some lived in grand wealth; others in deep poverty. England lay on the edge of Europe; but was tightly connected to wider worlds. These connections brought both opportunities and threats to Elizabeth and her people.

Your enquiry

Historians once viewed Elizabethan England as isolated and cut off by the Reformation. But we now know that this was not the case. In this enquiry, you will study the connections between Elizabethan England and wider worlds. You will consider the effects of these connections on:

- diverse peoples in and beyond England
- Elizabeth herself as ruler and stateswoman.

In 1590, Bess of Hardwick, the Countess of Shrewsbury, began building Hardwick Hall in Derbyshire. Visitors marvelled at the sparkling expanses of fragile Venetian glass and walls adorned with tapestries from the Netherlands.

Securing the kingdom, 1558–1561

It is 15 January 1559. Snow lies everywhere. Despite the cold, thousands line the streets. Today the new queen will be crowned.

The queen's procession is magnificent. Around her, hundreds of horses carry noblemen and noblewomen, glittering in their finery. Processing to Westminster Abbey in a golden litter, Elizabeth waves at her people.

All along her route, plays and pageants predict her future greatness. These dramatic spectacles compare Elizabeth's new reign to the decay of her sister's, poor Mary Tudor. During one play, the queen herself is given the Bible in English. Tearfully, she kisses it before clutching it to her chest. She raises the Bible in the air. The crowd roars.

Despite Elizabeth's grand coronation, she had never been sure of gaining the throne. Elizabeth I was daughter of Henry VIII and his second wife, Anne Boleyn. After Henry VIII had had Anne executed in 1536, Elizabeth's status had been downgraded. Her siblings, Edward and Mary, had been placed ahead of her in line to the throne. Let's look at Elizabeth's long and uncertain road to the crown. It would make her a cautious queen.

September 1533: Elizabeth was born to Henry VIII and his second wife, Anne Boleyn.

May 1536: Henry VIII had Anne Boleyn beheaded. Elizabeth was no longer 'Princess Elizabeth' but 'Lady Elizabeth'.

1536–1547: Elizabeth was brought up in the Protestant faith. Her exceptional education made her fluent in French, Italian, Spanish, Latin and Greek by age 11. She even translated an entire religious book from Latin into French.

January 1547: Henry VIII died. The 14-year-old Elizabeth went to live with Henry's widow, Katherine Parr, and Katherine's new husband, Thomas Seymour.

1548–1549: Seymour was accused of plotting to marry Elizabeth in order to secure power. 15-year-old Elizabeth was questioned to see if she was guilty too.

July 1553: Edward VI died. Protestant nobles put Lady Jane Grey on the throne for nine days, until Mary Tudor's supporters overthrew them.

July 1553: Mary Tudor took the throne.

March 1554: Accused of plotting to overthrow Mary, Elizabeth was imprisoned in the Tower of London.

1554–1558: Elizabeth was kept under house arrest.

November 1558: Mary died childless. At last, Elizabeth became queen.

England, France and Scotland in 1558

As queen, Mary Tudor had agreed to join her husband, Philip II of Spain, in a war against France. When Elizabeth became queen in 1558, England and France were still at war. Mary Tudor's war with France had not gone well. England had lost its last lands in France. War was expensive. England was in debt.

Worse, France now allied with Scotland! The Queen of Scotland was Mary Stuart, Elizabeth's Catholic cousin, often known as Mary, Queen of Scots. In April 1558, Mary Stuart had married the heir to the French throne. What if the French were to help the Scots invade England?

Elizabeth had to act. She worked to gain peace with France while keeping Spain as an ally.

Tackling religious division

You will remember from studying the village of Morebath that the English had suffered bewildering religious change. Even more change was now inevitable because Elizabeth was a committed Protestant with powerful Protestant supporters. During Mary Tudor's Catholic reign, wealthy Protestants had fled to the Protestant German states or to Switzerland. They expected Elizabeth to make England Protestant again.

Yet Morebath's story shows just how much some areas hated Protestantism, especially the extreme Protestantism of Edward VI.

So how could Elizabeth return England to Protestantism without making enemies of English Catholics?

A new Church for everyone?

At this time, it was accepted that rulers should decide a country's religion. It was unthinkable for people to worship as they pleased. Yet Elizabeth needed to reassure her people. They had endured so much change, as well as rebellion, bloodshed and hatred. She needed a religious settlement that would unite as many of her subjects as possible. She needed Parliament to help her achieve it.

It was clear that Elizabeth would make England Protestant again. But would it be *extremely* Protestant, like Switzerland, or would Elizabeth choose a gentler, Lutheran Protestantism?

Helped by her most trusted adviser, William Cecil, Elizabeth built a middle way. It was Protestant, but the moderate kind, with some Catholic ways kept. It became known as the Elizabethan Religious Settlement.

These were its main points:

Elizabeth's Religious Settlement
- Elizabeth will be supreme governor of the Church of England.
- All clergy and royal officials must swear an Oath of Allegiance to the new Church of England.
- Everyone is to attend the new Church, or else be fined.
- A new prayer book in English will be used by all.* It will be carefully written to satisfy most Catholics and most Protestants.
- Church music will be allowed.
- Priests will wear vestments.
- Priests may marry.

*Soon there was a Welsh prayer book and a Welsh bible too.

You can guess the two very different groups in Parliament who gave this a frosty reception! Many Catholics hated Elizabeth's changes. More extreme Protestants hated them too.

Yet, in 1559, Parliament still passed laws that made Elizabeth's religious settlement a reality.

The marriage question

Elizabeth's councillors begged her to consider marriage. Rule by a single woman felt unnatural. Elizabeth refused. She never married, but she made the most of the offers! When King Philip II of Spain proposed, Elizabeth was slow to decline. Elizabeth wished to secure peace with him. Keeping suitors guessing was a clever way to protect England.

Step 1

Using pages 175–178, look for connections between Elizabethan England and wider worlds. We have started you off.

Political connections
(Hint: look for Elizabeth's relationships with other rulers)
Economic connections
(Hint: trade)
Religious connections
The young Elizabeth studied new Protestant ideas and read books in many languages.

Growing confidence, growing threat, 1562–1585

It is October 1562.

In France, civil war rages between Catholics and Protestants. Elizabeth has pledged to aid the French Protestants (known as Huguenots).

English traders seek new routes to the silk markets of India and China. In Plymouth, John Hawkins prepares to sail to Africa. He hopes to break into the Spanish and Portuguese slave trade. An uneasy alliance continues with Philip II of Spain.

At home, England settles into Elizabeth's moderate Protestantism.

So why does fear hang over London?

The queen is deathly ill. A German doctor is summoned. Seeing her blistering rash, he announces his diagnosis. Smallpox! Elizabeth is wrapped head-to-toe in red cloth.

What if the childless queen dies? The queen's councillors are gripped by fear of invasion or civil war. What if the Catholic Queen of Scotland, Mary Stuart, seizes the throne?

Catholic challenges and Elizabeth's response

Elizabeth survived. But trouble now came from abroad. In 1568, Scotland overthrew its Catholic queen, Mary Stuart (Mary, Queen of Scots). Mary then fled to the worst possible place: her cousin Elizabeth's kingdom.

Mary Stuart's timing couldn't have been worse. It was not a good moment for Elizabeth to be sheltering a refugee Catholic queen! That same year a wealthy English Catholic set up a college in France for training Catholic priests to convert English Protestants to Catholicism. This was Elizabeth's nightmare. Would Catholics at home and Catholic rulers abroad unite to put Mary Stuart on the English throne? Elizabeth promptly imprisoned Mary Stuart. Mary would spend nineteen years locked in English castles.

In November 1569, some Catholic earls marched to Durham Cathedral, ripped up the English prayer book and celebrated mass. By January 1570, Elizabeth's forces had crushed the revolt, exacting terrible punishment on the rebels and on the ordinary people of Yorkshire.

Elizabeth looks to Islamic worlds

Two months later, a dangerous document appeared in London – a Papal Bull. In the Bull, the Pope had declared Mary Stuart the rightful Queen of England. Then, in 1571 another plot was discovered. It involved the Pope, Mary Stuart, Philip II of Spain and an Italian Londoner called Ridolfi. The plan? To put Mary Stuart on the throne.

Once again, Elizabeth fought back. She executed over 450 rebels. To the King of Spain's fury, she now sheltered Protestant rebels from the Spanish Netherlands.

Philip II, however, was too busy to respond. He was fighting the Turkish Ottomans. The Ottomans ruled a vast Muslim empire, encircling the eastern Mediterranean. Together with the Pope and Venice, Philip won a big naval victory over the Ottomans in the Mediterranean Sea. This was the Battle of Lepanto in 1571. Even Elizabeth sent her congratulations!

But Elizabeth's congratulations were hollow. Elizabeth was already seeking connections with the Muslim world.

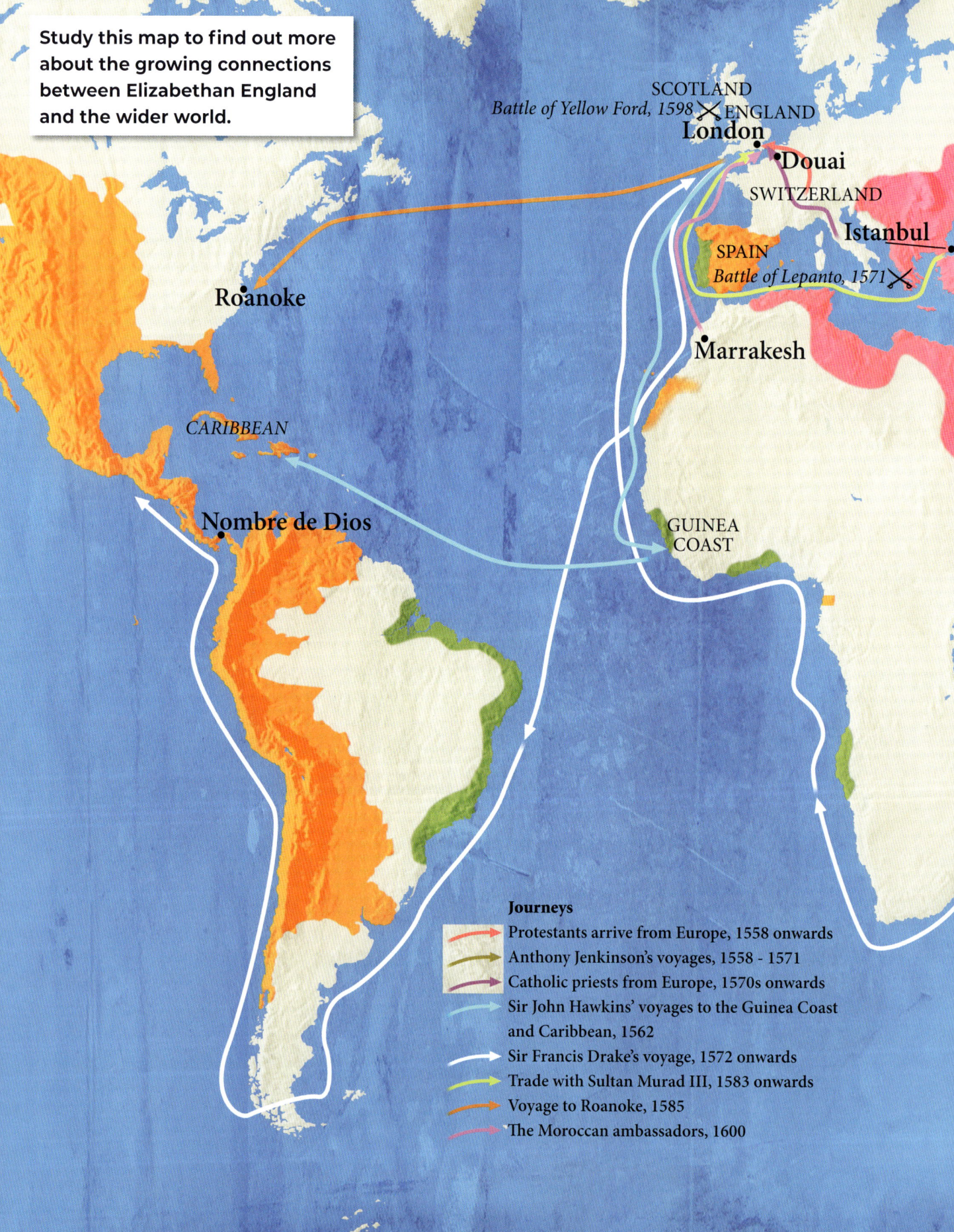

Elizabeth looks beyond Europe

Elizabeth now began to export tin and lead to the Ottoman Sultan, Murad III. Murad used this metal and lead for guns and ammunition to fight his Catholic enemies. Unfortunately for Elizabeth, rumours then spread that Elizabeth had stripped the tin and lead from England's old Catholic monasteries! Catholic hatred of Elizabeth grew and grew.

Elizabeth also built relations with another Muslim enemy of Spain – Morocco's ruler Ahmad al-Mansur. Al-Mansur's empire stretched across African lands, some of which were once ruled by Mansa Musa.

These connections were strengthened by trade. By 1569, England was importing 250 tons of Moroccan sugar a year, while selling the Moroccans guns and cloth. New words, such as 'turquoise' from Khurasan and 'algebra' from Baghdad, entered the English language.

Meanwhile, far away in the Americas, Elizabethans were challenging Spain. England's first transatlantic trader in enslaved people, John Hawkins, was infuriating Spanish traders.

Empires
- Ottoman
- Spanish
- Portuguese

Drake and the Cimarron

In the early 1570s, Hawkins' cousin Francis Drake heard that the Inkas' gold and silver was flowing into the King of Spain's pockets. This treasure travelled by ship from Peru to Panama. From there it was loaded onto two hundred donkeys for a trek across mountains and through jungles. Drake decided that he would steal it.

To ensure his success, Drake worked with the Cimarron. The Cimarron were enslaved African people who had escaped Spanish slavery. They lived in the hills and mountains of Panama. Drake (although a slave trader himself) worked with the Cimarron to seize the treasure. One Cimarron, called Diego, joined Drake's crew and sailed with Drake around the globe. Find Drake's routes, in white, on the map.

Drake's exploits infuriated Philip II of Spain. They delighted Elizabeth so much that she knighted him.

Arguments for colonies

All this activity abroad led English writers to find reasons for having English colonies. In 1584, Richard Hackluyt wrote a book on the subject. Here are Hackluyt's four main arguments for having colonies. Of course, it did not occur to Hackluyt to consider what people already living in the Americas might have thought about this.

- England should develop colonies so that it can compete with Spain.
- English colonies will provide employment for the poor of England.
- English colonies will bring wealth to England.
- It is our moral duty to share our Protestant ways with the indigenous people of America. If they resist, violence is justified.

A stained-glass window in Bristol Cathedral showing Richard Hackluyt.

The first colony: Roanoke

As English sailors became familiar with the waters around the Americas, Sir Walter Raleigh dreamed of an English **colony** there.

To help his mission, two young Native Americans, Manteo and Wanchese, were brought to England. They stayed with Raleigh and taught him their language – Algonquian. After a year, in 1585, they returned to their homeland with a small group of English settlers. The settlers now founded a new English colony called Roanoke.

Sir Walter Raleigh sent an artist on the expedition. The artist was called John White. White's task was to paint the plants, animals, landscape and peoples that the colonists found. White's watercolour paintings are the first English images of Native Americans.

Tensions in Europe

Philip II was angry. Not only were the English raiding his ships but now they had a base in America too! This alongside Elizabeth's connections with Morocco and with the Ottomans was too much.

Worse, in 1585, Elizabeth sent English troops into the Spanish Netherlands to help the Protestants fight their Spanish rulers. England and Spain were now at war.

Step 2

Using pages 179–182, add to your table. Remember to name specific individuals and groups.

An Algonquin village, one of many images of indigenous life and peoples painted by John White.

The Battle for England, 1585–1588

The execution of 'Mary, Queen of Scots'

It is February 1587. Mary Stuart is dressed in deep black. Her famed beauty has not left her.

Evidence has been found that, while imprisoned, she plotted to kill her cousin, Queen Elizabeth of England. She has been sentenced to die as a traitor.

At Mary Stuart's waist lies a golden crucifix; in her hands, her rosary beads with her Latin prayer book. Even now, on the scaffold, Elizabeth's men still try to goad Mary into accepting Protestantism. She drowns them out with Latin prayers.

As she approaches the executioner's block, the crowd gasps. They have seen a bright scarlet underdress beneath Mary Stuart's black gown! Red is the colour of martyrs.

Today, Mary Stuart will find freedom at last. She says her last prayers confident that her soul is in the Lord's hands.

Mary Stuart had become Queen of Scotland in 1542, when she was just six days old. By the time of her execution in 1587, however, Mary Stuart was no longer Queen of Scotland. In 1567, she had been forced to abdicate in favour of her one-year-old son, who became King James VI of Scotland.

Many Catholics in Europe had placed their hopes on Mary Stuart as the monarch who could fight back against Protestantism. Her first cousin, the Protestant Queen Elizabeth, had never met Mary Stuart. But Elizabeth knew that Mary Stuart was a grave threat to her own security on the English throne. Elizabeth had kept Mary in captivity in order to stop her plotting with foreign Catholic powers, but plots and rumours of plots showed Elizabeth that Mary Stuart was still a threat. A plot uncovered in 1586 was the last straw for Elizabeth. In 1587, Elizabeth signed Mary Stuart's death warrant.

Mary Stuart's execution infuriated European Catholic rulers, including Philip II of Spain. Philip II now developed a plan to invade England.

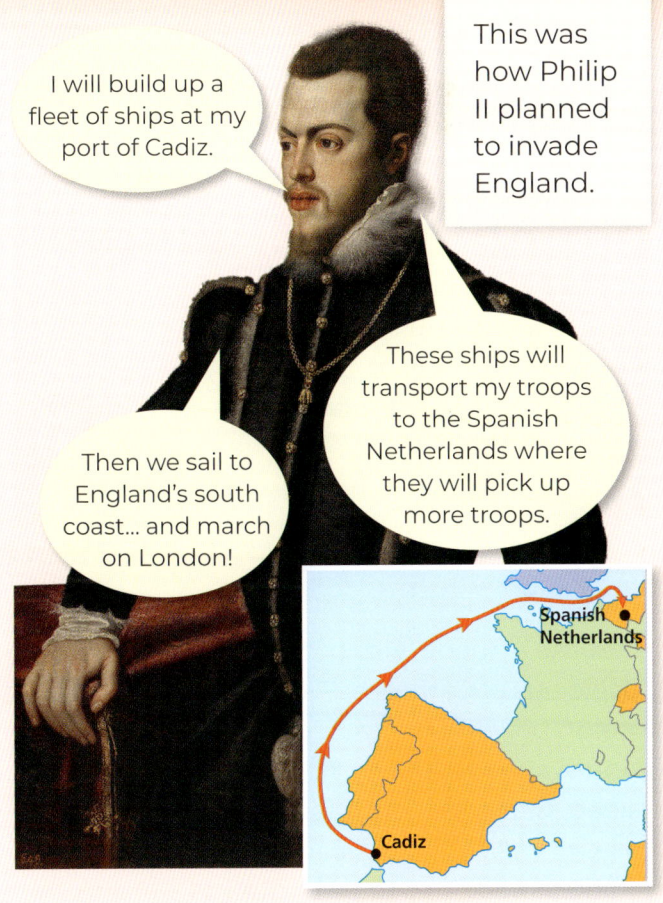

This was how Philip II planned to invade England.

I will build up a fleet of ships at my port of Cadiz.

These ships will transport my troops to the Spanish Netherlands where they will pick up more troops.

Then we sail to England's south coast... and march on London!

Defeating the Armada

The first part of Philip's plan was scuppered by Sir Francis Drake. Drake raided and destroyed Philip's ships in Cadiz. But Philip did not give up. He moved his remaining ships to Lisbon in Portugal. From Lisbon, in May 1588, the Spanish fleet set sail for England.

It was off the Cornish coast on 19 July 1588, that someone first saw it, stretching for miles. Arranged in a crescent shape, this was the Spanish Armada.

Outnumbered and outgunned, the English needed clever tactics. They used fireships – small ships packed with explosives.

The Spaniards panicked. The crescent formation broke. Many ships were sunk. Then a storm blew the Armada north towards Scottish waters where many more Spanish ships sank.

To Elizabeth, the Armada's defeat was a miracle. She commemorated it with this painting, her Armada portrait.

Punishing Catholics and Puritans

After the Armada, Elizabeth was even more suspicious of Catholics. Fearing their links with foreign powers, she passed harsh laws to control and punish them. Catholic homes were raided. Catholics now had to stay within five miles of their homes. Hearing the Mass or hiding a priest was to be treated as **treason**.

Meanwhile, more extreme Protestants, known by this time as **Puritans**, thought that England was not Protestant enough! They feared Catholic influence everywhere. Back in 1579, a Puritan called John Stubbs had criticised Elizabeth for her marriage negotiations with a French Catholic prince. Stubbs was sentenced harshly. His right hand was cut off.

Puritans loathed practices which they deemed to be too Catholic, such as priests wearing vestments, congregations kneeling to receive the bread and wine or the playing of organ music in church. Puritans wanted simple worship and sermons about the Bible.

Many Puritans hated bishops. Some even wanted the Swiss practice of church congregations choosing their own ministers! All this threatened Elizabeth's government and authority, as well as the peaceful unity that she had sought in her religious settlement.

Puritans tried to push reforms through Parliament. They failed, but new tactics kept coming. In 1588, mysterious Puritan tracts (pamphlets) appeared on London streets. Gossipy, witty and amusing, they called bishops 'scorpions' and 'ministers of damnation'. The tracts only stopped when government spies discovered the printing press (they never found the author). Meanwhile, Puritanism grew in East Anglia and in London, where lawyers and merchants shared Protestant books from abroad.

Step 3

Read through this section again and add to your table.

Elizabeth's final years, 1588–1603

The defeat of the Armada was not the end of Elizabeth's troubles.

Supply ships to Roanoke, the colony settled by Sir Walter Raleigh, had been delayed by the Armada. In 1590, English ships finally reached the colony. Aboard was John White. He'd travelled back to England in 1587 and left behind his family, including his newly-born granddaughter, Virginia. Can you guess what John White found?

A fort, freshly built. Some footprints. Abandoned possessions. The English settlers had vanished.

The English would make no further attempts at colonisation in the Americas until 1607.

Controlling Ireland

Elizabeth would now focus her colonising closer to home. After the Reformation, most of Ireland had remained loyal to Catholicism. Elizabeth therefore feared that Ireland might become a place where the Spanish looked for support to overthrow her. Ireland was led by Gaelic-speaking families in the north and west. To the south and east lay areas under English control.

Brutality and violence against the Irish people now became increasingly normal. Elizabeth sent troops to Ireland to try to force English law and Protestant ways on the population. She also reduced the power of the Gaelic chieftains. One of these was Hugh O'Neill.

Educated like an English nobleman, Hugh O'Neill had been loyal to Elizabeth. When his lands and traditional title were threatened, however, he turned against her. In 1598, he led troops to victory over the English.

Elizabeth and Essex

In 1599, Elizabeth sent the Earl of Essex to Ireland with 17,000 men. In 1596, Essex had raided Cadiz, just as Drake had done. Viewed as a hero, it was hoped that Essex would successfully crush O'Neill too.

Yet Essex, who was often rash, did the opposite. Instead of fighting O'Neill, he made a truce with him! When she heard this, Elizabeth flew into a rage.

Returning to England, Essex stormed into Elizabeth's private chamber to plead his case. Unfortunately for Essex, breaching Elizabeth's privacy enraged her more. Knowing punishment was unavoidable, Essex planned to overthrow her. When he failed, Elizabeth had him beheaded.

Some Englishmen in Ireland chose to have portraits painted in Irish style dress. Captain Thomas Lee is here shown bare-legged just like Gaelic kerns (Irish warriors).

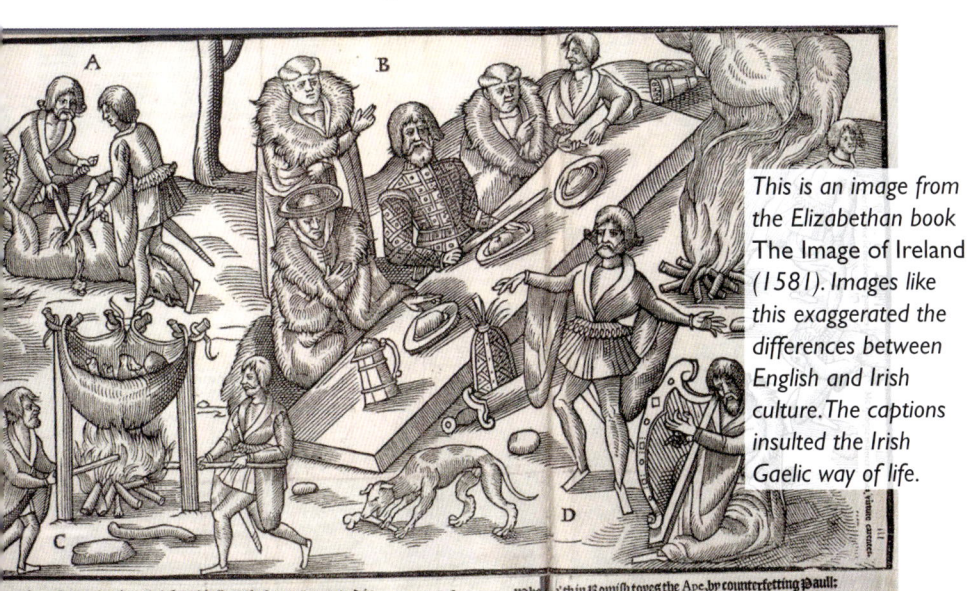

This is an image from the Elizabethan book The Image of Ireland *(1581). Images like this exaggerated the differences between English and Irish culture. The captions insulted the Irish Gaelic way of life.*

Visitors from Morocco

In 1600, the same year as Essex's rebellion, London had new visitors. The Moroccan ruler Ahmad al-Mansur had been impressed by Elizabeth's defeat of the Armada. In 1600, al-Mansur sent a delegation led by Abd el-Ouahed ben Messaoud to secure a military and trading alliance with Elizabeth.

Messaoud, a man of great political skill, secured the alliance. The two monarchs proposed to invade Spain together. Elizabeth was promised vast quantities of Moroccan sugar and half the Spanish empire.

Neither monarch lived to see the proposal become reality. In March 1603, Elizabeth sickened. She refused to lie down, lest she couldn't get up again. She took to standing for hours before collapsing onto the floor which her ladies-in-waiting had covered with cushions. There she lay for four days before being persuaded to get into bed.

When her councillors asked if her successor should be James VI of Scotland (son of Mary Stuart) she managed a faint hand gesture.

On 24 March, in Richmond Palace, she died.

This is Abd el-Ouahed ben Messaoud, the leader of the Moroccan embassy. He had this portrait painted while in London. It is one of the first images in English art history of a Muslim figure.

On her deathbed, Elizabeth was thin and frail, her teeth blackened by Moroccan sugar. In her portraits, however, Elizabeth was 'Gloriana' to the end. The 'Rainbow Portrait' on page 176 was painted after 1600.

Step 4

Use pages 185–86 to complete your table.

Shaping your argument

You now know how Elizabethan England was linked to the world. You have seen alliances shift and merchants seek new markets. You have seen the English challenge the Spanish and plan their own colonies. You have seen Protestant countries influence English Puritans and Catholic nations alarm Elizabeth.

Your completed table is your plan for an essay answering the question: 'What connected Elizabeth and the Elizabethans to the wider world?' You can either write a paragraph for each Step or write a longer paragraph on each theme.

First write an introduction. Begin it like this:

Historians once viewed England as isolated. In fact, England was connected to wider worlds. This essay explains these connections by… (Now tell your reader whether you will shape your essay as a narrative across time [a paragraph on each Step] or using themes [writing a paragraph on each theme in your table: politics, economics and religion].)

For your conclusion, you can either tell the reader which theme was most important in connecting Elizabethan England with wider worlds or you can explain how these three themes mingled together.

29 Meanwhile, in the National Archives

Uncovering the lives of African Tudors

In the cool, dark library, the desks are lit by little lamps. Under their light, Miranda rereads the source that the historian has quoted: '…divers blackamoors crept into this realm'. Her mind races. If so many Black people had come to Tudor England, surely there must be other traces of them in the sources?

A few weeks later, in the autumn of 2004, Miranda steps off the train at Kew Gardens. She walks towards the National Archives. She is determined to know more. How many Black people were in Tudor England? Why were they there? What was their status?

Miranda had studied the Tudors at school and at university. No one had told her about African people living in Tudor England! Surely, among the millions of documents stored at the National Archives, something could be found?

'You won't find anything about that here,' says the archivist.

Undeterred, Miranda heads to the online catalogue. Minutes later, she finds a record of an African person living in Elizabethan Gloucestershire. She is now determined to learn more.

Dr Miranda Kaufmann is a historian. Miranda soon realised that she was not the only historian interested in the topic. She found several books, dating back to the 1960s, which no one had shown her when she was at university. One historian, Marika Sherwood, helped Miranda by sharing over 100 references.

What follows is just some of what Miranda learned.

John Blanke, a Black Tudor

This picture is part of the Westminster Tournament Roll, which is a long scroll stretching to 60 feet. It is a picture record of a jousting tournament that Henry VIII held to celebrate the birth of a son to Catherine of Aragon in 1511. One of the six trumpeters in the scroll is Black.

The Treasurer's accounts refer to a John Blanke, the 'blacke trumpeter'. The trumpeter shown in the scroll is therefore almost certainly John Blanke.

Other historians had already used this source as evidence to conclude that:

- there were Black people in sixteenth-century London;
- some Black people took part in important royal events;
- some were skilled musicians.

But Miranda wanted to know more. She joined another historian, Michael Ohajuru, who was on the same quest. Miranda and Michael studied the treasurer's list of payments made to royal musicians. There it was: 'John Blanke, the blacke trumpeter', was paid eight pence a day – three times as much as an average servant. John Blanke was clearly a valued member of Henry's court.

The more Miranda learned about John Blanke, the more he fascinated her. His pay showed his status. A further document in the National Archives showed that he had successfully asked Henry VIII for a pay rise. In her book *Black Tudors* (pp.21–22), Miranda commented:

> The petition shows that Blanke was ambitious and keen to grasp the opportunity for promotion that the death of his fellow trumpeter provided. There also seems to be some rivalry with the other trumpeters: he wanted to live in the same style as his peers and claims that his previous wage of 8d a day was insufficient for this.

Edward Swarthye, Black Tudor

That day at Kew, Miranda had ignored the archivist and typed into the National Archives search engine different words that Tudor people might have used for Black people. Little came back, but one record caught her eye. It read, 'Buck vs Wynter, Swarthye alias Negro, 1597, Court of the Star Chamber.'

Miranda asked to see the papers. She saw that a Black servant, Edward Swarthye, had given evidence in a court in Gloucester. His testimony was read out to leading Tudor noblemen.

This is a photograph of the document recording Edward Swarthye's testimony.

The rest of the writing was hard to read, but one word stood out: 'whip'. Miranda had seen images of Black people in the Caribbean being whipped by white enslavers. At first, she assumed that Swarthye was the one being whipped. But enslaved people could not give evidence in court. So Edward Swarthye could not have been enslaved.

Later, Miranda deciphered more of the document. Here is an extract:

> Edward Swarthe als Nigro of servant to Sir Edward Wynter kt sworne and examined. To the first Interrog [question] he sayth that he was commanded by the said Sir Edward Wynter his master on the Sodden [suddenly] to whipp the sayd Guy but was not prepared of his roddes before Guyes cominge to his m[aste]r's house as is proposed. Neyther dyd he this dep[onent] before the sayd Guyes cominge know that he his dep[opent] should whip the s[a]id Guye as ys also supposed.
>
> To the 2 Interrog…he…dyd whip the sd Guy in the hall of the sd house & [there were many] persons there [including] Sir Edward Wynter, Mr William Wynter, his brother…& [20] others.

Miranda discovered that the Tudors seemed unconcerned about the colour of Swarthye's skin. Rather they were troubled by his social status: Edward was several ranks below the man he had whipped, causing the whipped man great shame. Edward was a porter, living in the Gloucestershire town of Lydney.

But how had Edward Swarthye ended up working as a porter in Lydney, Gloucestershire? Do you remember Drake and Diego in Chapter 28? Miranda learned that Edward Swarthye's employer had sailed with Francis Drake in 1585 on a voyage to raid Spanish colonies in the Caribbean. Enslaved African people had boarded their ships hoping to flee their Spanish masters. It was likely that this was how Edward Swarthye came to be in Gloucestershire.

Mary Fillis, Black Tudor

Helped by historian Marika Sherwood, Miranda now examined something very rare indeed. She was now used to finding glimpses of Black Tudors in parish registers: a baptism with 'blackamoor' next to the baby's name, the date of a marriage, a burial. But this document was different. It had detail. It had a sense of occasion.

The document included a long description of the baptism of Mary Fillis, an African Tudor. Miranda could almost see the 20-year-old woman, born in Morocco, walking towards the font to be baptised. She could hear her voice repeating the Lord's Prayer. Silently she found herself thanking the parish clerk who, over 400 years ago, had written the record. In her book, Miranda used the document to write an account of the event. Here it is:

Mary Fillis would have been baptised in a font like this one, in a London church.

'The articles of her belief' means the statements that new Christians had to learn by heart.

'Of his great Providence' is referring to a belief in the goodness and mercy of God. It can also mean God's plan for all Christian believers.

> 'Our Father, which art in heaven…' The strange words echoed around the church. 'Hallowed be thy name…' Mistress Porter had helped her learn this verse, and what it meant, in preparation for the day. When she'd reached the end of the Lord's Prayer, Reverend Threlkeld asked her to rehearse the articles of her belief and she did so, carefully and fluently. Then he asked, did she desire to be baptised? 'Aye' she replied. And so they went to the font. The whole congregation called on God the Father through the Lord Jesus Christ to receive her into Christ's Holy Church. She had been in London thirteen or fourteen years now, since she was six or seven. She had seen the church spires every day, towering over the city streets. She had heard these people speak of their God, of his great Providence, of his Heaven. And of his wrath. Finally, Reverend Threlkeld said 'I baptise thee in the name of the Father, and of the Son, and of the holy Ghost. Amen.' And it was over. She was a Christian, and she could go forth and 'daily proceed in all virtue and godliness of living'.

Reverend Threlkeld is the minister who led the baptism service. 'Reverend' is a title for a priest or minister.

'Wrath' means anger.

An extract from Miranda Kaufmann's book, Black Tudors, *p.134, for which she used the parish clerks' account of the baptism of Mary Fillis at St Botolph's, Aldgate, 1597.*

Apart from her baptism record, there are no other known documents referring to Mary Fillis, so Miranda drew on other historians' work and other documents about other Black Tudor people living in the same part of London. In this way, she was able to make inferences about Mary Fillis's life.

As the years went by, Miranda gathered and analysed evidence of some 200 African Tudors. Miranda wanted the knowledge about African people living in Tudor England to reach as wide an audience as possible. In 2017 she published her book, *Black Tudors: The Untold Story* – the result of years of researching in archives, reading other historians' work and collaborating with other scholars.

30 Meanwhile, in the Mediterranean
Travelling through connected worlds

It is May 1600. It is the start of the 'fine season' for travel, when the strongest winds stop blowing. A lone traveller sets out on a long journey. He begins in Venice. In 1600, Venice is less powerful than it once was. Portugal and Spain have taken over its Mediterranean trade. The Portuguese now control the spice trade with the Indies. Spain is an even bigger problem. Spain now controls much of Italy. Spain and the Ottoman empire squeeze Venice between them. The Ottomans are Turkish Muslims. Their empire extends into Asia, Africa and Europe.

Sicily is our traveller's first destination. He goes ashore in Palermo. Busy streets and buildings reveal peoples who have lived here over the centuries: Jewish, Muslim and Christian people; Byzantines, Arabs and Normans. In the markets of the old Arab quarter, he sees perfumes, spices, figs, dates, silks and carpets. Today, Sicily is ruled by King Philip III of Spain. Sicily seems prosperous, but will it last? In the end, reflects our traveller, wherever Philip rules, trade ends up benefiting Spain. The silver coins in our traveller's hand are Spanish. They are accepted everywhere he goes.

Another sea journey, this time in a heavily-armed ship, takes the traveller to Cyprus. Cyprus used to belong to Venice. Now it belongs to the Ottoman Turks. That great sea battle of Lepanto in 1571, a Christian victory, came a year too late for Cyprus. Cyprus is now in Turkish Muslim hands. It would be unwise to land here. The Ottomans discourage landings by non-Muslims, especially Venetians! The Ottomans encourage Turkish farmers and craftsmen to settle in Cyprus. Cyprus will soon have a Muslim majority.

By the end of May, our traveller has arrived in the capital of the Ottoman empire. It was once called Constantinople. In 1050, the Byzantine Empress Zoe believed her city could not be conquered. She was wrong.

Zoe's city is now called Istanbul. On 29 May 1453, the army of the Ottoman sultan, Mehmed II, had smashed through Constantinople's triple walls. A six-week siege had seen over a hundred ships, seventy thousand men and a terrifying cannon bombardment. Mehmed had studied all the earlier, failed attempts to take Constantinople. By 1452 he had developed a plan that could not fail.

Inside Constantinople's walls, during the siege, every citizen had played their part. Lines of women and girls had passed rocks to one another, to throw over the city's walls. But Mehmed prevailed.

The greatest city in Europe was now in Muslim hands. The last Byzantine emperor was dead.

The Ottomans had not stopped at Constantinople. By 1529, their armies were approaching Vienna (though Vienna did not fall). The Ottomans conquered other Muslims too. In 1517, they captured Cairo. They hanged the last sultan of Egypt from the city gates.

Last year (1599), Queen Elizabeth of England sent a ship to Istanbul. It was loaded with presents for Sultan Mehmed III. This was a sign of Elizabeth's desire for trade. It was also a sign of England's growing power at sea. England's seapower worries the Ottoman sultan. Despite the presents – which included an organ and a horse-carriage – this new relationship is unlikely to last. This pleases our traveller. An alliance between England and the Turks wouldn't be good for Venice.

Our traveller does not spend long in Istanbul. He visits its sprawling, impressive Topkapi palace, but he does not see the sultan. He would like to have seen the greatest church in Christendom, Hagia Sofia. But it is now a mosque. Non-Muslims may not enter. So he spends his day in the Büyük Çarşı, a vast covered market. Here, in over three thousand shops, he sees the world's produce: spices, metalwork, furs, textiles, carpets, slaves. Here no one cares about our traveller's religion: he is just another customer.

But he leaves without buying a thing.

From Istanbul, the traveller sails south. He plans to reach north Africa and sail west. The ship's crew is anxious. All along the coast are the lairs of the Barbary pirates. Their fleets prey on any passing vessels. Anyone captured could end up in the Ottoman slave-markets. These pirates raid and plunder their way through the Mediterranean and beyond, even as far as Iceland. From his ship, our traveller can see stretches of fertile land that is uncultivated. Pirates make it too dangerous to settle near the coast. But it is still early in the fine season; the pirate raids have not begun.

Eventually, our traveller sails along the north coast of Morocco. The port of Larache, glaring white in the sun, welcomes his ship. Everyone disembarks. From here, it will be a long and uncomfortable journey by camel to the capital, Marrakesh. It will take a month. Our traveller knows that Marrakesh is a large slaving-depot.

This map shows the Mediterranean in 1600. Follow the Venetian traveller's journey using the red arrows.

The sultan of Morocco, Ahmad al-Mansur, is one of the most powerful rulers in the Mediterranean. In 1578, this Moroccan sultan took part in a victory over the Portuguese. Thousands of captured Portuguese soldiers were enslaved and forced to row in Moroccan galleys. But if the traveller sees a galley, he will not see a Portuguese slave. That battle with the Portuguese was over twenty years ago and, besides, galley slaves do not live that long.

What else does our traveller know about Ahmad al-Mansur? A few years ago, the Moroccan sultan's army crossed the Sahara and destroyed the Songhai empire, the African state that had replaced the empire of Mali. When the Moroccans captured the city of Timbuktu, they used English cannons. England and Morocco are trading partners: Elizabeth obtains sugar, ostrich feathers and saltpetre for gunpowder; Morocco obtains modern guns.

Elizabeth and Ahmad al-Mansur share a common enemy: the Ottomans. Our traveller has heard that a Moroccan ambassador will soon travel to London.

Our traveller would like to see more of Marrakesh. Famous for its advanced medicine and hospitals, there are even women doctors, something he finds hard to believe. But he must push on to his final destination: Seville. Again, he leaves without buying a thing.

To reach Seville, our traveller's ship must pass through the narrowest point of the Mediterranean between Africa and Europe, and then sail up the Guadalquivir river. Seville is still wealthy, which is what our traveller is there to investigate: no sign, yet, of Spain's slowly declining wealth. He notes the galleons in the harbour, some just arrived from the Americas. These ships have brought silver from the mines of South America (it is a long time since Spanish ships brought Inka gold). The silver will be melted down and turned into coins, the sort in our traveller's purse. But most of these coins will leave Spain. They will go to the banking-houses of Brabant, to repay loans that King Philip III has taken out to finance his endless war against the Dutch.

So much wealth coming in – and yet Spain now benefits little. The value of silver has dropped, since so much has arrived in Europe. This will cause problems for everyone, and well beyond Spain.

And why has our traveller undertaken this long, expensive but successful journey? He is no tourist – travel is much too risky for tourism. Perhaps you guessed? Our traveller is a spy for his city of Venice. Venice is struggling. Its rulers need information about rivals and neighbours. Luckily for our Venetian spy, no one guessed his real purpose: spies are unwelcome everywhere.

A map of the eastern Mediterranean Sea made in 1595 by Abraham Ortelius, a Dutch map maker.

We have not invented the idea of a Venetian spy. Venice had a secret service, known as the Council of Ten. Its spies found out about changes in the region.

But even the best-informed spy couldn't have predicted the changes that would occur in the three centuries after 1600. Wars and conquest will continue, but new technology will make them yet more devastating. Trade will remain important. So will empire, but empire will change; our traveller could scarcely have predicted how much. Worlds will expand in unexpected ways. Do you remember how the Muslim Arabs and Persians connected with India's ancient learning about mathematics? The power that connects with India in the next century will be Britain. Britain will turn that connection into control. Within two centuries, India will be part of a vast empire that our traveller could never imagine.

That 'endless' war between Spain and its Dutch rebels will end. Spanish power will decline, but the Dutch will build a vast empire. The map above is the work of a Dutch map maker.

In 1600 France was recovering from decades of civil war between Protestants and Catholics. In 1789, revolution will turn France upside down. Huge revolutions, shattering the old order, will now become common. Britain, like France, will execute its king. But revolutions in thinking will be just as important.

Europe will dominate much of the world by 1900. This would have seemed unlikely in 1600, when Spain was the only European world power. The others were China and India. And in 1900, Venice will be just one city in a new kingdom of Italy.

Now that would have surprised our traveller most of all.

Glossary

Abbot the monk in charge of other monks in a monastery

Archaeologist a person who studies past peoples, usually by digging for remains they have left behind, such as buildings or tools

Archbishop bishop of the highest rank, in charge of all the bishops and priests in a large area

Astrologers people who studied the movement of stars and planets and interpreted their influence on the world

Astronomy the study of space, stars and planets

Baptism a Christian ceremony in which water is poured over a person's head or the person is briefly covered completely by water, and is named as a Christian

Baron a powerful lord who was granted land by the King

Byzantine empire the Greek-speaking eastern Roman Empire

Caravan a large group of people travelling together over long distances, usually in desert environments, with goods carried by camels

Christendom Christian people or countries as a whole

Civil war armed conflict between two opposite sides in the same country

Colony a country under full or partial control of another, and occupied by settlers from that country

Crusade a holy war to conquer the Holy Land declared by Christians during the Middle Ages

Dynasty a series of rulers or leaders who are all from the same family

Excommunicate to expel from the Roman Catholic Church

Heir someone who will inherit money, goods, land or a title (for example King of England) from another person once that person dies

Heresy An opinion or belief that challenges the key beliefs of the Church

Indulgences papers, given by the Roman Catholic Church upon payment of a sum of money, which guaranteed the forgiveness of sins and a fast track into heaven

Knights skilled warriors on horseback

Longbow A tall bow that could fire arrows over 300 metres and pierce armour

Manor a large piece of land belonging to a lord, often including a whole village

Minister an advisor to a monarch/ a term for a Protestant church leader

Monastery a community of monks living together

Muslim a follower of the religion of Islam

Nobility a group of people who were seen as very important and respected in the medieval period. Members of the nobility were landowners, knights and people related to and under the monarch, either through blood or royal service

Oath a formal promise of loyalty to a person or country

Orthodox Christianity the name given to the Christian Church that grew and flourished in the eastern regions of the late Roman Empire. Orthodox means 'correct belief/ worship'.

Pagan people who did not follow Christianity, Judaism, or Islam. Pagans worshipped many gods and goddesses

Pestilence a deadly, fast spreading disease such as bubonic plague

Pilgrims people who travel to a holy place

Pope head of the Roman Catholic Church

Protestant followers of the Christian movement that began in north Europe in the 16th century. During the time of Martin Luther, protestants were those who protested against the Roman Catholic Church

Puritan an extreme Protestant who wanted churches to be very plain without decoration and wanted simple services with no music

Rebellion armed resistance to a government or ruler

Reformation the religious revolution which divided the Church in Europe during the sixteenth century

Relic remains of a saint's body or belongings

Reliquary a container or shrine in which holy relics are kept

Renaissance a revival of Classical learning and wisdom in fifteenth and sixteenth century Europe

Rhetoric the art of persuasive speaking or writing

Saint a person whom the Church has said lives a life of great holiness

Scholar a learned person with great knowledge

Sovereign a gold coin/a person who has supreme power or authority, such as a king or queen

Sultan the ruler of a Muslim country

Treason plotting against the monarch

Tribe a large community of people who are all distantly related

Tyrant a cruel and unjust ruler

Villan a word used before the Norman Conquest meaning 'man of the vill' or 'man belonging to the land'

Villein the term in use by the twelfth century for a tenant tied to the land and paying money and services to a lord in return for that land

Index

Adelard of Bath 62–5
Armada defeat 183–4
arts and music 6, 55, 61, 112, 150–3, 186
Baghdad 4–5, 8–15, 43, 76–82
Bayeux Tapestry 28–9, 47
Becket, Thomas 60
Black Death 100–14
Black Tudors 187–9
books and literacy 8, 10–13, 36–7, 44, 51, 64, 76, 86, 137–9, 147–9, 155, 185
Byzantine empire 2–3, 6, 14, 42, 45–51, 57
Catholic Church 17–27, 38–40, 49–50, 60, 71, 135–41, 143, 149, 154–64, 178–9, 183–5
Chinggis Khan 77–80
Christianity see Catholic Church; Eastern Orthodox; Protestantism
Conques 16, 20–6
Constantinople 2–3, 10, 42, 45–51, 57, 190–1
Copernicus, Nicolas 145
crusades 49–51, 57–8, 63–4, 67
Dado the Hermit 20–1, 24
de Montfort, Simon 73–5
Domesday Book 36, 102–3
Eastern Orthodox Church 17
Edward I 92–7
Edward IV 123
Edward VI 158–9
Egypt 5–6, 14, 19, 67, 85–6, 191
Eleanor of Aquitaine 54–61, 93
Elizabeth I 162, 176–86, 191
Foy 16–27
France 16, 18, 20–6, 43, 59, 61–3, 71, 74, 104, 106, 115–17, 141, 177, 179, 193
Galileo 149
Great Revolt 1381 113
Guiscard, Robert 43, 47
Harold, King of England 28–9
Henry I 52, 68
Henry II 53, 58–61
Henry III 69, 72–5
Henry V 115–16, 118
Henry VI 118–21, 123, 125–6
Henry VII 133–4
Henry VIII 142–4, 157, 177
Hundred Years War 115–17
Inkas 166–74
Ireland 185
Islam 4–9, 42, 44, 45, 49–50, 58, 65–7, 88, 179
Italy 43–4, 46–7, 146, 150–3, 190, 193
Jerusalem 49–51, 57–8, 66–7
John, King of England 61, 69–72
Komnenos, Alexios 45–51
Llywelyn ap Gruffydd 92
Louis VII 56–8
Luther, Martin 135–41
Magna Carta 70–3
Makkah 5, 44
Mansa Musa 83–90
Mary Stuart 183
Mary Tudor 161, 164–5, 177–8
Matilda 53, 58
Michelangelo 152
miracles 25–6
Mongols 76–82
Muhammad 5–7
Norman Conquest 28–40, 52–3
Normandy 28–9, 43, 55
Palestine 13, 19
Persian empire 6–8, 44, 88
Philip II 66–7, 70–1, 177, 182
pilgrims 5, 11, 19, 21, 23–6, 62–3, 83–7
Poma, Guamán 170–1
Protestantism 140–1, 157–63, 178, 183, 185
Raleigh, Walter 182
Reformation 135–41, 144, 154–63
Renaissance 150–3
Richard I 61, 66
Richard II 113
Richard III 127–8
Richard of York 119
Roger II of Sicily 42, 63
Roman empire 17–18, 27, 137–8, 141
science and mathematics 8, 10, 13–14, 48, 64–5, 145–9
Scotland 94–9
Shakespeare 115, 175
Sicily 41–4, 63–4, 190
slavery 5, 12, 34, 36–8, 40, 191
Sofonisba 150–3
Stephen, King of England 53, 58–9
Syria 6–8, 10, 19, 44, 63–4, 67
Timbuktu 89–90
Vikings 29, 32, 43
Wales 91–4
Wars of the Roses 118–28, 133–4
William Duke of Normandy 28–40, 52
Zoe 2–3, 45

Photo credits

p.iii © Christine Counsell; **p.2** background © DeliDumrul (2018, January 17). Constantinople. World History Encyclopedia. Retrieved from https://www.worldhistory.org/image/7956/constantinople/; **p.2** sarymsakov.com/stock.adobe.com; **p.4** b © BlueOrange Studio, background © JEFF DAI / SCIENCE PHOTO LIBRARY, inset © Wikiwand.com/Public Domain; **pp.8–9** © JEAN SOUTIF / LOOK AT SCIENCES / SCIENCE PHOTO LIBRARY; **p.9** r © pop_gino/stock.adobe.com; **p.10** © Heritage Image Partnership Ltd / Alamy Stock Photo; **p.11** b © Edinburgh University Library. With kind permission of the University of Edinburgh / Bridgeman Images, t © Peter Nahum at The Leicester Galleries, London / Bridgeman Images; **p.12** t © Science History Images / Alamy Stock Photo, b © Wikipedia.com/Public Domain; **p.13** © Science History Images / Alamy Stock Photo; **p.14** bl © Zoonar GmbH / Alamy Stock Photo, tr © The Metropolitan Museum of Art. 13.152.6 Rogers Fund, 1913/Public Domain; **p.15** © CPA Media Pte Ltd / Alamy Stock Photo; **p.16** © Dominique REPERANT/Gamma-Rapho via Getty Images; **p.18** t © Ian G Dagnall / Alamy Stock Photo, b © British Library Board. All Rights Reserved / Bridgeman Images; **p.19** t © British Library Board. All Rights Reserved / Bridgeman Images, b © Bridgeman Images; **p.20** © Olivier Klencklen/Stock.adobe.com; **p.21** © Bridgeman Images; **p.23** © Paul Maeyaert. All rights reserved 2023 / Bridgeman Images; **p.24** t © MIMOHE/Stock.adobe.com, bl © Mahaux Charles/AGF/Universal Images Group via Getty Images, br © Photononstop/Alamy Stock Photo; **p.26** © Svintage Archive / Alamy Stock Photo; **p.27** © Dominique REPERANT/Gamma-Rapho via Getty Images; **p.28** t © Album / Alamy Stock Photo, b © Bridgeman Images; **p.29** © With special authorisation of the city of Bayeux / Bridgeman Images; **p.30** background © allouphoto/stock.adobe.com, b © PA Images / Alamy Stock Photo; **p.31** © CADW; **p.32** © Stephen Baxter; **p.36** c © PA Images / Alamy Stock Photo, b ©

Mary Evans / The National Archives, London. England; **p.37** © CC-BY-SA licence/Professor John Palmer, George Slater and opendomesday.org; **pp.38–39** background © AVTG/stock.adobe.com; **p.38** b © REDA &CO srl / Alamy Stock Photo; **p.40** © Christina Bollen / Alamy Stock Photo; **p.41** b © mauritius images GmbH / Alamy Stock Photo, t © imageBROKER / Alamy Stock Photo; **p.42** © JEROME LABOUYRIE/stock.adobe.com; **p.43** background © dtatiana/stock.adobe.com, br © Robert Guiskard/Wikimedia/Public Domain; **p.44** © Konrad Miller (1844-1933)/Wikimedia Commons/Public Domain; **p.45** © Public Domain/Wikimedia Commons; **p.47** t © Public Domain/Wikimedia Commons, b © funkyfood London – Paul Williams / Alamy Stock Photo; **p.48** © The Picture Art Collection / Alamy Stock Photo; **p.49** © The History Collection / Alamy Stock Photo; **p.50** © Science History Images / Alamy Stock Photo; **p.51** © Sailko/Wikimedia Commons/CC BY 3.0; p.52 © Pictorial Press Ltd / Alamy Stock Photo; **p.53** tl © British Library/Wikimedia/Public Domain, cl © Public Domain/Wikimedia Commons; **p.54** © rysan34/stock.adobe.com; **p.55** b © The Archives of the Planet / Alamy Stock Photo, cr © The Picture Art Collection / Alamy Stock Photo; **p.56** © Peter Willi/Bridgeman Images; **p.57** © GRANGER – Historical Picture Archive / Alamy Stock Photo; **p.59** tr © Axis Images / Alamy Stock Photo, cr © Mattis Kaminer / Alamy Stock Photo, bl © agefotostock / Alamy Stock Photo; **pp.60–61** background © Nigel Blacker / Alamy Stock Photo; **p.61** inset tl © History and Art Collection / Alamy Stock Photo Commons, inset tr © INTERFOTO / Alamy Stock Photo, inset bl © Public Domain/Wikimedia Commons, inset br © Public Domain/Wikimedia Commons; **p.64** background, c © archiv.onb.ac.at/Wikimedia Commons/Public Domain; **p.65** l © Nigel Blacker / Alamy Stock Photo, r © StarTigerJLN/Wikimedia/Pubic Domain; **p.66** © LianeM/stock.adobe.com; **p.67** t © The History Collection / Alamy Stock Photo, r © Bibliotheque Municipale de Lyon, Ms 828 f33r/Domeniu public/Wikimedia Commons; **p.68** all © Bridgeman Images; **p.70** © Look and Learn / Bridgeman Images; **p.72** l © Bridgeman Images, r © Bridgeman Images; **p.73** background © acceptfoto/stoc.adobe.com; **p.74** © Ivan Smuk / Alamy Stock Photo; **p.75** © Bridgeman Images; **p.76** © Sayf al-vâhidî et al/Wikimedia Commons/Public Domain; **p.77** © Татьяна Мельникова/stock.adobe.com; **p.78** bl © Mieszko9/stock.adobe.com, r © Urtnasan/stock.adobe.com; **p.80** © dsaprin/stock.adobe.com; **p.81** l & r World History Archive / Alamy Stock Photo; **p.82** © Sayf al-vâhidî et al/Wikimedia Commons/Public Domain; **p.84** © World Archive / Alamy Stock Photo; **p.85** © Dmitry Rukhlenko/stock.adobe.com; **p.86** © The Granger Collection / Alamy Stock Photo; **p.87** © Heini Schneebeli / Bridgeman Images; **p.89** © Gavin Hellier / Alamy Stock Photo; **p.90** t © GRANGER - Historical Picture Archive / Alamy Stock Photo, b © Professor Toby Green; **p.93** © Dextra Visual; **p.94** © Kristian Bond / Alamy Stock Photo; **p.96** © Angelo Hornak / Alamy Stock Photo; **pp.96–97** background © Duncan Andison/stock.adobe.com; **p.97** © Atlaspix / Alamy Stock Photo; **p.98** Image CC BY 4.0 © National Library of Scotland; **p.101** © Photo Josse / Bridgeman Images; **p.103** © Katie Chan/CC BY-SA 4.0/Wikimedia Commons; **p.104** © History and Art Collection / Alamy Stock Photo; **p.105** tr © Jim Monk / Alamy Stock Photo, b © Art Collection 3 / Alamy Stock Photo; **p.106** © GRANGER - Historical Picture Archive / Alamy Stock Photo; **p.107** © SPK / Alamy Stock Photo; **p.110** © North Wind Picture Archives / Alamy Stock Photo; **p.111** © Bridgeman Images; **p.112** t © Hansard Collection / Alamy Stock Photo, b © mrallen/stock.adobe.com; **p.113** t © The Picture Art Collection / Alamy Stock Photo, b After the Black Death by Mark Bailey cover © Oxford University Press (Reproduced with permission of the Licensor through PLSclear.); **p.114** t © GRANGER – Historical Picture Archive / Alamy Stock Photo, c © Mark Bailey, b © Claire Kennan; **p.115** © Desintegrator / Alamy Stock Photo; **p.116** © Pictorial Press Ltd / Alamy Stock Photo; **p.117** © The Picture Art Collection / Alamy Stock Photo; **p.118–128** background © xenial/stock.adobe.com; **p.119** t & b © xenial/stock.adobe.com; **p.120** © Helen Castor; **pp.122–123** © Art Collection 3 / Alamy Stock Photo; **p.123** r © DianaHirsch/E+/Getty Images; **p.124** © The History Collection / Alamy Stock Photo; **p.127** © naumoid/123RF.com; **p.128** t © Public Domain/Wikimedia Commons, b © Helen Castor; **p.129** © British Library / Bridgeman Images; **p.130** © Historic Images / Alamy Stock Photo; **p.131** © CC by 4.0. James Mindham/www.thisispaston.co.uk; **p.133** t © The Picture Art Collection / Alamy Stock Photo; **p.133** © xenial/stock.adobe.com; **p.134** © CMA/BOT / Alamy Stock Photo; **p.135** background © death_rip/stock.adobe.com, r © Artefact / Alamy Stock Photo; **p.136** © Bettmann / Getty Images; **p.137** © caifas/stock.adobe.com; **p.139** t © Public Domain/Wikimedia Commons, bl © History and Art Collection / Alamy Stock Photo, br © Domini públic/Wikimedia Commona; **p.140** t © public domain/Wikimedia Commons, b © Eraza Collection / Alamy Stock Photo; **p.141** l & background © Artokoloro / Alamy Stock Photo, r Public Domain; **p.142** t & b © public domain/Wikimedia Commons; **p.143** l © Bridgeman Images, r © IanDagnall Computing / Alamy Stock Photo; **p.144** © Leighton Collins/Shutterstock.com; **p.145** © Forum / Bridgeman Images; **pp.145–147** background © incamerastock / Alamy Stock Photo; **p.148** © lukszczepanski/stock.adobe.com; **p.147** t © Bridgeman Images, c © GRANGER - Historical Picture Archive / Alamy Stock Photo, b © Arterra Picture Library / Alamy Stock Photo; **p.149** t © Public Domain/Wikimedia Commons, Portrait of Nicolaus Copernicus, half length holding astronomical device. © Wellcome Collection. (Attribution 4.0 International (CC BY 4.0)); **p.150** © Axis Images / Alamy Stock Photo; **p.151** © Marie-Lan Nguyen/public domain/Wikimedia Commons; **p.152** t © IanDagnall Computing / Alamy Stock Photo, b © Bridgeman Images; **p.153** t © Web Gallery of Art/Public Domain/Wikimedia Commons, b © CBW / Alamy Stock Photo; **p.154** tl © Alainara/Shutterstock.com, tr © Gribanov/stock.adobe.com, bl © Arsgera/stock.adobe.com, bc © gomolach/stock.adobe.com, br © Dave Kelly/Wikimedia Commons/CC BY-SA 2.0; **p.155** © Courtesy of St. George's Church, Morebath/Devon Archives, Devon Heritage Centre; **pp.158–9** © History and Art Collection / Alamy Stock Photo; **p.161** © IanDagnall Computing / Alamy Stock Photo; **p.162** wartburg.edu/Wikimedia Commons/Public Domain; **p.163** t © Dmitry Naumov/stock.adobe.com, b © Andrey/stock.adobe.com; **p.166** © Sebasti/stock.adobe.com; **p.167** tr © Wikimedia Commons/Public Domain; **pp.167/171/173** background, **174** cr © Bridgeman Images; **pp.167–171/173–174** background, **171** t © Sabine Hyland; **pp.168–171/174** background, **174** c © Artokoloro / Alamy Stock Photo; **p.169** cl (Copyright unknown). Taken from University of Texas Press; **p.170** l © Historic Images / Alamy Stock Photo, c © Volgi archive / Alamy Stock Photo, r © Det Kgl. Bibliotek/Royal Danish Library; **p.171** b © Sabine Hyland; **p.172** © Belikova Oksana/Shutterstock.com; **p.173** both © Sabine Hyland; **p.174** l © Daniel Prudek/stock.adobe.com, tr © Bridgeman Images; **p.176** t © Bridgeman Images, b © A.P.S. (UK) / Alamy Stock Photo; **p.177** wartburg.edu/Wikimedia Commons/Public Domain; **p.178** © Album / Alamy Stock Photo; **p.179** © Mechanical Curator collection/Flickr Commons/ British Library; **p.182** t © Paula Worth, b © The Print Collector / Alamy Stock Photo; **p.183** t © MAXPPP / Alamy Stock Photo, b © Public Domain/Wikimedia Commons; **p.184** © Niday Picture Library / Alamy Stock Photo; **p.185** l © Public Domain/Wikimedia Commons, r © ART Collection / Alamy Stock Photo; **p.186** © Public Domain/Wikimedia Commons; **p.187** © College of Arms; **p.188** © Miranda Kaufmann; **p.189** © Jim Batty / Alamy Stock Photo; **pp.190–3** background & **193** © Jimlop collection / Alamy Stock Photo.

Text permission pp.108–9 John Hatcher, *The Black Death, The Story of a Village 1345-1350*, 2008. Weidenfeld & Nicolson. Reproduced with permission of the Licensor through PLSclear.